# WOMEN'S RETIREMENT

Volume 6
Sage Yearbooks in WOMEN'S POLICY STUDIES

# WOMEN'S RETIREMENT
## Policy Implications of Recent Research

Edited by

# MAXIMILIANE SZINOVACZ

SAGE PUBLICATIONS
Beverly Hills / London / New Delhi

*For information address:*

SAGE Publications, Inc.
275 South Beverly Drive
Beverly Hills, California 90212

SAGE Publications India Pvt. Ltd.
C-236 Defence Colony
New Delhi 110 024, India

SAGE Publications Ltd
28 Banner Street
London EC1Y 8QE, England

Printed in the United States of America

**Library of Congress Cataloging in Publication Data**

Main entry under title:

Women's retirement.

    (Sage yearbooks in women's policy studies ; v. 6)
    Bibliography: p.
    1. Women—United States—Retirement—Addresses, essays, lectures.
I. Szinovacz, Maximiliane.  II. Series.
HQ1064.U5W62  1982        305.4'890696'0973        82-16758
ISBN 0-8039-1894-1
ISBN 0-8039-1895-X (pbk.)

FIRST PRINTING

*To my retired parents*

# CONTENTS

Preface                                                                9

1. Introduction: Research on Women's Retirement
   MAXIMILIANE SZINOVACZ                                                13

**PART I: Employment Status, Work History, and Life
   Situation of Older Women**                                          23

2. Midlife Work History and Retirement Income
   ANGELA O'RAND and JOHN C. HENRETTA                                  25

3. Life Satisfaction Among Aging Women: A Causal Model
   CAROL CUTLER RIDDICK                                                45

4. Employment Status and Social Support: The Experience
   of the Mature Woman
   CHARLENE DEPNER and BERIT INGERSOLL                                 61

5. Working Women Versus Homemakers: Retirement
   Resources and Correlates of Well-Being
   PAT M. KEITH                                                        77

**PART II: Preparing for Retirement: Attitudes and Plans**             93

6. Preretirement Preparation: Sex Differences in Access,
   Sources, and Use
   NAOMI KROEGER                                                       95

7. Retirement Expectations and Plans: A Comparison of
   Professional Men and Women
   EVELYN S. NEWMAN, SUSAN R. SHERMAN,
   and CLAIRE E. HIGGINS                                               113

8. Attitudes Toward Retirement: A Comparison of
   Professional and Nonprofessional Married Women
   SHARON PRICE-BONHAM and
   CAROLYN KITCHINGS JOHNSON                                           123

9. Retirement Plans and Retirement Adjustment
   MAXIMILIANE SZINOVACZ                                    139

**PART III. Adjusting to Retirement: The Female Experience**   151

10. The Process of Retirement: Comparing Women and Men
    ROBERT C. ATCHLEY                                       153

11. After Retirement: An Exploratory Study of
    the Professional Woman
    RUTH HATHAWAY JEWSON                                    169

12. Professional Women: Work Pattern as a Correlate of
    Retirement Satisfaction
    MARILYN R. BLOCK                                        183

13. Personal Problems and Adjustment to Retirement
    MAXIMILIANE SZINOVACZ                                   195

14. Responsibility for Household Tasks: Comparing
    Dual-Earner and Dual-Retired Marriages
    TIMOTHY H. BRUBAKER and CHARLES B. HENNON               205

15. Conclusion: Service Needs of Women Retirees
    MAXIMILIANE SZINOVACZ                                   221

Bibliography                                                235
About the Contributors                                      269

# PREFACE

*Women's Retirement: Policy Implications of Recent Research* is the sixth volume of Sage Yearbooks on Women's Policy Studies. To my knowledge, this volume constitutes the first book-length publication of research specifically devoted to women's retirement. All the contributions to this volume are original publications, although several are based on papers presented at scientific meetings. The primary objectives of the book are to extend our knowledge base on this widely neglected issue and to discuss policy implications derived from this evidence.

Given the extensive literature on male retirement, it may very well be asked why a volume on female retirement is necessary. Obviously, if men and women experienced retirement in a similar fashion, special studies of women's retirement would be of little scientific or applied value. There is, however, good reason to believe that men's and women's retirement experiences and adjustment differ in substantial ways, and previous research as well as evidence presented in this volume tend to confirm this assumption. Not only does society place a different value on men's and women's work and their occupational roles, but we may also expect that sex differences in socialization and other gender-based variations in men's and women's roles impact on their adaptation to life transitions in general and the retirement transition in particular. Furthermore, women's retirement may be of special policy relevance. The population of aged individuals consists to a large degree of women, many of whom are retirees, and the number of retired women can be expected to rise substantially in the future. Also, aging women are among the economically most disadvantaged population groups, and women retirees have been found to experience more problems in their adjustment to this life transition than men. However, current retirement programs tend to focus on the situation of male retirees, partially because so little is known about women retirees' problems and needs. Empirically founded recommendations for the development of programs and policies specifically designed to facilitate

9

women's retirement transition and to enhance their retirement adjustment are thus urgently needed.

As will be discussed in detail (see Chapter 1), research on female retirement has not gone far beyond an exploratory stage. Not only are there relatively few studies that address women's retirement, but the existing investigations are often restricted in regard to sample size and representativeness. And nationally representative data bases that are now available (such as the Social Security Administration's Retirement History Study) tend to portray relations between general population characteristics and the timing and economic aspects of retirement, but fall short of exposing individuals' personal attitudes and reactions to retirement (see Schwab and Irelan, 1981). Although some contributors to this volume present nationally representative data, these research limitations also apply to several studies reported here. While findings based on small and selective samples may not be generalizable and often contain inherent methodological problems (e.g., in regard to significance tests and some violations of statistical assumptions), they do play an important role in theory construction. Grounded theory (Glaser and Strauss, 1967) relies on the accumulation of empirical evidence from various sources, and the theoretical assumptions generated by initial exploratory investigations are only later submitted to more stringent empirical tests. In this sense, the primary orientation of this volume remains within the theory generating, rather than the theory testing, realm.

It would obviously be premature to offer definite policy recommendations on the basis of such exploratory research. Thus, while authors were encouraged to discuss policy implications of their findings, additional research will often be necessary to substantiate their results before specific policies can be developed or implemented. Nevertheless, the results presented in this volume provide guidelines for future policy-relevant research, and in some cases cumulative evidence from several studies already suggests specific directions for policy applications. Some policy implications are outlined in the concluding sections of each contribution and further elaborated in the final chapter of the book.

The essence of this volume consists of three parts, arranged by major research themes. The first part concerns itself with the impact of work history and employment status on the life situation of the older woman. Thus, chapters contained in this section center on differences within the population of older women in terms of their employment status and work patterns. Attitudes toward retirement and retirement preparation among women are addressed in the second section of the book. Various studies are presented that examine retirement attitudes and plans of various population groups and explore the effects of retirement planning on retirement adjustment. The third part is devoted to analyses that deal more specifically with the determinants and consequences of retirement for women. Contributions to this section compare retirement adjustment processes of men and women, as well as of selected groups of female retirees. The bibliography presented at the end of the book contains, in addition to the authors' references, a broad range of materials on the life situation of older women in general and female retirement in particular. Specifically, it includes most of the publications on women's retirement published within the last decade. However, no claims are made that the reference list exhausts the existing literature on female retirement.

As is usually the case with edited works, this volume is the result of collaborative efforts by many individuals. I would like to extend special thanks to the contributors to this volume not only for their hard work, but particularly for their patience and cooperation with my many and often pedantic requests for revisions. My own empirical contributions to the book, as well as the editorial work, were supported by funds from the NRTA-AARP Andrus Foundation, Washington, D.C. Two graduate students, Barbara Fletcher and Brien Sorne, helped with the compilation of the bibliography, and Janet Roberts typed several chapters and the bibliography in record time.

*—Maximiliane Szinovacz*

# 1

# INTRODUCTION: RESEARCH ON
# WOMEN'S RETIREMENT

## Maximiliane Szinovacz

**Despite increasing interest in** retirement issues, women's retirement has been widely neglected by social scientists. This introductory chapter presents some documentation on the prevalent gender bias in the retirement literature and examines reasons for this trend. A programmatic statement regarding the development of policy-relevant research concludes the chapter.

## DOCUMENTATION

While it is generally recognized that research on women's retirement is lacking (Beeson, 1975; Atchley and Corbett, 1977; Lehr, 1977; Fox, 1977), evidence for this conclusion is usually restricted to citations of the few better-known studies on women's retirement. In order to further illustrate and more adequately document this gender bias in the retirement literature, a survey of papers presented at the meetings of the Gerontological Society between 1970 and 1981 was undertaken. These meetings constitute the most likely forum for research presentations on retirement issues, and materials on retirement presented at these conferences probably provide a better representation of research efforts than articles published in scientific journals (owing to the high rejection rate of papers submitted for publication, as well as the time lag between paper presentation and publication). The present survey does not exhaust the existing research on women's retirement, but it should provide a fairly representative comparison of research efforts on male and female retirement.

Abstracts of papers published in the Gerontological Society's Annual Meeting programs (also reproduced in *The Gerontologist*) were used for the comparisons. All abstracts whose titles clearly identified them as retirement research and/or that appeared in sessions on retirement were selected, including paper and poster sessions, but excluding symposia and discussion sessions. A few papers on retirement which neither referred to retirement in their titles nor appeared in retirement sessions may have been omitted from this survey.

The classification of papers in regard to sex of respondents relied on the brief sample descriptions given in the abstracts. Since many authors failed to identify sex of subjects in these abstracts, a relatively high proportion of the abstracts could not be categorized. Many of these studies used employees from selected industries or companies, some of which were clearly male-dominated (e.g., rubber workers, university faculty). It can thus be assumed that a good portion of these unclassifiable papers used male subjects. Indeed, the mere fact that authors fail to identify the sex of their respondents in sample descriptions might in itself be viewed as an indication that some researchers consider the gender of subjects in retirement studies as given. All other abstracts were classified as covering only males, only females, both sexes, or couples. Papers dealing with retirement issues but which were not based on studies of the retirees themselves (e.g., investigations of employers or review papers) were excluded from this survey.

The results from this brief survey are shown in Tables 1.1 and 1.2. It is evident that research specifically concerned with female retirement was practically unheard of before 1975. From 1970 to 1975, about one-third of the papers relied entirely on male samples, and a majority of the unclassified papers were probably also male-centered. Although "male only" samples still prevailed in the later 1970s, the gender bias had become somewhat less severe. For 1981, we observe heightened interest in women's retirement and also a relatively higher proportion of studies which included both sexes.

Not only was past research on retirement male-oriented, but investigations on women's retirement were further limited by their reliance on small, nonrepresentative samples. As shown in Table 1.2, nearly one-third of the studies dealing specifically with women's retirement were based on samples of less than 100 subjects, as compared to only 12 percent of the investigations on retiring males. One-quarter of the studies on women's

**TABLE 1.1**   Sex of Subjects in Research Papers on Retirement Presented at the Annual Meeting of the Gerontological Society, 1970-1981

| Year | | Male Only | Female Only | Both Sexes | Couples | Unclassi- fiable | (N) |
|---|---|---|---|---|---|---|---|
| 1970 | | 2 | – | 1 | – | 1 | (4) |
| 1971 | | 2 | – | 2 | – | 2 | (6) |
| 1972 | | 1 | 1 | – | 1 | 2 | (5) |
| 1973 | | – | – | 2 | – | – | (2) |
| 1974 | | 2 | – | – | 1 | 3 | (6) |
| 1975 | | 3 | – | 1 | – | 5 | (9) |
| 1976 | | 1 | 3 | – | 1 | 2 | (7) |
| 1977 | | 3 | 2 | 4 | – | 2 | (11) |
| 1978 | | 1 | – | 2 | 1 | 2 | (6) |
| 1979 | | 1 | – | 3 | 1 | 8 | (13) |
| 1980 | | 6 | 4 | 1 | – | 8 | (19) |
| 1981 | | 4 | 6 | 9 | 2 | 12 | (33) |
| 1970-1975 | % | 31 | 3 | 19 | 6 | 41 | (32) |
| 1976-1980 | % | 21 | 16 | 18 | 5 | 39 | (56) |
| 1981 | % | 12 | 18 | 27 | 6 | 36 | (33) |
| 1970-1981 | % | 21 | 13 | 21 | 6 | 39 | (121) |

retirement used university employees, whereas only 8 percent of the research on male retirees focused on this population group.

Overall, this survey clearly confirms the emphasis on male retirement in the past literature, a trend that has only begun to change within the last couple of years. The existing evidence on women's retirement is clearly restricted owing to small and selective samples used in investigations of female retirees.

## REASONS

It is probably appropriate to state that women's retirement was not studied because it was not considered to constitute a salient social or research issue. It is questionable, however, whether the implicit or explicit assumptions that underly the gender bias in the retirement literature have been justified on theoretical or empirical grounds and whether they are currently applicable.

TABLE 1.2    Sample Size and Population by Sex of Subject in Research
Papers Presented at the Annual Meetings of the Gerontological Society, 1970-1981

| Sample Size/ Population | Male Only % | Female Only % | Both Sexes % | Couples % | Unclassi- fiable % |
|---|---|---|---|---|---|
| Under 100 | 12 | 31 | 8 | 43 | 28 |
| National | 42 | 38 | 44 | 43 | 11 |
| Other | 46 | 31 | 48 | 14 | 61 |
| (N) | (26) | (16) | (25) | ( 7) | (47) |
| University Employees | 8 | 25 | 16 | 14 | 13 |
| Other | 92 | 75 | 84 | 86 | 87 |
| (N) | (26) | (16) | (25) | ( 7) | (47) |

One obvious argument concerns the incidence of labor force participation and retirement among men and women. Nationally representative
figures on the number of retired women are difficult to obtain because
census data treat the non-employed as a homogeneous group, thus com-
bining women retirees and homemakers. However, some estimates can be
derived from statistics on the labor force participation of middle-aged and
older women.

Female labor participation rates have undergone drastic changes during
this century, and this trend also applies to middle-aged and older women.
In 1940, 24.3 percent of women aged 45-54 years were working outside
the home, as compared to 95.5 percent of the men in this age group. By
1976, these proportions had changed to 54.6 percent and 90.6 percent,
respectively. A similar tendency applies for the 55-64 age group. In 1940,
only 18.7 percent of the women in this age group were members of the
labor force, but this proportion increased to 40.7 percent in 1976. The
respective percentages for men were 87.2 percent and 73.5 percent. For
persons aged 65 years and over, labor force participation rates for males
decreased from 45.0 percent in 1940 to 19.4 percent in 1976, whereas the
proportion of working women remained relatively stable at about 7-8
percent (Foner and Schwab, 1981: 3, Table 1.1). These statistics suggest
that by the mid-1970s a substantial proportion of women entered old age
as retirees rather than homemakers, and further increases in women's labor

force participation rates indicate a continuation of this trend into the 1980s.

Further support for this argument is provided by Pampel's (1981) analysis of data from the Survey Research Center of the University of Michigan. According to the nationally representative SRC data, less than one-third (28 percent) of women aged 57 years or more were either employed, unemployed, or retired in 1952. All other women were classified as homemakers. By 1978, these proportions were reversed, with only 40 percent of the women classified as homemakers and 60 percent either actively employed, seeking employment, or retired (Pampel, 1981: 71, Table 4.1).

Thus, at least since the mid-1970s, women retirees have represented a noteworthy and growing proportion of the population of older women. Since women clearly outnumber men among aged persons, the proportion of women retirees within the total population of older individuals is certainly not negligible, and thus deserving of scientific investigation.

A second assumption responsible for the neglect of women's retirement in the literature concerns the relative salience of work and retirement to men and women (Beeson, 1975). Even recent college texts contain statements supportive of such assumptions. For instance, Eshleman (1981: 527) argues: "Retirement for women, traditionally at least, represented a less drastic shift in roles, since domestic roles often supplemented work roles." Scanzoni and Scanzoni (1981: 614) quote an early and certainly not representative study by Blau (1973) when they state: "Because of the traditional meaning of the breadwinner role, retirement is experienced much more demoralizing to males than is the case with females who retire from the work force." While both authors note that increases in women's labor force participation may change this pattern, it is certainly interesting to observe that such statements still appear in 1981 texts despite long-existing empirical evidence to the contrary (see Streib and Schneider, 1971).

It is obviously presumed that employment represents a central life interest for men, whereas women are expected to be less committed to work and to rank their work lower in the hierarchy of life interests. However, research renders such assumptions highly questionable. Studies on career women clearly indicate that work outside the home can become a central life interest to women (Epstein, 1970; Fogarty et al., 1971; Holmstrom, 1972; Pepitone-Rockwell, 1980). Even among women in less specialized and nonprofessional occupations, work motives are not restricted to financial incentives. Rather, multidimensionality of work motives prevails (Haller and Rosenmayr, 1971; Lindenstein-Walshok, 1979; Szinovacz, 1979a, 1982a). Also, work is not always men's central life interest (Fogarty et al., 1971; Bailyn, 1970; Dubin, 1956; Friedman and Orbach, 1974; Maddox, 1966), since both sexes derive important satisfactions from various roles (Campbell et al., 1976; Markides and Martin, 1979; Palmore and Kivett, 1975; Larson, 1978).

While it is certainly true that women's work patterns are more discontinuous than men's and that, on the average, women spend a smaller proportion of their adult lives in gainful employment (see chapter 2), time spent with work should not be identified with work commitment or salience of the work role. Women who enter or reenter the labor force after their childrearing years may develop a strong commitment to their work and perceive it as an important if not *the* central role in their lives. Quite frequently, and in some cases more so than men, older working women have been shown to anticipate various retirement problems, including missing social contacts, feelings of uselessness, or failure to achieve work-related goals (Laurence, 1961; Atchley, 1971, 1976b, 1976c; Streib and Schneider, 1971; Prentis, 1980). Also, a "decrystallization of women's life patterns" (Lopata and Norr, 1980) has been observed, with women spending increasing proportions of their lives outside familial roles and more time in the labor force and in their preretirement jobs (Mallan, 1974; U.S. Bureau of the Census, 1976).

These assumptions concerning gender differences in the salience of work further led to the belief that the retirement transition will be more severe and demoralizing to men than to women. Loss of their work role, it is argued, deprives men of their central life interest and therefore often results in a sense of status loss and low self-esteem which cannot be easily overcome by involvement in retirement activities (see Rosow, 1974; Blau, 1973; Burgess, 1960; Cavan, 1962). Women, on the other hand, are expected to experience less retirement stress than men, not only because they are supposedly less committed to work, but also because society offers them an equally acceptable role in the position of full-time housewife. Thus, retiring women are expected to reassume happily the role of a full-time homemaker, whereas retiring men are left with a role truly void of meaningful content. This argumentation is questionable because it implies full substitutability of work and family roles. Furthermore, with increasing numbers of retirees, the retiree role has become socially acceptable and less threatening than might have been the case several decades ago (Sussman, 1972; Friedman and Orbach, 1974; Bell, 1976; Maddox, 1966; Taylor, 1972; Sheppard, 1976). The assumption that women can easily substitute former work activities with increased involvement in household activities also disregards the fact that many women choose to work in order to escape a full-time household routine or because they are not fully occupied with household and family tasks once the children have reached school age or left the parents' home (Sobol, 1974). Indeed, current research evidence suggests that women retirees may experience more retirement problems than men (Streib and Schneider, 1971; Jaslow, 1976; Fox, 1977) and that they show no particular interest in homemaker activities after retirement (Szinovacz, 1980).

In addition, adjustment to retirement is not entirely a function of previous work commitment or length of employment. Their participation in the labor force provides individuals with resources and gratifications beyond the immediate rewards gained from work itself. Loss of these resources and benefits can constitute a significant barrier to retirement adjustment. Women seem particularly vulnerable to economic and social losses associated with retirement. Since women's emotional well-being seems to be more contingent than men's on the maintenance of social contacts outside the family (Candy, 1977), loss of contacts with co-workers could present a serious problem for women retirees. Owing to their discontinuous work histories, as well as a series of other factors, women experience marked decreases in income upon retirement, a condition that is clearly reflected in the disproportionate number, particularly of nonmarried women, with incomes below the poverty level (Fox, 1979; Thompson, 1971; Friedman and Sjogren, 1981; Muller, 1980; Beller, 1980; Pampel, 1981; see also Chapter 2). Also, because of their shorter preretirement employment history, women may not be as able as men to achieve their occupational goals, thus rendering retirement a particularly disruptive experience (Atchley, 1976b, 1976c; Atchley and Corbett, 1977).

The majority of retirement research also neglects the fact that most retiring persons are married. Since individuals' work roles have a major impact on their family lives, we may expect the retirement of one spouse to have important implications for the marital relationship. The few studies dealing with retirement effects on marital relations were restricted to investigation of the husband's retirement on wives (Fengler, 1975; Kerckhoff, 1964, 1966; Heyman and Jeffers, 1968; Lipman, 1960, 1961; Keating and Cole, 1980; for an exception, see Szinovacz, 1980). This trend is particularly regrettable, because couples are known to plan retirement together and to opt for joint timing of the retirement transition (Anderson et al., 1980; Clark et al., 1980; Henretta and O'Rand, 1980). Research on the husband's retirement effects on the couple usually did not control for wife's employment status, probably resulting in biased results. For instance, frequent complaints about the retired husband's interference with household tasks and "having the husband underfoot" may be typical reactions of housewives, but not of presently employed or retired wives (Darnley, 1975; Fengler, 1975; Keating and Cole, 1980; Szinovacz, 1980).

Finally, major life transitions of women have been treated as independent events. This tendency is particularly evident in the almost total empirical and theoretical separation of research on retirement and widowhood. Failure to view women's life transitions as unrelated experiences cannot be justified on theoretical grounds nor on the basis of prevailing demographic trends. Indeed, it is quite likely that aging women encounter retirement and widowhood within a relatively short time period. The literature on critical life events emphasizes that adjustment to one life transition is contingent on antecedent life circumstances, as well as on the specific conditions under which life events occur. Specifically, the synchronization of life events and/or the accumulation of major life transitions within a relatively short time period has been shown to hinder successful adaptation (Bengtson, 1973; Neugarten et al., 1975; Seltzer, 1976; Morgan, 1977; Lowenthal, 1977). Thus, having to face retirement and widowhood within a few years may also enhance women's vulnerability to either event. Retired women who become widows could also be deprived of feelings of accomplishment derived from their homemaker roles. Many household tasks may lose their gratifying value if they are no longer performed for others, but only for oneself (Matthews, 1979).

To summarize, general assumptions concerning the frequency and importance of women's participation in the labor force have led to an overemphasis on male retirement and a one-sided approach to retirement adjustment. It is argued here that the increased labor force participation of women has rendered female retirement a socially significant phenomenon, and it is precisely those characteristics underlying the neglect of women's retirement in the literature (e.g., discontinuous work histories, the importance of the empty nest, and widowhood) that may contribute to women's demonstrated vulnerability to the retirement transition (see also Atchley and Corbett, 1977). Therefore, women's retirement would also seem to constitute a policy-relevant issue, and retirement programs need to be adjusted to serve the divergent needs of male and female retirees.

## FUTURE RESEARCH

Effective social policies and programs require representative research that contributes to the identification of potential risk groups and pinpoints the specific problems most likely encountered by selected population groups. In order to obtain such information, longitudinal and comparative retirement studies are most needed. Such investigations should follow representative samples of older employees through the retirement transition years, including postretirement-age workers and housewives as control groups. In order to assess the short- and long-term effects of retirement, postretirement subjects should be studied well beyond their retirement, and the occurrence and timing of other life events should be considered. Only such comparative and longitudinal studies will enable the researcher to differentiate between the effects caused by retirement and those attributable to other life changes.

The identification of specific problems experienced by retirees further necessitates analyses of the impact of retirement on diverse life spheres, including health, economic conditions, social contacts, family relations, and leisure activities, as well as personal adjustment and emotional well-being. Development of efficient retirement programs and policies will also require evaluation studies of existing programs. While some evaluation studies have been carried out, their results are inconsistent, and potential differences in the effects of programs on male and female retirees were ignored.

Finally, most of the retirement literature (including research on males) focuses on blue-collar and even more frequently on white-collar employees. A comprehensive evaluation of the life situation of retirees cannot rely on selective samples. Research is especially needed on the retirement experiences of self-employed professionals, small business and private service workers, and the rural population. Additional efforts should also be made to investigate retirement effects on minorities, who are overrepresented among low-income occupations and thus particularly susceptible to the negative effects of loss of income at retirement. The following contributions may aid in decreasing the knowledge gap on women's retirement, but they may very well raise more questions than they answer.

# I

# EMPLOYMENT STATUS, WORK HISTORY, AND LIFE SITUATION OF OLDER WOMEN

Given the meager empirical evidence on female retirement, it remains virtually unknown to what extent and in which ways the life situation of women retirees diverges from that of other groups of aging women. If gainful employment outside the home constitutes a salient experience for women, we may certainly expect retirees' life styles to differ from those of either older employees or homemakers. Furthermore, the group of women retirees is in itself quite heterogeneous. It is thus essential to investigate which preretirement conditions account for variations in the postretirement situation of women, for instance, in regard to their economic resources or social contacts. The following chapters attempt to shed some light on these questions.

Retirement involves a significant reduction in income for most individuals, but this financial loss is particularly pronounced for women in general and for nonmarried women in particular (Spector, 1979; Fox, 1979; Friedman and Sjogren, 1981; Schwab and Irelan, 1981; Pampel, 1981). Indeed, national statistics suggest that 60 percent of the nonmarried women aged 65 years and over have incomes below the poverty level (Thompson, 1971). In order to alleviate this problem, information is needed on those conditions which prevent women from achieving adequate retirement incomes. Angela O'Rand and John Henretta address this problem in Chapter 2 by isolating those factors which affect unmarried and married women's retirement incomes.

Women have been often shown to leave the labor force before age 65 and to retire at younger ages than men (Foner and Schwab, 1981; Palmore, 1965; Mallan, 1974). Because of this trend, little is known about the effect of continued employment beyond age 65 on women's life situations. Carol Riddick raises this question in Chapter 3 and investigates the relative importance of employment status and other "mutable" characteristics for the life situations of older women.

There can be little doubt that older women's emotional well-being is contingent upon their ability to maintain satisfactory social contacts (Powers and Bultena, 1976; Candy, 1977; Lowenthal and Haven, 1968). Gainful employment outside the home provides women with an important source of social contacts, and the loss of co-workers upon retirement is perceived as a negative consequence of this life transition (Sheldon et al., 1975; Fox, 1977; Szinovacz, 1980, 1982a). However, research evidence concerning the social networks of retired women is lacking. In Chapter 4, Charlene Depner and Berit Ingersoll contribute a comparative analysis of the social network extension and composition of retired women, retired men, employed women, and homemakers.

In the concluding chapter of this section (Chapter 5), Pat Keith offers further evidence concerning the importance of social ties for the well-being of female retirees. Specifically, her study compares the social activities of retirees and homemakers and provides information on the relative salience of social and other resources for these women's life evaluations and death perceptions.

# 2

# MIDLIFE WORK HISTORY AND RETIREMENT INCOME

## Angela O'Rand and John C. Henretta

**Women face special problems** of income maintenance in later life. These problems stem from two related demographic and labor force participation trends during this century. One trend is the persistent and widening differential life expectancy between the sexes, with women the growing numerical majority in the older population (Maddox, 1979). For many women, the cost of living longer includes the greater incidence of poverty income levels characteristic of older single persons (O'Rand, 1981).

A second trend in this century has been the variable labor force participation of women across the life span, with women displaying relatively more interruptions in their work histories and following more diverse schedules in the timing and incidence of their labor force behavior than men (Elder and Rockwell, 1976; Polachek, 1975). Such diverse labor force patterns by women result from their family roles and labor market positions and influence their expected retirement income from work. Consequently, large numbers of single (usually widowed) women with "atypical" work careers, in addition to many who have never been attached to the workforce in a sustained way, are constituting the elderly population.

*AUTHORS' NOTE: Support for the research reported here was provided in part by grants from the Social Security Administration (10-P-97004-4-02) and the National Institute on Aging (NIH AG02136).*

In this chapter, we will examine the influence of the diverse work history patterns of older unmarried and married women on their estimated levels of retirement income from work. These influences will be considered within a life-span framework that also includes the effects of early family and work roles and later labor market positions on retirement income. Data will be drawn from the Longitudinal Retirement History Study (LRHS) and the Earnings Records (ER) of the Social Security Administration for a sample of unmarried and married women on the threshold of retirement in 1969.

## WOMEN'S WORK CAREERS AND RETIREMENT POSITIONS

A work career that results in adequate retirement income is likely to have several important characteristics. First, it tends to be characterized by steady work over many years. Since private pensions typically require a number of years of uninterrupted service to one employer to qualify for benefits and often base dollar amounts of pensions on number of years of service, an uninterrupted career is important. Second, one should work in an occupation characterized by high wages and fringe benefits. Pension coverage is more likely in such occupations, and higher wages are often directly tied to pension payments in benefit formulas. Finally, one should work in an industry with good pensions. A good pension not only has high benefit levels but also can be transferred from one employer to another. Uninterrupted service and high wages also lead to higher dollar amounts in Social Security benefits. These criteria are obviously closely related to each other, and overall, women are disadvantaged, compared to men, on each of them.

First, work careers can be classified into three general participation patterns: continuous labor force participation, or extended attachment to work throughout adulthood; interrupted participation, or in-and-out-of-work patterns over time; and nonparticipation (see Chenoweth and Maret, 1980). The category of interrupted work includes a diverse set of career schedules, such as midlife career entry after children begin school, intermittent labor force participation throughout life, and frequent job changes that are more typical of women than of men. For example, Polachek (1975) found that women with a high school education spend an average of 37 percent of their working life at work, and women with a college education work 41 percent of their work life. This relatively low level of work experience can account for up to 50 percent of the hourly wage gap between men and women. These in-and-out schedules affect retirement income sources and levels by slowing the progress toward pension vesting and increasing the risk of never achieving pension coverage, as well as leading to lower wages on which retirement income is based (Clark, 1980; O'Rand and Henretta, 1981).

The second feature of women's work careers is their tendency to be concentrated in only a few occupations, such as sales, clerical, and domestic service (Blaxall and Reagan, 1976) and limited to a few professions, such as teaching and social services (Oppenheimer, 1970). This segregation process confines women of diverse educational and job experience backgrounds to a restricted set of occupations with limited opportunities for mobility (Rosenfeld, 1979). Occupational sex segregation, in turn, is tied to lower levels of earnings and fringe benefits (including pension coverage), with typically female-dominated ones less advantaged than typically male-dominated ones (Blau and Jusenius, 1976). Furthermore, predominantly female occupations are characterized by a relatively high labor turnover rate that is, in part, a function of the interrupted lifetime work patterns of women in these occupations and, in part, of low wage and benefit structures that encourage labor turnover (Wolf and Rosenfeld, 1978).

The final aspect of women's career patterns is the tendency for women workers to be concentrated in particular industries, in addition to particular occupations, that are distinguished by high rates of labor turnover, lack of unionization, small firm size, and low wages and fringe benefits (Edwards et al., 1975; Beck et al., 1978). For example, Beck et al. (1978) found that 47 percent of workers in these peripheral industries are female, while only 37 percent of workers in the better paid primary sector are female. Along these lines, pension coverage in industries can be classified into favorable and unfavorable categories according to the extent and promise of final pension coverage (Schulz et al., 1979; Kolodrubetz and Landay, 1973). Industrial sectors in which more workers achieve pension coverage and receive high pension incomes include government and public administration; finance, insurance, and real estate; manufacturing; wholesale trade; transportation, communications, and utilities; and professional and related services. In these sectors, pension plans are more likely to include vesting and portability criteria that offer more flexibility to mobile workers, who may transfer pension contribution credits from one employer to the next. Where such portability exists, workers have better retirement income security. Women workers are underrepresented in these sectors; instead, they are likely to be concentrated in retail trade, and in personal and other service sectors where pensions are generally not as available or attainable, even for workers with continuous patterns of labor force participation.

In short, interrupted and delayed work careers combine with occupational locations in lower-paid jobs and in industries without favorable pensions to produce a large number of retirement-aged women with very low retirement incomes. Interrupted work means that many women never work for one employer long enough to qualify for a pension. This problem is exacerbated by the industrial location of many women in industries that have poor pension coverage. Finally, the low earnings of many women mean that the pensions they do receive are likely to be low. These problems can be particularly acute for those who are not married. Since this latter category of women comprises the fastest-growing population subgroup in our society (Ross and Sawhill, 1975; Masnick and Bane, 1980), it warrants special attention.

While the life-span occupational characteristics of interrupted work, difficulties in achieving pension coverage, and poor jobs characterize women as a group, there is nevertheless a great deal of individual variation. Some women work steadily, while others do not. Some are in industries with good pension coverage, while others are not. It is important to examine differences in retirement income that result from differences in these factors in order to suggest solutions to the low levels of retirement income among women in general.

## THE STUDY

The Longitudinal Retirement History Study (LRHS) of the Social Security Administration is a ten-year, biennial panel study of 11,153 men and unmarried women aged 58 to 63 in 1969 when the study began (see Irelan, 1972a, for the fullest description of this sample). For the unmarried female respondents and for the wives of male respondents, survey data are available on selected aspects of family background, work history, and prospective retirement status. Quarterly Social Security Earnings Records (ER) are also available for the period since 1955 for both wives and unmarried women. In the following analysis, unmarried women respondents and wives of married male respondents in 1969 are compared. The effects of background, work history, and husband's characteristics (for wives) on preretirement income status, measured as estimated annual retirement income from Social Security and private or government pensions, are examined for each set of women. Of particular concern will be the influence of the midlife work patterns of these women on their preretirement income status. The specific variables in the study are described in Table 2.1.

## MIDLIFE LABOR STATUS PATTERNS

Life-span models of attainment in later life have come increasingly to emphasize adulthood and midlife development as opposed to adolescent or childhood events (Neugarten, 1964, 1968; Chenoweth and Maret, 1980; Rossi, 1980). The pattern of work through adulthood is of major importance for the study of retirement within this framework. Midlife labor patterns can be classified easily as continuous or discontinuous using the LRHS and ER data. Since at least 85 percent of all workers sampled in the LRHS have worked in jobs covered by Social Security, their quarterly work patterns since 1955 can be fairly precisely categorized. Those who have worked in jobs not covered by Social Security do not appear in the ER but can be identified with relative success in the LRHS using self-reports of current and previous work. Noncovered workers are quite diverse in their occupational locations. In general, they fall into two groups: those in relatively high-status private employment or local, state, and federal government positions including, for example, teachers who have participated in pension plans largely outside the Social Security system until the 1970s, and those in relatively low-status positions, such as personal services and temporary work for cash wages, for whom Earning Records and self-reports are very unreliable indicators of work history. In this study, workers in jobs since 1955 not covered by Social Security are generally distributed occupationally in the way indicated earlier. Among unmarried older women in 1969, those who have worked in jobs not covered are either in professional, managerial, or clerical jobs (38 percent) or in private household or other service work (29 percent). Among wives in 1969, the distribution is 46 percent in the three higher-status categories and 19 percent in the lower.

In Tables 2.2 and 2.3, the average characteristics of unmarried women and wives are reported separately by midlife labor status patterns. The midlife patterns include those "usually in" the labor force between 1955 and 1969 (having worked under Social Security three or more quarters per year since 1955); those "usually out" (having worked less than one quarter per year since 1955); those "in-and-out" of covered work (having worked between one and three quarters annually since 1955); and finally

**TABLE 2.1  Major Variables for Unmarried and Married Women in LRHS (1969)**

| Variable | Description | Source[a] |
|---|---|---|
| Age | Age in 1969<br>Unmarried women and husbands = 58 to 63<br>Wives = 24 to 80 | LRHS |
| Race | White = 1<br>Other = 0 | LRHS |
| Years of Education | Range = 0 to 18 years,<br>with 18 years including all graduate degrees | LRHS |
| Number of Children | Total number of children ever had by women, reported in 1971<br>Unmarried women = 0 to 10<br>Wives = 0 to 10 | |
| First Job After 35 | Self-reported age of first full time job<br>After Age 35 = 1<br>Age 35 or younger = 0 | LRHS |
| Average Annual Quarters Worked Under Social Security | Total Quarters Worked Under Social Security in three periods divided by 5: 1955-59, 1960-64, 1965-69 | ER |

*Midlife Labor Status (1955-69)*

| | | |
|---|---|---|
| 1. Usually in Labor Force | Worked three or more quarters annually in 1955-1959, 1960-64, and 1965-69 in jobs covered by Social Security | ER |
| 2. In and Out of Labor Force | Worked between one and three quarters annually in 1955-59, 1960-64, and 1965-69 in jobs covered by Social Security | ER |
| 3. Usually Out of Labor Force | Worked less than one quarter annually in 1955-59, 1960-64, and 1965-69 in jobs covered by Social Security | ER |
| 4. Worked between 1955 and 1969, but in jobs not covered by Social Security | Zero quarters covered by Social Security between 1955 and 1969, but self-report of current and/or previous job during this period | ER & LRHS |
| SEI Last Job | Duncan SEI score of major occupational grouping of 1969 occupation of current workers or previous occupation of nonworkers in 1969: range = 7 to 75. Included also is a dummy variable equal to 1 if the woman did not report an occupation | LRHS |
| Last Job in Favorable Pension Industry | Industrial sector location of last job reported by respondent | LRHS |
| | Favorable Industry = 1, if last job in public administration; manufacturing; communication; transportation and public utilities; finance, insurance and real estate; or professional and related services | |
| | Favorable Industry = 0, if last job in mining; construction; wholesale, or retail trade; entertainment and recreation; or other services | |

*(continued)*

**TABLE 2.1** Major Variables for Unmarried and Married Women in LRHS (1969) (continued)

| Variable | Description | Source[a] |
|---|---|---|
| Widowed in 1969 (unmarried women only) | Widowed in 1969 = 1<br>Other = 0 | LRHS |
| Retirement Income | Estimated annual retirement income based on respondent's calculated Social Security benefit at age 65 *plus* expected annual pension income from private and/or government pensions. For wives, Social Security benefit based on 1.5 times of husband's benefit at age 65 or the sum of husband's and wife's retired worker benefits, whichever is greater | |

a. Source abbreviations are: LRHS Longitudinal Retirement History Study; ER Earning Record. Data sources are discussed in the text.

32

**TABLE 2.2  Means of Background, Work History, and Preretirement Characteristics Among Unmarried Older Women, By Midlife Labor Status Patterns (1955-1969)**

| | All Unmarried Women (N = 2873) | Midlife Labor Status Patterns Under Social Security | | | Worked in Jobs Not Covered by Social Security (N = 389) |
|---|---|---|---|---|---|
| | | Usually In (N = 1322) | In and Out (N = 528) | Usually Out (N = 734) | |
| Age in 1969 | 60.6 | 60.5 | 60.6 | 60.6 | 60.8 |
| Race (White) | 86.1 | 88.6 | 86.8 | 83.7 | 83.1 |
| Years Education | 9.8 | 10.4 | 10.0 | 8.5 | 9.8 |
| Number of Children | 2.1 | 1.6 | 2.0 | 2.7 | 2.4 |
| First FT Job After Age 35 | 13.5 | 14.6 | 18.2 | 10.6 | 10.4 |
| Ave Ann Qrts Worked, 1955-59[a] | 1.8 | 3.4 | 1.8 | .3 | 0 |
| Ave Ann Qrts Worked, 1960-64[a] | 1.9 | 3.8 | 1.1 | .2 | 0 |
| Ave Ann Qrts Worked, 1965-69[a] | 1.9 | 3.5 | 1.5 | .4 | 0 |
| SEI Last Job[b] | 34.6 | 37.9 | 30.6 | 30.5 | 34.4 |
| Last Job in Favorable Pension Industry | 49.7 | 62.2 | 48.6 | 30.6 | 50.3 |
| Widowed in 1969 | 63.6 | 55.9 | 64.3 | 70.3 | 71.2 |
| Estimated Annual Retirement Income from Social Security and Priv/Govt Pensions | 1886.1 | 2369.5 | 1697.1 | 1367.6 | 1724.9 |

a. Average annual quarters worked under Social Security coverage for each five-year period.
b. Based only on those cases with occupations reported for current or previous job.

**TABLE 2.3** Means of Background, Work History, and Preretirement Characteristics Among Older Wives, By Midlife Labor Status Patterns (1955-1969)

| | All Wives (N = 6411) | Midlife Labor Status Patterns Under Social Security | | | Worked in Jobs Not Covered by Social Security (N = 1493) |
|---|---|---|---|---|---|
| | | Usually In (N = 1709) | In and Out (N = 1180) | Usually Out (N = 2029) | |
| *Wife's Characteristics* | | | | | |
| Age in 1969 | 56.3 | 55.8 | 55.6 | 56.2 | 57.4 |
| Race (White) | 91.8 | 92.4 | 90.0 | 91.3 | 93.2 |
| Years Education | 10.4 | 10.8 | 10.4 | 9.8 | 10.7 |
| Number of Children | 2.6 | 2.3 | 2.7 | 3.0 | 2.5 |
| First FT Job After Age 35 | 3.8 | 5.6 | 6.9 | 2.4 | 1.3 |
| Ave Ann Qrts Worked, 1955-59[a] | 1.2 | 3.1 | 1.7 | .3 | 0 |
| Ave Ann Qrts Worked, 1960-64[a] | 1.4 | 3.8 | 1.7 | .2 | 0 |
| Ave Ann Qrts Worked, 1965-69[a] | 1.4 | 3.4 | 2.1 | .3 | 0 |
| SEI Last Job | 35.6 | 37.2 | 33.7 | 33.4 | 36.9 |
| Last Job in Favorable Pension Industry | 48.1 | 64.7 | 49.9 | 26.7 | 56.5 |

*Husband's Characteristics*

| | | | | | |
|---|---|---|---|---|---|
| Age in 1969 | 60.3 | 60.3 | 60.3 | 60.4 | 60.4 |
| Years Education | 10.0 | 10.2 | 9.8 | 9.5 | 10.6 |
| SEI Last Job | 35.9 | 34.2 | 35.0 | 34.4 | 40.8 |
| Last Job in Favorable Pension Industry | 61.7 | 65.9 | 59.5 | 58.0 | 63.6 |
| *Couple's Estimated Annual Retirement Income from Social Security and Priv/Govt Pension* | 4763.2 | 5338.1 | 4464.4 | 4330.9 | 4928.7 |

a. Average annual quarters worked under Social Security coverage for each five-year period.
b. Based only on those cases with occupations reported for current or previous job.

"uncovered workers." Among unmarried women (Table 2.2), continuous workers under Social Security (column two) and workers in jobs outside the Social Security system (column five) tend to have higher-status jobs, to be in more favorable pension industries, and to expect higher annual retirement incomes from their work.

Workers with discontinuous patterns under Social Security (column three), on the other hand, have lower-status jobs and lower expected retirement incomes from their work, though the difference between discontinuous workers and noncovered workers is not large. In addition, discontinuous workers are the most likely of all four groups to have entered the full-time labor force at midlife; nearly one-fifth of these workers (18.2 percent) began their first full-time jobs after the age of 35. The reasons for this probably include early childbearing or midlife marital status changes, such as divorce or widowhood. While these women appear to have higher education levels and fewer children on the average than women who usually never work (column four), they do not achieve higher-status jobs.

Among wives (Table 2.3), the patterns are approximately the same as those among unmarried women, although as a group wives are slightly less attached to work, and the average expected retirement income of couples is more than twice that of unmarried women. Continuous workers under Social Security (column two) and workers outside the Social Security system (column five) have higher-status jobs before retirement, are likely to be located in favorable pension industries, and can expect higher pension incomes. However, the preretirement income status of wives cannot be separated from their husband's work-related characteristics. Accordingly, these are included in Table 2.3. Interestingly, husbands and wives tend to be similar to each other in the distributions of education and SEI of last job, but husbands are generally more favorably located in pension programs. This is probably due to their more typical work careers. But couples appear to benefit by wives' continuous work or their location in favorable employment outside the system. The couples with the highest average expected retirement income fall into the two latter groups (columns two and five).

## THE DETERMINANTS OF PRERETIREMENT EXPECTED INCOME

### UNMARRIED WOMEN

The importance of occupation, industrial location, and life-span labor patterns in the determination of retirement income from work is described in Tables 2.4 and 2.5, where unstandardized multiple regression coefficients of major life-span variables are reported. A regression coefficient is the estimated difference in income (expressed in dollars) between two persons who differ by one unit on the particular variable being considered but who are otherwise identical.

The effects for women who were unmarried in 1969 are reported in the equations of Table 2.4. Generally, early work history and preretirement occupational location variables have significant effects on retirement income levels. Years of education and number of children have persistent effects on retirement income levels in all three equations, though these effects decline in magnitude as work history and preretirement status variables are introduced. In equation three, with all variables in the model, the net effect of each year of education is approximately $46 in retirement income annually, while each additional child leads to a decline in annual retirement income of $36.

The coefficients for midlife status patterns represent the differences between each pattern reported and the continuous or "usually in" pattern. In equations two and three, continuous work and uncovered work both yield higher retirement incomes than the interrupted and nonwork patterns. Women with interrupted employment can expect $666 less and nonworkers $577 less than those following the "usually in" pattern under Social Security. In the uncovered group, income is wholly accounted for by non-Social Security sources; on average, these women will receive $445 less per year than continuous workers under Social Security. In short, women following the continuous pattern of work during midlife find themselves with an advantage on the threshold of retirement.

Furthermore, late career entry continues to have a negative effect on expected income even after the effects of children and midlife patterns of continuity are introduced. Starting full-time work after the age of 35 reduces annual retirement income by $142. Thus, timing as well as continuity has an impact on womens' retirement income levels. Late starts penalize women, probably by making them "off-time" in pension vesting and, perhaps, as a result of age discrimination.

The final three preretirement status variables in Table 2.4 also have significant net effects on retirement income. Each increment in socioeconomic status of last job among workers makes a difference of $18 in annual retirement income. Location in a favorable pension industry approaches the pattern of continuous labor force status in the magnitude of its effect on income; being in a favorable sector increases income by $571 per year. Finally, widowed status in 1969 decreases income by $171 per year. This effect may represent the unmeasured effects of lifetime patterns of interrupted work. However, widows are more likely to be

**TABLE 2.4  Determinants of the Level of Retirement Income Among Unmarried Women in 1969**

| Independent Variables | (1) b | s.e. | (2) b | s.e. | (3) b | s.e |
|---|---|---|---|---|---|---|
| Age in 1969 | -13.63 | 15.75 | -9.02 | 15.22 | -1.88 | 14.50 |
| Race (White) | 264.63** | 81.03 | 274.91** | 78.48 | 57.56 | 76.28 |
| Years of Education | 134.56** | 8.19 | 117.38** | 8.07 | 46.22** | 9.25 |
| Number of Children | -83.03** | 12.07 | -56.06** | 11.90 | -36.29 | 11.58 |
| First FT Job After 35 | | | 278.03** | 74.09 | -142.48* | 71.88 |
| Midlife Labor Status Pattern[a] | | | | | | |
| In and Out of Labor Force | | | -828.65** | 72.53 | -666.72** | 69.58 |
| Usually Out of Labor Force | | | -731.85** | 68.78 | -577.47** | 71.33 |
| Worked, No Social Security Coverage | | | -481.01** | 82.30 | -445.23** | 78.44 |
| SEI Last Job[b] | | | | | 18.35** | 1.64 |
| Last Job in Favorable Pension Industry | | | | | 571.09** | 54.43 |
| Widowed in 1969 | | | | | -171.02** | 53.77 |
| Intercept | 1402.42 | | 1655.81 | | 1171.70 | |
| R$^2$ | .150 | | .211 | | .289 | |
| (N) | (2603) | | (2602) | | (2602) | |

a. Omitted category consists of women Usually In the Labor Force working under Social Security between 1955 and 1969 (incl.).
*p < .05; **p < .01

b. This coefficient is only for women who report an occupation, though other coefficients in the equation include nonworkers as well. For a description of the technique involved, see Cohen and Cohen (1975: 274-288). The arbitrary dummy coefficient is not reported.

dependent on their deceased husband's resources for retirement than on their own work-related resources, and some of these resources, particularly Social Security benefits based on the deceased husband's work record instead of the widow's record, are not reflected in the retirement income measures.

## MARRIED WOMEN

Table 2.5 reports the effects of both wives' and husbands' characteristics on the expected retirement incomes of older couples. Three equations summarize the effects of wives' background, work history, and husband's characteristics. Table 2.5 shows a persistent net effect of education level of wives on final retirement income in all three equations. However, race has a larger persistent effect among wives than among unmarried women. This race effect may be largely attributable to the husbands' rather than the wives' work-related experience. Still, in equation three, couples' retirement income is $409 higher for whites.

Starting the first full-time job after age 35 has a persistent negative effect on income, even net of husbands' characteristics. A wife's late entry into full-time work costs the retired couple an estimated $411 per year in the third equation. The midlife labor force status variables show the same pattern among wives as among unmarried women. Compared to wives who are "usually in" the labor force, wives with an "in-and-out" pattern have a family retirement income that, on average, is predicted to be $667 lower. Wives who are "usually out" have average retirement incomes $610 lower.

The contrast between being in uncovered employment versus the "usually in" pattern under Social Security yields a similar effect to that observed among unmarried women. Workers in jobs not covered by Social Security have retirement incomes $419 lower than those following the interrupted pattern.

Wife's SEI in last job increases annual income significantly; each increment in SEI yields a $9 increase in retirement income. Also, location in a favorable pension industry by wives increases income by an average of $374 for couples. Finally, all four of husbands' characteristics introduced in equation three have significant effects on income, with the most significant being location in a favorable pension industry prior to retirement. Husbands in favorable pension industries contribute an average of $1035 more annually to retirement income from work than those less advantageously situated.

**TABLE 2.5  Determinants of the Level of Retirement Income Among Wives in 1969**

| | (1) b | (1) s.e. | (2) b | (2) s.e. | (3) b | (3) s.e. |
|---|---|---|---|---|---|---|
| *Wife's Characteristics* | | | | | | |
| Age in 1969 | 3.68 | 6.27 | 3.16 | 6.25 | 1.45 | 6.31 |
| Race (White) | 762.57** | 127.38 | 672.92** | 126.33 | 409.33 | 123.22 |
| Years of Education | 232.20** | 11.36 | 176.85** | 13.30 | 69.26** | 15.03 |
| Number of Children | −67.98** | 16.26 | −42.71** | 16.20 | −21.81 | 15.73 |
| First FT Job After Age 35 | | | −611.16** | 171.81 | −411.18* | 166.12 |
| Midlife Labor Status Pattern[a] | | | | | | |
| In and Out of Labor Force | | | −684.14** | 103.71 | −667.55** | 100.19 |
| Usually Out of Labor Force | | | −601.25** | 102.95 | −610.44** | 99.62 |
| Worked, No Social Security Coverage | | | −325.06** | 97.48 | −419.48** | 95.00 |
| SEI Last Job[b] | | | 11.48** | 2.29 | 9.39** | 2.25 |
| Last Job in Favorable Pension Industry | | | 528.46** | 75.97 | 374.86** | 74.05 |

*Husband's Characteristics*

| | | | |
|---|---|---|---|
| Age in 1969 | | | −60.75** 20.01 |
| Years of Education | | | 120.20** 12.89 |
| SEI Last Job | | | 8.91** 2.03 |
| Last Job in Favorable Pension Industry | | | 1035.17** 69.23 |
| | | | |
| Intercept | 1733.85 | 2110.53 | 5180.50 |
| $R^2$ | .095 | .124 | .185 |
| (N) | (5716) | (5716) | (5671) |

a. Omitted category consists of women Usually In the Labor Force working under Social Security between 1955 and 1969 (incl.).

*p < .05 **p < .01

b. This coefficient is only for women who report an occupation, though other coefficients in the equation include nonworkers as well. For a description of the technique involved, see Cohen and Cohen (1975: 274-288). The arbitrary dummy coefficient is not reported.

The results of the analysis are very similar for unmarried women and wives. Discontinuous work throughout life, a late age at first job, and industrial location have important and large effects on expected retirement income. In the case of unmarried women, disadvantage on one of these factors may be very serious, since their average expected income is very low. The problem is not so severe for married women, yet their work histories can have a surprisingly large effect on the couple's retirement income.

## POLICY IMPLICATIONS

Zero-population-growth societies characterized by low fertility and increased longevity face special problems of dependency among the elderly. The trend toward extending the legal age of retirement beyond 65 is a direct effort to confront this problem. As such, it is not by accident that private and public pension structures and transfer payment programs are coming under increased scrutiny. Part of this examination will require a better understanding of the relationship between diverse individual lifetime patterns of work and the public and private structures of retirement funding. This will necessarily involve an emphasis on women's lifetime work patterns and pension status, since this segment of the population is increasing its labor force attachment across the life cycle and maintaining a dominant role as the numerical majority in older populations. Both these trends among women have gone unanticipated by pension structures and must now be addressed.

Older women are a heterogeneous group. They vary by marital status, though most will survive to widowhood in later life, and by family and work history. Early work pattern has an important effect on expected retirement income, as do midlife and late life occupational patterns and industrial locations. For both unmarried women and wives, starting work after age 35 and being in a favorable pension industry have important effects on expected retirement income. In addition, continuity of work has an important effect on retirement income for both groups.

The policy implications of these findings relate primarily to unmarried older women, since the greatest incidence of poverty among the aged is found among this group. Indeed, nearly three-quarters of the elderly poor are unmarried women (President's Commission on Pension Policy, 1980). The analysis presented here traces part of that problem to the work histories of these women. There are, of course, other causes of poverty among older unmarried women, such as lack of survivor benefits in deceased husbands' pensions, and the longevity of women. Yet at least part of the problem lies in the nature of their work histories and career opportunities. In addition to intermittent work, these work histories have several other important characteristics. Presence in certain industries and occupations, lack of pension coverage, low wages, and midlife career entry are some of them. Together, they lead to lower retirement incomes. The related policy questions deal with ways of alleviating these problems.

Some changes that have occurred over the past several years may in time help alleviate the problems of older unmarried women. The Employee Retirement Income Security Act of 1974 (ERISA) provides for some minimum survivor benefits in private pensions (Schulz, 1980). Recent changes that allow persons covered under other pensions to save for retirement in Individual Retirement Accounts (IRAs) will also help workers who ordinarily might have been covered by a private pension but who will never receive retirement income from it. However, many women are in low-wage jobs, and the evidence until now is that only those with high incomes have utilized IRAs very extensively (President's Commission on Pension Policy, 1980). Therefore, changes in the IRA program may have little effect on single women.

In addition to these recent changes, current Social Security law favors those with low income in that they receive higher replacement rates. That is, their Social Security benefits are a higher percentage of their preretirement earnings than is true for higher wage earners. This higher replacement rate, however, may mean a very low dollar benefit. However, further increases in benefits for these low-income workers relative to other workers are not likely.

Possible policies can be divided into short-range and long-range ones. Short-range policies include greater income support for older women who have already completed their careers. In the long run, better pension coverage and better job opportunities for women should lead to higher retirement incomes. However, even then it must be remembered that, to a great extent, intermittent work patterns are required of women in order to have time to devote to their families. While more recent cohorts may have fewer interruptions in their work, these problems will remain. For unmarried women who have been divorced, the President's Commission on Pension Policy (1980) suggests one solution: the splitting of Social Security "credits" in families, with half going to the husband and half going to the wife. This or a similar solution would help update Social Security's treatment of the family, but the size and persistence of the problem of intermittent careers among women, as well as the amount of poverty among unmarried older women, suggest that the problem of income support will not easily be solved.

# 3

# LIFE SATISFACTION AMONG
# AGING WOMEN: A CAUSAL MODEL

## Carol Cutler Riddick

**Since older women,** who are or have been employed, occupy a unique status in society, one might wonder how well these individuals have adjusted to work and nonwork—or leisure—roles. Efforts have been directed at ascertaining the satisfaction older persons experience in their lives and the possible factors that might account for the level of feeling expressed (Larson, 1978). However, for a variety of reasons, most of the previous research is inadequate.

One problem with a bulk of the past studies is that the life satisfaction of older females simply has not been studied. Many sampling designs have omitted older females altogether. Furthermore, in the few studies allegedly examining the life satisfaction of males and females, older female workers or ex-workers have been ignored for the most part. Instead, the norm has been to compare mean differences in adjustment scores of female home-makers to employed or retired males. In short, these studies reveal nothing specific about older females who are employed or retired from the labor force. It is unclear whether older women who have a history of labor force

AUTHOR'S NOTE: This research was supported by Sigma Kappa sorority. The data used in this study were made available in part by the Inter-University Consortium for Political and Social Research. The data were originally collected under funding provided by the National Council on Aging. Neither the original source or collectors of the data nor the Consortium bear any responsibility for the analyses or interpretations presented here.

involvement share similar backgrounds, experiences, and attitudes when compared to female homemakers or employed males.

In summary, the external validity of studies focusing on working men or homemakers is limited. The concern evolves around the soundness of extending generalizations about one group (employed males or female homemakers) to another group (older females with working experience outside the home). It remains to be seen if the patterns of relationships responsible for the life satisfaction of working men or female homemakers are similar to those for working and retired women.

Moreover, much of the research conducted up to and through the 1970s tends to oversimplify relationships among life satisfaction determinants. Typically, relationships have been examined by using bivariate analyses. The problem with this approach is that no controls are exerted in order to measure the influence of other relevant variables on life satisfaction. Even when the research design has used a multivariate analysis approach, typically the interrelationships among the correlates have been left unspecified.

One purpose of this chapter is to suggest a theoretical model, based on the literature, for the life satisfaction of older females with labor force backgrounds. As noted earlier, this is a particular age, gender, and occupational group overlooked in past research. The second purpose of this chapter will be to examine the efficacy of the proposed model. In order to overcome analytical shortcomings found in some of the previous life satisfaction research, the path analysis technique (Duncan, 1966) will be used in testing the proposed model. This technique seems appropriate for the task at hand. Basically, it enables one to: (a) verify a proposed causal flow of events leading to life satisfaction, and (b) determine the independent effect of variables (specified in the model) on life satisfaction.

## RATIONALE FOR VARIABLE SELECTION AND REVIEW OF LITERATURE

One approach for selecting variables that could contribute to the understanding and explaining of life satisfaction is to concentrate on those which are "mutable." Mutability refers to the extent to which a factor has the potential for being altered to influence the key dependent variable under study. In other words, a mutable factor is one which is changeable. This concept of mutability provides a criterion for identifying policy-relevant variables. To show that factors amenable to intervention affect life satisfaction is to provide policymakers with directly applicable guidelines for intervention.

In contrast, some variables can be termed "immutable" or nonchangeable. Using this framework, examples of immutable variables are age, gender, marital status, and racial status. Some variables (such as age) are considered immutable because nature prevents them from being considered alterable by policymakers. Other variables (for instance, marital status) may be categorized immutable because social mores would inhibit any attempts by policymakers to change the "natural state of affairs." Still other variables are immutable for natural and social reasons. For example, suppose hair color was reported as being related to life satisfaction. From a social policy perspective, hair color would have to be considered an immutable variable. In other words, it would be ludicrous to advocate, as a means for improving the psychological well-being of the nation, that everyone in the country have the same color hair!

Using the mutability criterion, the correlates chosen for inclusion in the review are: employment status; perceived health problems; income; transportation barriers; and the leisure roles of friendship interactions, voluntary association affiliations, and solitary recreational activities. In addition to being mutable, from a social change perspective many of these chosen variables have previously been correlated to life satisfaction. For instance, Larson (1978), after reviewing 30 years of gerontological research, pointed out that health, socioeconomic status, and activity have consistently been related to well-being.

## EMPLOYMENT STATUS

Findings from studies examining the effects of retirement suggest that separation from work is not a smooth, trouble-free transition. Thompson (1973) reported that the variations in morale of male workers versus male retirees could be explained almost entirely by systematic differences in the two groups' income, health, and age. Fox (1977) also reported that the lower psychological well-being of female retirees relative to female workers was attributable to lower income, subjective health status, and perceived level of social contact of retirees. Similarily, Hoyt et al. (1980) found that after controlling for the independent effects of health and socioeconomic status, retirement was an insignificant factor on the life satisfaction of Midwesterners.

Conversely, Jaslow (1976), controlling for the significant differences existing between employed and retired females in regard to age, income, and health, found that employed women still had significantly higher morale than female retirees. However, this situation reversed itself among women with annual incomes of $5000 or more; that is, in this income group retirees had better morale than workers. Elwell and Maltbie-Crannell (1981), controlling for a number of variables including health and income, found that role loss (as measured in part by having undergone retirement) had a direct negative effect on the life satisfaction of older women.

## HEALTH PROBLEMS

Perceived health status has been positively linked to adjustment in old age (Sauer, 1975; Bild and Havighurst, 1976; Cutler, 1975; Zeglen, 1976; Hawkins, 1976; Fox, 1977; and Palmore and Kivett, 1977). Several analyses (Medley, 1976; Markides and Martin, 1979; Shapiro et al., 1980; Hoyt et al., 1980; Elwell and Maltbie-Crannell, 1981) have been designed to control for the influence of socioeconomic status and found that a positive relationship emerged between reported good health and adjustment. In contrast, Kutner et al. (1956) and Bultena (1969) reported that self-defined poor health had a greater negative impact on the well-being of older persons of lower socioeconomic status than on those of higher socioeconomic status.

## INCOME

With a few exceptions, studies have found that the income of older persons positively affects subjective well-being. This association has been maintained when the relationship was evaluated simultaneously with control variables such as health status, social contacts, gender, and age (Edwards and Klemmack, 1973; Fox, 1977; Chatfield, 1975; Medley, 1976; Hoyt et al., 1980; Shapiro et al., 1980).

In contrast, Hutchison (1975) reported no significant relationship between income and life satisfaction among low-income urbanites. Furthermore, Markides and Martin (1979), Liang et al. (1980), and Elwell and Maltbie-Crannell (1981), when examining the causal order of variables, found that income had no significant direct effect on life satisfaction.

## TRANSPORTATION BARRIERS

The few investigations conducted on the relationship between transportation availability and adjustment suggest that transportation affects quality of life. In one set of studies, Cutler (1972) reported that availability of personal transportation was associated with higher life satisfaction among older residents of a rural community. Developing his pioneer work further, Cutler (1975) conducted a longitudinal analysis on the relationship between the availability of personal transportation and changes in life satisfaction. After simultaneously controlling for a number of variables, it was found that individuals experiencing transportation problems had low life satisfaction scores. Holley (1978), too, found that transportation availability was linked to life satisfaction.

## FRIENDSHIP INTERACTIONS

No clear pattern emerges as to the overall effects of friendship interactions on well-being. Some studies (Havens, 1968; Graney, 1971; Hawkins, 1976; Elwell and Maltbie-Crannell, 1981) have reported a significant positive relationship between these two variables. Indeed, Elwell and Maltbie-Crannell (1981) found that role loss (which included retirement) indirectly affected life satisfaction due to a negative effect on friendship interactions. Different investigators (Palmore and Luikart, 1972; Lemon et al., 1972; Rosen, 1973; Edwards and Klemmack, 1973; Sauer, 1975; Hoyt et al., 1980; Shapiro et al., 1980) have found no significant relationship between friendship interactions and morale.

Others have suggested that a more complex relationship exists between friendship interactions and adjustment. Smith and Lipman (1972) reported a significant positive relationship between peer contacts and life satisfaction for individuals experiencing health and financial constraints. Along the same lines, Kutner et al. (1956) also found that social contacts had a positive and significant relationship on the morale of individuals with low socioeconomic status.

## VOLUNTARY ASSOCIATION AFFILIATION

In general, most of the research conducted on the relationship between well-being and involvement in voluntary association affiliations reports these two variables as being positively related (Zibbell, 1971; Graney, 1971; Hawkins, 1976; Hoyt et al., 1980). Elwell and Maltbie-Crannell (1981) concluded that voluntary service activities were significantly and positively correlated with the life satisfaction of older women. On the other hand, several other investigators (Lemon et al., 1972; Cutler, 1973; Edwards and Klemmack, 1973; Bull and Aucoin, 1975) have suggested that participation in voluntary associations has a much weaker relation to well-being when controls for health and socioeconomic status are introduced.

Some researchers have investigated how factors indirectly affect life satisfaction through organizational activity. Markides and Martin (1979) found that income was indirectly and positively related to life satisfaction by means of an activity measure that included, among other things, participation in formal organizations. In regard to employment status, Elwell and Maltbie-Crannell (1981) reported that role loss (which was measured in part by recent retirement) had no indirect effect on life satisfaction via participation in formal organizations. In contrast, Videback and Knox (1965) reported that retirement tended to produce increased participation in voluntary associations.

## SOLITARY RECREATIONAL ACTIVITY

Overall, there appears to be a link between recreational activity pursuits and adjustment. For example, Maddox and Eisdorfer (1962), as well as Zibbell (1971), reported a positive relationship between "activity level" (which included specific recreational activities) and life satisfaction of the elderly. Markides and Martin (1979) found that activity emerged as a strong predictor of life satisfaction among a low-income, elderly, female sample. Palmore and Kivett (1977) also found a positive association between participation in solitary recreational activities and well-being. By the same token, Sears (1975) recorded a significant positive relationship between participation in solitary recreational activities (e.g., television viewing, radio listening) and life satisfaction.

A handful of studies have identified either a negative or no relationship between recreational activity and life satisfaction. Filsinger and Sauer (1978) found that poorly adjusting females were more likely to engage in the informal activities of "18 behaviors such as taking walks, watching television, or going to the movies" than moderately adjusting females. At least one study (Hoyt et al., 1980) found no significant correlation between solitary activity participation and life satisfaction.

## LIFE SATISFACTION MODEL OF OLDER WOMEN
## WITH LABOR FORCE EXPERIENCE

The life satisfaction model underlying this study is based largely on the preceding literature review and is depicted in Figure 3.1. It is assumed that employment and participation in leisure roles by older females are ante-cedent to rather than the consequence of life satisfaction.

Employment status, health, income, and transportation barriers are considered as mutable, exogenous (or predictor) variables that have a direct effect on the endogenous (i.e., dependent) variable, life satisfaction, as well as an indirect effect via their influence on the intervening and endogenous variable, leisure roles. In other words, it is hypothesized that employment status, health problems, income, and transportation barriers influence life satisfaction indirectly through leisure roles, as well as di-rectly by their effects on life satisfaction.

## METHODS

### SAMPLE

The data used in this study are from a survey consisting of five separate national samples, each designed to draw representative groupings from the total U.S. population. One sample was drawn from persons 18 years of age and over; three samples were drawn from among persons 65 years and over; and another sample was drawn from blacks 65 years and over (Harris and Associates, 1975). The survey was conducted during June and July, 1974, under commission by the National Council of Aging.

The criteria for inclusion of a respondent from the Harris survey in the present study were these: the individual was a female, either employed or retired from the labor force, 65 years of age or older, and not residing in an institution. The women in the sample were distributed among the age groups in about the same pattern found in the American population (U.S. Bureau of the Census, 1973). The sample was divided among the following age categories: 39 percent were 65-69 years old, 28 percent were 70-74 years old, 17 percent were 75-79 years old, and 16 percent were 80 years and older. Furthermore, approximately 12 percent of the total sample were employed in the labor force at the time of the study, compared to the 10 percent national older women (i.e., 65 years and older) employ-ment rate (U.S. Bureau of the Census, 1974).

### PROFILE OF THE SAMPLE

A majority of the 753 sampled women reported that health was either a "somewhat serious problem" or a "very serious problem." In addition,

TABLE 3.1    Demographic Characteristics of the Sample

| Demographic Characteristic | No. (N = 753) | % |
|---|---|---|
| *Extent Health is a Problem* | | |
| Hardly a problem | 60 | 8.0 |
| Somewhat serious problem | 358 | 47.5 |
| Very serious problem | 355 | 44.5 |
| *Income* | | |
| $2,999 or below | 269 | 35.7 |
| $3,000 − $6,999 | 305 | 40.6 |
| $7,000 and over | 179 | 23.7 |
| *Extent Public Transportation is a Problem* | | |
| Hardly a problem | 191 | 25.4 |
| Somewhat serious problem | 254 | 33.7 |
| Very serious problem | 308 | 40.9 |
| *Time Spent Socializing with Friends* | | |
| Hardly any | 91 | 12.1 |
| Some but not a lot | 274 | 36.4 |
| A lot | 388 | 51.5 |
| *Time Spent Reading* | | |
| Hardly any | 185 | 24.6 |
| Some but not a lot | 274 | 36.4 |
| A lot | 294 | 39.0 |
| *Participation in Voluntary Associations* | | |
| Hardly any | 426 | 56.6 |
| Some but not a lot | 170 | 22.6 |
| A lot | 157 | 20.8 |

approximately three-quarters of the surveyed older women reported a total annual household income falling in the "$6,999 or less" category. Roughly 75 percent of the queried group viewed public transportation as being "somewhat to a very serious problem."

In regard to leisure role pursuits, approximately one-half of the interviewed women spent "a lot" of time socializing with their friends. When examining time devoted to a solitary recreational activity, most of the sampled group reported that they had spent "some" to "a lot" of time reading. In contrast, the majority of the sample reported participating very little in voluntary associations (Table 3.1).

INSTRUMENTATION

Life satisfaction was measured by the 18-item version (Wood et al., 1969) of the life satisfaction index originally proposed by Neugarten and Havighurst (1961). Scoring procedures allow two points for each response in agreement with a positive statement or disagreement with a negative statement, one point for each "not sure" response, and zero for each disagreement response with a positive statement or agreement with a negative statement. Wylie (1970) reported this scale as having relatively high validity and reliability.

Employment status was determined by response to the interview question: "What is your current employment status?" Those answering "employed full time," "employed part time," and "retired and employed part time" were classified as workers. Those who said they were retired were categorized as "retiree." This classification yielded 110 workers and 643 retirees.

Health problems were assessed by the respondent's answer to the question: "How serious a problem is your general health?" Similarly, transportation barriers confronted by the respondent were estimated from the answers given to the question: "How serious of a problem is not having buses or subways available for where you want to go?" Responses to the questions relating to perceived seriousness of health and transportation barriers were scored one to three, corresponding respectively to "hardly a problem at all," "somewhat serious problem," and a "very serious problem."

Income was based on the reported figure for the respondent's household. Scoring for household income ranged in valued from 1 to 11, corresponding to ordinal income categories beginning with "under $1,000" and ending with "$25,000 and over."

Leisure role activity regarding friendship interactions, solitary recreational activity, and voluntary association activity was sought by direct, simple questions: (1) "How much time do you personally spend socializing with friends?" (2) "How much time do you personally spend reading?" (3) "How much time do you personally spend participating in fraternal or community organizations or clubs?" Possible responses to these questions were: "hardly at all," "somewhat but not a lot," and "a lot." A response of "hardly at all" received a score of one, "somewhat but not a lot" was scored two, and "a lot" received a score of three. Theses three leisure activities showed intercorrelations for the total sample ranging from $r = .21$ to $r = .37$. Since parsimony would make the path analysis more readily interpretable, a Leisure Role Index was formed by summing the responses to the three questions. The coefficient alpha for this index was .53, suggesting some degree of internal consistency (Cronbach, 1951).

## ANALYTICAL PROCEDURES

Since the proposed model established causal priority among an array of variables, paths of direct as well as indirect influence were assessed by using the path analysis procedure (Duncan, 1966). Path analysis is a method that tests diagrammed temporal and cause-effect linkages for the specified variables. Arrows indicate direction of influence. Path coefficients (standardized partial regression coefficients) indicate the proportion of change in the dependent variable for which a predictor (i.e., independent) variable is responsible while simultaneously taking into account and controlling for all other specified variables. In addition, the indirect effect and joint association of each predictor variable on life satisfaction was calculated.

In performing path analysis, multiple regression equations must be solved, which requires the input of interval scaled data. The responses for questions measuring health problems, income, transportation barriers, and leisure pursuits were treated as interval in nature. Arguments for adjusting ordinal data to interval scaling have been set forth by Boyle (1970) and Labovitz (1967). The remaining independent variable, employment status, was entered into the regression equation using the method of dummy variables (Blalock, 1972). Life satisfaction was entered into the regression equation as interval-level data. In cases where missing values existed, the individual was eliminated from all calculations through listwise deletion procedures.

Once all the path coefficients in the model were calculated, some criterion for judging the utility of each path was needed. Heise (1969) refers to this approach as "theory trimming." Two kinds of criteria may be used in theory trimming: statistical significance and meaningfulness (Kerlinger and Pedhazur, 1973). As has been pointed out, the problem with a significance criterion is that minute path coefficients may occur when the analysis is based on fairly large samples (Kerlinger and Pedhazur, 1973: 318). Therefore, given the size of the present sample, the criterion of meaningfulness was adopted.

Meaningfulness involves establishing a particular criterion with regard to the absolute size of the standardized partial regression coefficient. In the absence of firmly rationalized guidelines, as is presently true, some researchers (for example, Land, 1969) recommend that path coefficients less than ±.05 be treated as not meaningful. Such a criterion was applied in this research. Thus, if the regression coefficient between an independent variable and a given dependent variable was equal to or greater than ±.05, the relationship was deemed noteworthy.

## FINDINGS

As evidenced by the coefficient of multiple determination ($R^2$), the entire set of antecedent variables accounted for 25 percent of the measured variation in the life satisfaction of older women (Figure 3.1). The coefficients shown in Figure 3.1 are path coefficients (standarized partial regression coefficients) and are also presented in Table 3.2 (see column B).

Of all the variables considered, leisure roles had the strongest positive relationship (b = .397) with life satisfaction. Women who were more active in their leisure pursuits were more likely than inactive women to experience greater satisfaction in their lives. Separate examination of each of the three leisure activities (components of the Leisure Roles Index) suggests that friendship interactions had the strongest association (r = .37) with life satisfaction, followed by reading activity (r = .30) and voluntary association participation (r = .26).

Reported health problems (b = −.142) and income (b = .124) also emerged as strong predictors of life satisfaction. The beta coefficients indicated that a lower incidence of health problems and an increase in income resulted in greater life satisfaction. Not surprisingly, income was correlated (r = −.14) with employment status. In other words, being employed was associated with a higher income level.

Furthermore, retirement status was negatively linked (b = −.089) to the life satisfaction of older women. Retired women had a mean life satisfaction score of 23.2; employed women had a mean life satisfaction score of 26.5. In addition, employment status had an intricate and summative effect on life satisfaction through a substantial joint association (Table 3.2, column D) with some of the other variables specified in the model.

Transportation barriers emerged as a meaningful but somewhat weak predictor (b = −.059) of life satisfaction. Unavailability of public transportation was associated with lower life satisfaction. When examining what contributes to public transportation barriers, health problems emerged as having a relatively strong positive correlation (r = .24). That is, a high level of health problems was related to the experiencing of transportation barriers, which in turn was related to a lowering in life satisfaction.

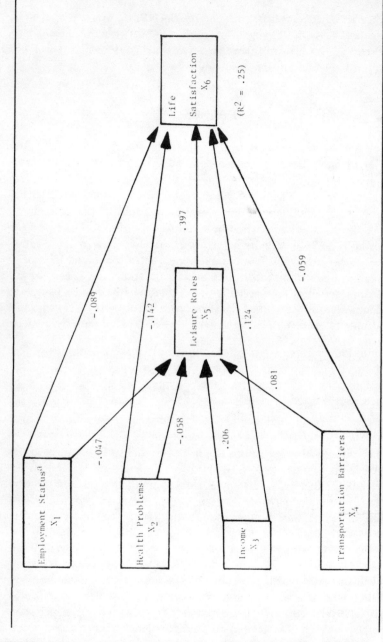

**Figure 3.1   Path Model on Life Satisfaction of Older Women (N = 753)**

a. Employment coded: 0 = employed; 1 = retired

**TABLE 3.2  Decomposition Table of the Effects of Variables**

| Relationship | Total Association[a] (A) | Direct Effect (B) | Indirect Effect (C) | Joint Association (D) |
|---|---|---|---|---|
| $X_6X_5$ | .435 | .397 | . . . | . . . |
| $X_6X_4$ | -.064 | -.059 | .032 | -.037 |
| $X_6X_3$ | .233 | .124 | .082 | .027 |
| $X_6X_2$ | -.195 | -.142 | -.023 | -.030 |
| $X_6X_1$ | -.146 | -.089 | -.019 | -.038 |
| $X_5X_4$ | .068 | .081 | . . . | -.013 |
| $X_5X_3$ | .217 | .206 | . . . | .011 |
| $X_5X_2$ | -.058 | -.058 | . . . | .000 |
| $X_5X_1$ | -.082 | -.047 | . . . | -.035 |

NOTE: $X_6$ = Life satisfaction; $X_5$ = Leisure roles; $X_4$ = Transportation barriers; $X_3$ = Income; $X_2$ = Health problems; $X_1$ = Employment status (coded 0 = employed, 1 = retired)

a. The correlation coefficient

In addition to their direct effects, the four exogenous predictor variables indirectly exerted, via leisure roles, varying levels of influence on life satisfaction. Among the four variables, income had the most indirect influence (.082) on life satisfaction (Table 3.2, column C). About one-third of the total influence of income (r = .23) on life satisfaction can be traced indirectly through leisure roles. In other words, income had a direct positive effect on life satisfaction and a substantial indirect positive effect through leisure roles.

A different pattern of relationships emerged between transportation barriers and the endogenous dependent variables. The total effect of transportation barriers (r = -.06) on life satisfaction was derived from its direct effect (b = -.059), its indirect effect via leisure roles (.032), and its joint association with other exogeneous predictor variables (-.037). Although transportation barriers had a direct negative effect on life satisfaction, this variable had a slight indirect positive effect on life satisfaction via leisure roles.

Health problems had a small indirect negative effect (-.023). Not surprisingly, a negative relationship existed between health problems and leisure roles (b = -.058). That is, as the incidence of health problems went up, leisure role pursuits declined.

Employment status did not indirectly affect life satisfaction via leisure roles (-.019). This was due to employment status' direct relationship (b = -.047) with leisure roles. The direction of the relationship did suggest, however, that women who were employed were more active in leisure roles than those who were retired.

This latter finding, combined with other results, suggests that retired women are triply disadvantaged. First, retirees when contrasted to employed women had lower life satisfaction. Second, retirees had lower incomes than their employed counterparts. Third, a concomitant effect of retirement was a lower level of leisure activity.


## CONCLUSION

The findings of this study suggest that causal relationships among life satisfaction determinants are more complex than previous research indicated. Although life satisfaction has been the topic of numerous research undertakings, a review of the literature located no study that specifically examined the life satisfaction of older women with a labor force background while simultaneously controlling for the effects of leisure roles, employment status, health problems, income, and transportation barriers.

Leisure roles were the most important explanatory variable of older women's life satisfaction. A positive relationship existed between leisure roles and satisfaction with one's life. Health problems had the second most direct (negative) impact on life satisfaction. However, health problems had a small indirect negative effect via leisure roles. In contrast, income had a direct positive effect on life satisfaction and a sizable indirect positive effect via leisure roles. Apparently, income is one of the keys for permitting or preventing individuals from engaging in some leisure roles. Employment status, though not having much of an indirect effect on life satisfaction via leisure roles, had a significant direct effect on life satisfaction. Employed women were more likely than retired women to experience greater life satisfaction. Additionally, employment status exerted other influences on life satisfaction by its correlation with income (retirees' income was lower than the employed) and its joint association effect. Transportation barriers had a direct negative effect on life satisfaction, coupled with a slight indirect positive effect via leisure roles. It appears that older women do not necessarily need access to public transportation in order to socialize with friends, read, and participate in organizations and clubs.

Based on the findings presented here, the explanatory framework from which life satisfaction has been viewed needs to be examined. This expansion might proceed along several lines. Since the secondary data used for this study permitted neither the examination of the perceived importance of various leisure roles nor the impact of a variety of activities on life satisfaction, it may prove worthwhile to include these factors in future studies. Also, it is unclear whether or not activity in general or specific types of activities are linked to life satisfaction. Finally, it is essential to determine how well the model explains age, period, and cohort effects.

The findings have implications for public policy. Mutable or policy-relevant variables were selected for testing. The factors that appear to have the greatest impact on the life satisfaction of older women are leisure roles, health problems, income, employment status, and transportation barriers. Furthermore, the findings suggest that retired women are in triple jeopardy. Besides experiencing lower life satisfaction, retirees when compared to employed women tend to have a lower income. Retirees also appear to be less active in leisure role pursuits.

In conclusion, social policies in regard to activity programs for the elderly (e.g., senior centers), compulsory retirement, guaranteed income, national health insurance, and public mass transportation may act to influence the life satisfaction of older women. Consequently, national, state, and local policies addressing these issues appear to have considerable potential for reducing unhappiness and increasing satisfaction with one's life. In summary, decisionmakers should direct their attention on how best to meet the activity, health, financial, employment, and transportation needs of the older female population.

# 4

# EMPLOYMENT STATUS AND SOCIAL SUPPORT: THE EXPERIENCE OF THE MATURE WOMAN

## Charlene Depner and Berit Ingersoll

**Retirement is a life transition** that can be highly stressful. It is characterized by several changes—in status, income, and daily routine (Back, 1977; Donahue et al., 1960). Equally stressful is the fact that supportive relationships established within the job context may decline or need to be reformulated on a different basis after retirement (Back and Guptill, 1966; Elwell and Maltbie-Crannell, 1981; Mitchell, 1972; Stueve and Fischer, 1978). Research suggests that the social context in which retirement occurs has critical significance for the eventual adjustment of the retiree. That is, the retiree who has a rich network of social relationships will make the transition more smoothly.

It is our contention that the social support resources of women are affected by their labor force participation. That is, a woman's employment history will influence the kind of relationships she establishes and the forms of support that are exchanged within relationships. These structural and functional attributes of the support network may in turn affect her well-being in later life.

*AUTHORS' NOTE: This research was supported by the National Institute on Aging Research grant A60 1632-02. The authors wish to thank David Klingel for running the computer analyses and Toni Antonucci, Mary Lou Davis, Jim House, Robert Kahn, and Beth Spencer for reviewing earlier drafts of this manuscript.*

Social support theory views each individual as embedded in a network of social ties to significant others. Among the distinctive features of such networks are structural attributes (e.g., size), the kinds of relationships that make up the network (e.g., marriage, parenthood, friendship), and functions (i.e., the nature of interaction). This chapter investigates the social support networks of retired women. Specifically, we will examine network size, relationships, and functions of retired women in relation to retired men, employed women, and housewives.

Gerontological research has found that involvement in a supportive network can contribute to the aged person's sense of security, personal worth, and competence (Conner et al., 1979), as well as to life satisfaction (Bultena and Oyler, 1971; Graney, 1975; Lowenthal and Haven, 1968; Maddox, 1963; Markides and Martin, 1979; Pihlblad and Adams, 1972). Also, the presence of a close personal relationship can serve as a buffer against the effects of social losses which the elderly experience (Blau, 1973; Lowenthal and Haven, 1968). Although most of the social support literature is restricted to support that the individual receives from others, there is increasing awareness that it is of considerable importance that individuals have the opportunity to give as well as receive social support (Kuypers and Bengtson, 1973; Midlarsky and Suda, 1978).

Speculating about the distinctive features of the social support networks of retired women raises some interesting questions. Existing research evidence would lead us to suspect that women have larger, more supportive networks than men, but is this true only for traditional women who have invested themselves more exclusively in kinship bonds? When a woman enters the workforce, does she jeopardize kinship bonds? Does she form a greater range of relationships or is there no time available for relationships outside the time-pressured, job-family sphere? If she forms rewarding relationships with co-workers, are these ties severed with retirement? The following sections review the answers provided by existing data and theory on the social supports of retired women as compared to other groups.

## LITERATURE REVIEW

### RETIRED WOMEN VERSUS RETIRED MEN

The social support literature suggests that there may be differences in the kinds of social bonds retired men and women maintain, as well as in the ways in which important relationships function. Because the labor force experiences of men and women differ, their needs and opportunities for social relationships at home and on the job may also vary. Theoretical explanations for these differences have ranged from sex role socialization (Maccoby and Jacklin, 1974; Myerhoff, 1978; Powers and Bultena, 1976) to the different norms which operate in the social contexts of men and women (Bernard, 1981).

Men are characterized as having a wider circle of acquaintances than women, but fewer close relationships (Oxley, 1974). Further, researchers report that men often rely on one key relationship—usually their relationship with their spouse—as the source of confiding and as the nexus of a fuller range of social relationships (Keating and Cole, 1980; Lowenthal and Haven, 1968; Rossi, 1980).

In contrast, women's interactions tend to be more dyadic and intimate, and women seem to have more close personal relationships than men (Booth and Hess, 1974; Cantor, 1975; Depner and Ingersoll, 1980; Hess, 1979; Lowenthal et al., 1975; Powers and Bultena, 1976). Several studies show that women turn to mothers, sisters, and female friends for affection and intimate communication (Berardo, 1968; Blau, 1973; Longino and Lipman, 1981; Lopata, 1975; Lowenthal and Robinson, 1976; Myerhoff and Simic, 1978; Samuels, 1975). In a study of friendship among women aged 14 through 80, Candy et al. (1981) were struck by the consistency with which the function "intimacy-assistance" among female friendships was named. Myerhoff (1978) made similar observations concerning older adults in a Senior Center. She characterizes the women as "expressive leaders" who, in contrast to the men, are more intensely involved in personal interactions. The men seem much less connected. Accustomed to money as the typical medium of social exchange, they seem ill at ease within a social-emotional context.

In addition to gender-related differences in the likelihood that certain forms of social relationships will be established, important social losses are experienced by men and women at different points in the life span. Women are far more likely to enter retirement as widows. Whereas men may benefit from having a spouse who facilitates the retirement transition by helping to establish new routines and plan activities, women may suffer concomitantly from two major losses—the loss of a work role and the loss of a spouse. This brief review of the literature suggests that retired men and women will have differences in network structure, relationships, and function. This is one result of gender differences in the kinds of social bonds which are formed and in the timing of social losses.

RETIRED WOMEN VERSUS EMPLOYED WOMEN

Although women seem to have a more extensive range of supportive relationships, the loss of colleagues and business associates upon retiring may shrink the social support network. Employed women often mention people as a source of satisfaction on the job (Andrisani, 1978; Veroff et al., 1981). Levy (1980) concluded that one reason for women's reluctance to retire is that retirement involves the loss of work-based social ties and invokes the need to establish a new network outside the workplace. Indeed, Prentis's (1980) study of white-collar women shows that the greatest anticipated difficulty associated with retirement is the loss of friends and business peers. Women who identify their "real friends" as co-workers are most reluctant to retire (Jacobson, 1974).

Fox (1977) compared the social supports of employed and retired women and found that retired women report that they talk with fewer people in the course of the day. However, retired women have more contact with neighbors, friends, relatives, and voluntary associations than do their employed counterparts. We might hypothesize that retired women's networks reflect the loss of collegial relations and the formation of compensatory relationships with friends and neighbors. On the other hand, we might surmise that the relationships with friends and family may be longstanding rather than formed in response to the loss of co-worker relationships. In the latter case, retirement would result in a net loss in relationships.

RETIRED WOMEN VERSUS HOUSEWIVES

By comparing the social support networks of retired women and housewives, we can begin to learn whether the labor force experiences of retired women have had some lasting effects on the structure and functioning of their social support networks. There are conflicting notions about the relative social integration of housewives and women who have been employed.

One perspective portrays housewives as having an advantage, characterizing the home as the context of a rich network of extended family relationships and the nexus of close-knit community bonds. The employed woman is viewed as cut off from these important bonds. Employment reduces her opportunity for family and, as Booth (1972) and Lopata (1971a) suggest, limits the time available to participate in formal organizations.

Conversely, there is evidence that employment enriches the social lives of women. The friendship network established at work may prove extremely supportive. Veroff et al. (1981) report that employment enhances a woman's opportunity to form a wider circle of supportive friends. Further, the notion that the home remains a rich source of family and community bonds has been challenged, with the social isolation of the suburban housewife being noted by several investigators (Andre, 1981; Slater, 1970).

Although it is possible to cite arguments for beneficial as well as detrimental effects of labor force participation on women's social relationships, Fox (1977) finds few differences in the social interactions of housewives and retired women. Retired women report that they talk with more people on the average day, and housewives attend more voluntary association meetings but have similar numbers of relatives, friends, and neighbors in the vicinity. The two groups do not differ in the frequency with which they contact these people. It is possible, however, that differences between retired women and housewives may emerge with respect to more detailed measures of the structure and functioning of their networks. Such conflicting notions will be tested in the present investigation.

Our review of the literature suggests that retired women may be distinctive with respect to the structure, relationships, and functions that characterize their social support networks. The equivocal nature of the evidence, however, makes it impossible to derive any directional hypotheses. The present investigation attempts to clarify the issue. We conducted three parallel analyses, each employing a different comparison group (i.e., retired men, employed women, and housewives). By integrating the results of the three kinds of analyses, we are able to form a more comprehensive picture of the social support resources of the retired woman. The generalized research question may be stated as: What are the distinctive aspects of the structure, relationships, and functions of the social support networks of retired women?

# METHODS

**SAMPLE**

The data are taken from the "Supports of the Elderly" project funded by the National Institute on Aging. This study is based on a nationwide survey of 718 respondents aged 50 and over. Using the multistage procedure, we began with a random selection of households, followed by a sampling of residents aged 50 and over within households. This procedure resulted in a 70 percent response rate. To increase the number of "old-old" adults (Neugarten, 1974) in the sample, all residents of the sampled households aged 70 and over were interviewed, resulting in a response rate of 72 percent for all those aged 70 and over. The in-person interviews were approximately one hour in duration.

The analyses for this chapter focus on 543 men and women who were classified as working, retired, or housewives. There is currently much confusion in the literature over the operationalization of retirement. Defining retirement is particularly problematic among women, whose workforce participation is often discontinuous (Fischer et al., 1978; Fox, 1977). Our measure attempts to distinguish between the currently employed, the retired (those who have been employed in late adulthood and consider themselves retired), and housewives (those who have never been employed or who ceased their employment at very early ages). First, all respondents were asked to classify themselves as working for pay, unemployed, retired, or a housewife. Those who classified themselves as housewives were then asked whether they had ever been employed and whether they considered themselves retired. However, because some women said they had "retired" in their twenties or thirties to become housewives, we considered a woman retired if: (1) she said she stopped work at age 60 or above, or (2) she stopped work between the ages of 40 and 60, but the questions about retirement seemed applicable to her circumstances. Each of the interviews in question was reviewed by project staff. If a woman met neither of these conditions, she was considered a housewife. The employed were those who either: (1) defined themselves as employed, or (2) defined themselves as retired but continued to work 35 hours per week or more. These definitions resulted in groupings of 172 retired women, 146 retired men, 101 employed women, and 124 housewives.

**MEASURES**

The measures included:

*Support Structure.* A "bull's eye"-like diagram with three concentric circles was presented to respondents as a representation of their personal network. The total circle size was the total number of people in the social network. It was the sum of people listed in three concentric circles reflecting different levels of importance and closeness. The inner circle consisted of those to whom the person felt "so close that it's hard to imagine life without them." A measure of organizational involvement was based on a count of clubs and organizations with which the respondents were involved, including church, civic groups, and welfare organizations.

*Relationships.* For the first ten people in the diagram, the respondent was asked to indicate the relationship of each network member to them (for example, spouse, parent, child, sibling, grandchild, other relative, and friend).

*Functions.* Based on the first 20 network members listed in the diagram, the respondent was asked to identify which people provided different kinds of support, specifically: confiding, reassurance, respect, sick care, talking when upset, and talking about health concerns. Similarly, the respondent was asked to which of the network members he or she provided each of these functions. Based on a series of factor analyses, six indices were developed. These measures consisted of a count (from 0 to 40 people) of all those giving: (1) confiding and reassurance; (2) respect and sick care; and (3) talking when upset and about health concerns, and all those receiving: (4) confiding and reassurance; (5) respect and sick care; and (6) talking when upset and about health concerns.

## RESULTS

Three statistical procedures were used to determine significant differences among the groups. Chi square $(\chi^2)$ tests were used to evaluate demographic differences such as marital status. Analyses of variance (ANOVA) were used to make group comparisons on circle size and number of organizational memberships. To examine group differences in the relationships and functions within social support networks, a two-stage approach was employed. First, we tested for overall differences using Multivariate Analysis of Variance (MANOVA), which is advisable when numerous related dependent variables are used. If significant overall effects are observed using MANOVA, it is then acceptable to examine the results for specific dependent measures (in this case, specific relationships and specific functions) using univariate analysis of variance, or ANOVA (Lindeman et al., 1980). The results of each comparison are discussed below.

### RETIRED MEN VERSUS WOMEN

There were no significant differences in age between the two groups (M = 71.6 years for men and 71.7 for women). There were, however, significant differences in marital status ($X^2$ = 61.04, p < .001). Whereas 80 percent of the male retirees were married, this was the case for only 41 percent of the female retirees. The majority of retired women (51 percent) were widowed. These marital status differences were most pronounced after age 65.

Table 4.1 indicates the results of comparisons between retired men and women on measures of support structures. Women had larger social support networks (F = 9.65, p < .001). They had an average of 9.30 people in their entire network, while men had only about 7.66. Women also designated more people (M = 3.68) than did men (M = 2.75) in the inner circle of their network, indicating that they had a greater number of close relationships (F = 12.58, p < .001). Retired men and women belonged to a similar number of organizations. Men belonged to an average of 1.72 organizations and women to about 1.87.

Tables 4.2 and 4.3 provide information about the supportive relations and functions of retired men and women. There were overall differences in relationships (F = 9.04, p < .001). Men were significantly more likely to include a spouse in the network. Women, on the other hand, included more friends in the network (an average of 1.75 for women versus .99 for men; F = 11.49, p < .01). Otherwise, the network composition of retired men and women is quite similar. Most prevalent in the network are children, siblings, other relatives, and friends. As for exchanging support (Table 4.3), men and women were quite similar on most measures, but women reported that more people offer them confiding and reassurance (F = 7.76, p < .01) and that more people will talk with them about their health or about things that upset them (F = 5.05, p < .05). The significant sex differences hold when we control for age. Men and women were quite similar with respect to the number of people to whom they provided support.

## RETIRED VERSUS EMPLOYED WOMEN

As might be expected, the retired women in our sample were older than the employed women. Retired women had a mean age of 71.7 and employed women a mean age of 58.7. Employed women were heavily concentrated in the 50-64 age group. Because of this age difference, we repeated all analyses controlling for age. There were also significant overall marital status differences between the two groups ($X^2$ = 12.91, p < .05). More employed women were divorced or separated (17 percent versus 5 percent), and more retirees were widowed (50 percent versus 38 percent).

**TABLE 4.1**  Mean Number of Support Structures (Univariate Analysis of Variance)

| Support Structures | Retired Women | Retired Men | | | Employed Women | | | Housewives | | |
|---|---|---|---|---|---|---|---|---|---|---|
| | Unadjusted Mean | Unadjusted Mean | F-Ratio | F-Ratio With Age Covariate | Unadjusted Mean | F-Ratio | F-Ratio With Age Covariate | Unadjusted Mean | F-Ratio | F-Ratio With Age Covariate |
| Inner Circle | 3.68 | 2.75 | 12.58*** | 12.56** | 4.19 | 2.15 | 2.97 | 4.06 | 1.22 | 1.56 |
| Total Circle | 9.30 | 7.66 | 9.65*** | 9.66** | 10.60 | 3.68 | 1.19 | 9.35 | .01 | .04 |
| Count of Organizations | 1.87 | 1.72 | .82 | .82 | 1.67 | 1.07 | .01 | 1.45 | 6.43* | 5.69* |

\* $p < .05$
\*\* $p < .01$
\*\*\* $p < .001$

**TABLE 4.2  Mean Number of Social Support Relationships (Multivariate and Univariate Analysis of Variance)**

| | Retired Women | Retired Men | | | Employed Women | | | Housewives | | |
|---|---|---|---|---|---|---|---|---|---|---|
| | Unadjusted Mean | Unadjusted Mean | F-Ratio | F-Ratio With Age Covariate | Unadjusted Mean | F-Ratio | F-Ratio With Age Covariate | Unadjusted Mean | F-Ratio | F-Ratio With Age Covariate |
| Multivariate Tests | | | 9.04*** | 9.35*** | | 6.23*** | 1.87 | | 2.41* | 2.17* |
| Univariate Tests: | | | | | | | | | | |
| Spouse | .37 | .75 | 51.61*** | 53.95*** | .43 | .77 | 7.36** | .52 | 6.18* | 1.77 |
| Parents | .08 | .10 | .35 | .37 | .33 | 20.32*** | .50 | .15 | 2.14 | .09 |
| Children | 2.02 | 2.08 | .09 | .09 | 2.52 | 4.67* | 1.96 | 2.55 | 5.75* | 4.95* |
| Siblings | 1.03 | .97 | .16 | .17 | 1.60 | 9.09** | 1.60 | .93 | .42 | 1.21 |
| Grand-children | .70 | .57 | .80 | .83 | .20 | 12.36** | .07 | .90 | 1.35 | 5.90* |
| Other rel-atives | 1.33 | 1.19 | .65 | .66 | .23 | .24 | .97 | 1.20 | .44 | .66 |
| Friends | 1.75 | .99 | 11.49** | 11.46** | 1.60 | .32 | .14 | 1.10 | 7.68** | 7.47** |
| | (N = 172) | (N = 146) | | | (N = 101) | | | (N = 124) | | |

\*   p < .05
\*\*  p < .01
\*\*\* p < .001

**TABLE 4.3  Mean Number of Social Support Functions (Multivariate and Univariate Analysis of Variance)**

| | Retired Women | Retired Men | | | Employed Women | | | Housewives | | |
|---|---|---|---|---|---|---|---|---|---|---|
| | Unadjusted Mean | Unadjusted Mean | F-Ratio | F-Ratio With Age Covariate | Unadjusted Mean | F-Ratio | F-Ratio With Age Covariate | Unadjusted Mean | F-Ratio | F-Ratio With Age Covariate |
| Multivariate Tests | | 1.55 | 1.58 | | | 2.68* | 1.71 | | 2.21* | 2.75* |
| **Univariate Tests:** | | | | | | | | | | |
| *Receive* | | | | | | | | | | |
| Conf/Reassurance | 6.18 | 4.16 | 7.76** | 7.89** | 5.70 | .57 | 2.49 | 5.55 | 1.15 | 1.61 |
| Respect/Sick Care | 9.85 | 8.73 | 1.66 | 1.65 | 11.11 | 1.61 | 1.03 | 11.90 | 4.14* | 4.09* |
| Talk Hlth/Upset | 4.94 | 3.70 | 5.05* | 5.10* | 4.45 | .66 | 2.23 | 4.68 | .16 | .49 |
| *Provide* | | | | | | | | | | |
| Conf/Reassurance | 7.78 | 6.54 | 2.56 | 2.67 | 9.14 | 2.12 | .27 | 7.94 | .04 | .17 |
| Respect/Sick Care | 10.63 | 9.25 | 2.50 | 2.61 | 13.51 | 6.94** | .34 | 12.47 | 2.99 | 2.20 |
| Talk Hlth/Upset | 6.36 (N = 145) | 5.69 (N = 131) | 1.19 | 1.29 | 7.96 (N = 94) | 5.03* | .24 | 7.20 (N = 112) | 1.25 | .37 |

\*   $p < .05$
\*\*  $p < .01$
\*\*\* $p < .001$

However, when we stratify by age, this marital status difference is statistically significant only in the oldest age group.

Table 4.1 indicates that there were no significant differences in the support structures of retired versus employed women. Both the size of their networks and the number of organizations to which they belonged were remarkably similar. This finding holds when the means are adjusted for age.

As for supportive relationships (Table 4.2), there were overall differences in the networks of the two groups (F = 6.23, p < .001). The results of the univariate analyses indicate that the networks of employed women included more parents (M = .33 versus .08), children (M = 2.52 versus 2.02), and siblings (M = 1.60 versus 1.03). Retirees, on the other hand, listed more grandchildren in their networks (M = .70 versus .20). The picture changes quite radically, however, when age is controlled. The overall MANOVA test is no longer significant, and none of the differences noted above hold.

The overall MANOVA for network functions (Table 4.3) was significant before we controlled for age (F = 2.68, p < .05). Two univariate tests were significant: the amount of respect and sick care given to others (F = 6.94, p < .01), and the number of people to whom the respondents provide supportive talk about health or upsets (F = 5.03, p < .05). In each case, employed women provided these supportive functions to more network members than did retired women (M = 13.51 versus 10.63 for respect and sick care; M = 7.96 versus 6.36 for talk about health and upsets). When age is controlled, however, neither the multivariate test nor the univariate tests remain significant. The results of the age-controlled tests suggest that the differences observed between retired women and employed women were more a matter of age than employment status.

**RETIRED WOMEN VERSUS HOUSEWIVES**

There was a significant difference in age between the two groups. The mean age for housewives was 68.1 years and for retired women 71.7 years. More of the housewives fell into the 50-64 age group. Each analysis was repeated controlling for age. There was also a significant difference between housewives and retired women in marital status ($X^2$ = 10.59, p < .05). More housewives were married (57 percent versus 41 percent) and more retired women were widowed (51 percent versus 40 percent). When we examine these differences within age groups, however, the differences were not significant.

Turning to measures of support structures (Table 4.1), we find that retired women and housewives did not differ with respect to the size of their social support networks whether or not we control for age. However, there were differences in organizational involvement ($F = 6.43$, $p < .05$). Retired women belonged to an average of 1.87 organizations and housewives 1.45. This difference remains significant even when age is controlled.

As for the social support relationships and functions, both MANOVAS indicate overall significant differences. The MANOVA for relationships (Table 4.2; $F = 2.41$, $p < .05$) and the univariate tests show that housewives were more likely to include spouses and children in their networks, while retirees were more likely to name friends. When the data are controlled for the effects of age, the findings are altered somewhat. There is no longer a difference in the likelihood that a spouse is included in the network. The remainder of the differences in relationships remain significant. The overall MANOVA for the functions (Table 4.3) is also significant ($F = 2.21$, $p < .05$). The one significant univariate test indicates that housewives reported more people in their networks who respect them and care for them when ill. When we control for age, the multivariate test is still significant ($F = 2.75$, $p < .05$) and the same differences in functions hold.

## DISCUSSION

These results illustrate some distinctive features of the social support networks of retired women as compared with retired men, employed women, and housewives. The findings of this investigation show that, compared with the retired man, the retired woman has a larger social support network, with a larger inner circle of very close relationships. She is far less likely to be married, but she has more friends in her network. Although both retired men and women report that they provide various forms of support to numerous others, women say that more people provide them with certain kinds of support. But do these differences reflect the effects of gender or marital status? Do women have larger networks that provide more support because they have greater capacity and/or opportunity for the formation of close personal ties? Or is the size of the network an adaptation to unmarried status, reflecting the absence of one key personal tie and, consequently, greater reliance on an extended network of supportive others?

To answer these questions, we completed analyses comparing the networks of married retired men and women. The results indicate that the size of a retired woman's inner circle and total network is not a matter of marital status. The effect holds in comparisons of married retired men and women. However, there are no sex differences between married retired men and women in the types of relationships comprising the network. This suggests that friends are somewhat more prevalent in the networks of unmarried women (the effect approaches significance in the analysis of married retirees). The sex differences in functions hold in the married group, but new ones emerge as well. Married retired women provide confiding and reassurance to more people and listen to more people talk about their health and problems. We conclude that marital status affects sex differences observed in the relationships comprising men's and women's networks, as well as the support provided to others. The size of these networks and the amount of support received, however, is more a matter of gender. Married retired women still have larger networks, larger inner circles, and more network members from whom they receive support than do their male counterparts.

Are these network features unique to the retired woman's current employment status, or is there something to suggest that they reflect her long-term social interactions as an employed woman? Our data cannot offer a definitive answer to this question because they are not longitudinal. However, by comparing retired and employed women, we can see those network attributes which are shared by women in different points of the life span, all of whom have substantial labor force experience. The data show that employed women are more likely to have parents, children, and siblings in their networks, while retirees are more likely to have grand-children.

Again, we must ask whether these group differences are attributable to employment status or other exogenous variables such as age or marital status. As mentioned earlier, differences in the relationships and functions of retired versus employed women's networks do not hold when age is controlled. Further, when the analysis is confined to married respondents, some group differences remain significant, but only in regard to the number of parents and grandchildren in the network and the amount of respect and sick care they provide. Taken together, these results suggest that age is the most powerful factor affecting the network characteristics of retired versus employed women. Because retired women are substantially older than employed women, they have fewer parents and more grandchildren in their networks. This interpretation characterizes age rather than employment status as the critical factor that differentiates the networks of employed and retired women. This is not to say that the cessation of employment does not effect changes in the social networks of

women. Rather, it could be that important relationships are either renego-
tiated or replaced such that in the long run, retirement does not result in a
support deficit for a woman.

Finally, in comparing retirees and housewives, we are looking for
differences in the social relationships of the older woman associated with
more recent and long-term labor force participation. Our data show
differences in network composition rather than in size. Retired women
belong to more organizations and have more friends in their networks and
fewer children than do housewives. These differences hold when age is
controlled. However, when we repeat the analyses on married women
only, differences in organizational membership, number of friends in the
network, and types of support received do not remain significant. The
differences are in the same direction, however. This suggests that the
extended extrafamilial support network is particularly characteristic of
retired women who are unmarried. Thus, marital status emerges as the
critical variable that differentiates the networks of retired women and
housewives.

This triangulation of comparisons suggests that the social support of the
retired woman is a function of her age, gender, and her participation in the
labor force in later life. The size of her network and her inner circle is like
that of other women and larger than that of the retired man. Both her age
and her gender increase the likelihood that she will be widowed. The
composition and functioning of her network seem to reflect that fact. In
contrast to the housewives, her critical relationships include more friends
and fewer children, and she lacks the housewife's augmented number of
providers of respect and sick care. When age is controlled, the structure,
relationships, and functioning of the retired woman's network is not
unlike that of the woman still in the labor force. These data offer evidence
for strengths rather than weaknesses of retired women's networks of
support.

Further research should consider the qualitative aspects of support. Our
measures are limited to simple counts of the number of people with whom
support is exchanged, but it is also important to determine how individuals
assess the quality of support provided by their networks. Indeed, the
results of previous research (Fox, 1977) suggest that though the networks
of employed and retired women are very similar, their evaluations of the
adequacy of these networks are quite different. Additionally, research on
retired women should examine the relationship between network characteristics and the quality of their lives. That is, how does support affect
retirement adaptation? Research on social support suggests that it may
mediate the stresses associated with retirement. Supportive relationships

with family and friends may also enhance well-being, even when retirement is not experienced as a stressful event.

In addition, these findings have implications for practitioners and policymakers. The salience of friendship and organizational participation among retired women is particularly striking. Retired women have more friends than retired men and housewives, and they are involved in more organizations than housewives. These friendships are probably particularly important to retired women without a spouse.

The enhancement of friendships among the social networks of these women may improve the likelihood of positive adjustment to retirement. Preretirement trainers should consider including a session on the maintenance and improvement of friendships from work, as well as outside the work context. Employers can enhance the maintenance of work-related friendships among retiring women by providing them with alternatives to abrupt retirement, such as phased retirement or the opportunity to return to work on a substitute basis. The continued participation of retirees in work-related clubs and social activities can also be encouraged. Further, practitioners involved in counseling retired women who are facing the decision to relocate (e.g., moving to a warmer climate) should help such women carefully assess the content and value of their supportive network. If this network is comprised mainly of long-term friends, it may be irreplaceable in a new setting.

The fact that retired women are as engaged as they are in organizations suggests one possible avenue for service delivery to this population. Agencies providing services to retired women may advertise their services through such organizations, or they may provide their services in conjunction with these organizations. Further, they may work directly with professionals and paraprofessionals within such organizations helping them to respond to the needs of their retired female members.

Thus, while retirement can be a stressful experience for many women, the maintenance of a strong social support network may facilitate adaptation. Policymakers and practitioners can be involved in facilitating the strengthening of networks of women both before and after retirement.

# 5

# WORKING WOMEN VERSUS HOMEMAKERS: RETIREMENT RESOURCES AND CORRELATES OF WELL-BEING

## Pat M. Keith

This chapter compares the personal and social resources of very old retired women and homemakers and considers whether comparable factors promote psychological well-being. Without doubt, the structure of their lives and the schedules of full-time homemakers and women who work outside the home are quite different in early and midlife. Different values and economic constraints may have prompted initial choices between the two lifestyles. An intent of this research was to determine if their dominant work experience differentiated the lives of women in very old age.

Comparisons of employed women and homemakers have focused primarily on evaluations of life and psychological well-being of younger women for whom conflicts between work and family are presumed to be great. Consequently, little is known about the long-range outcomes of labor force involvement and homemaking on available personal and social resources and on the well-being of women in later life. With few exceptions (for example, Fox, 1977), studies of the influence of employment on older women have compared them with men rather than with women who have been full-time homemakers throughout adulthood. As a result, the literature indicating how the lives of retired women may differ in very old age, if at all, from those of women who have been full-time homemakers is sparse. Available research on younger women, however, is instructive in considering the differential influence of homemaking and employment on well-being.

Investigations of mental health and especially depression have suggested that for the most part, married women employed outside the home fare somewhat better than their counterparts who do not work outside the home (Bernard, 1972; Birnbaum, 1975; Burke and Weir, 1976; Gove and Geerken, 1977). Women who were employed and who had worked full-time for more than one year were the healthiest, while housewives who had never worked outside the home had better overall mental and physical health than housewives who had been employed previously (Welch and Booth, 1977). To explain the benefits of employment, Gove and Geerken (1977: 66) suggested that "married persons who hold a job are linked to two major social networks, one at home and one at work. These two networks serve as major sources of gratification for such persons and as a consequence they have a broader structural base than housewives who remain at home." While the benefits of multiple roles may offset some of the negative effects of role strain for employed women, a number of aspects of the homemaking role have been identified as stressful (Oakley, 1974).

Although homemakers may have somewhat more flexibility in their schedules which might permit more time to cultivate friendships and leisure activities, loneliness has been described as an occupational hazard for the housewife (Oakley, 1974). Also, the greater loneliness of women compared to that experienced by men has been attributed to their "house-bound role." Oakley (1974) found that limited social interaction and perceived monotony were linked to homemakers' dissatisfaction with their work.

Loneliness may also occur with role loss in old age, and its presence may indicate a deficit in social resources. Since opportunities to engage in social relationships at work are a valued aspect of employment outside the home (Veroff et al., 1981) and missing informal associations with co-workers is one of the losses associated with retirement, loneliness may accompany the withdrawal. Atchley (1976c), for example, reported that retired women more often than men described themselves as lonely.

Despite the contribution that employment may make to mental health, as indicated in research on depression, studies using global measures of happiness and life satisfaction have not indicated differences in the well-being of homemakers and employed women. Based on several national surveys, Campbell (1981) concluded that women who were homemakers were just as likely to say they were happy and completely satisfied with their lives as were employed women. He found no marked differences in general measures of well-being or in their satisfaction with specific areas of life.

Limited research examining the well-being of older retired women and homemakers, however, has produced conflicting results. Jaslow (1976), for example, found that women who had never worked had lower morale than women who were retired. In contrast, Fox (1977) reported that retirees had significantly lower affect balance than homemakers.

Furthermore, somewhat different factors may contribute to the well-being of homemakers and the retired (Fox, 1977). The well-being of retirees, for example, was influenced by various types of informal inter-action to a much greater extent than that of homemakers. Fox suggested the hypothesis that women who have been in the labor force for much of their lives may be more dependent on nonhome-centered contacts. How-ever, at the same time that work provides a contact with the larger community, it may also limit or preclude establishing extrafamily ties (Fox, 1977). It has been suggested that employed women, especially, because of both family and job demands may develop fewer leisure pursuits and perhaps may have fewer interpersonal ties outside the place of work. Presumably, limited time to develop leisure activities during the working years may hamper adjustment to retirement (Lowenthal and Chiriboga, 1973). One mode of adaptation to retirement may be to compensate for the loss of social ties at work by increasing opportunities for interaction with others.

Personal and social resources then may serve as a buffer against stressful events in old age. Four types of resources that the aged may draw upon have been identified: financial, health, education, and social and psycho-logical resources (George, 1980). Presumably, individuals with more access to these resources would make a positive adjustment to retirement and to old age. Furthermore, the literature suggests the hypothesis that retired women will increase their social resources outside the family and that nonhome-centered social ties will be more central to their psychological well-being than to that of homemakers (Fox, 1977).

## METHODOLOGY

### SAMPLE

Data were analyzed from structured interviews conducted with 114 retired women and 232 homemakers during the second phase of a longitudinal study of the aged in small towns. Respondents resided in towns of 250 to 5000 in a Midwestern state. In the initial study, respondents were randomly selected from a sample of towns drawn to be representative of small towns in the state (Pihlblad and Adams, 1972).

Respondents ranged in age from 72 to 97 years. The sample was Caucasian and was predominantly Protestant. Over one-half of the women had eight years or less of education, and their median income was $2041. About 20 percent of the women were married.

MEASURES

## Social and Personal Resources

Since personal and social resources may vary with employment status earlier in the life cycle, and are also believed to mitigate the negative effects of changes in old age, a number of these characteristics were assessed.

Four areas of personal resources were considered, namely, education, income, marital status, and health. Actual number of years of education were reported, and respondents indicated the amount of family income during the previous year. For the regression analyses, marital status was coded married (0) and widowed, never married, and divorced (1). Three measures of health from the second interview were used: (1) a general rating of health (good—3, fair—2, poor—1); change in health in the seven years since the first interview (better—3, same—2, worse—1); and comparison of health with others of the same age (using the same categories).

Measures of social resources involved both availability and use of formal and informal resources. Respondents reported number of living children, number of living siblings, number of closest friends, total number of friends, and total number of persons who visit. Frequency of face-to-face contact with closest friends was also reported. Response categories for frequency of contact with others ranged from never (1) to daily (8). To assess involvement in formal organizations, respondents reported the number of meetings of social, civic, or business organizations they attended in the previous year, coded none (0) to 52 or weekly (8). They also indicated the extent to which their informal contacts and church or religious organizational involvement (formal) were more (3), same (2), or less (1) than they were at the time of the first interview. Since social isolation and loneliness presumably reflect social resources and have been identified as potential problems for both homemakers (Oakley, 1974) and for retired women, respondents were asked to note how often they experienced loneliness (never—0, occasionally—1, often—2). The women in the present study indicated the extent to which they experienced loneliness at the time of two different interviews. It was then possible to examine the proportions of retired women and homemakers who were lonely at both times and to observe changes over a seven-year period.

A self-report was used to determine employment status. The retired defined themselves as such and described their previous employment outside the home as their major life's occupation. All had been retired seven years or longer. Homemakers identified "housewife" as their major occupation in life.

## Evaluations of Life and Death

Satisfaction with life was assessed by ten items (Wood et al., 1969). Response categories were "agree," "disagree," and "do not know." Scores were obtained by summing across the ten items, with higher scores indicating more positive perceptions of life. The coefficient of reliability was .67 (Alpha). Representative items include: "Do you agree or disagree that these are the best years of your life?" and "Do you agree or disagree that as you look back on your life, you are fairly well satisfied?"

Perceptions of death were examined by 12 Likert-type items reflecting the extent to which death was evaluated positively or negatively (Keith, 1979). Response categories were "strongly agree" to "strongly disagree" (0-4). Scores were obtained by summing across the items, with higher scores indicating more positive feelings about death. The coefficient of reliability was .71 (Alpha). Sample items include: "Do you agree or disagree that death is something to fear?"; "Do you agree or disagree that death is something to look forward to?" and "Do you agree or disagree that to die is to lose everything?"

Satisfaction with life and perceptions of death were used as indices of well-being. The evaluation of life entails an assessment of the past and the present, while perceptions of death focus on aspects of the future.

## RESULTS

### PERSONAL RESOURCES

Homemakers tended to be slightly older (80.6 years) than the retired (79.3 years). The retired had somewhat higher levels of education than did the homemakers; on the average, the retired had completed a little over

**TABLE 5.1**   Marital Status of the Retired and Homemakers (percentages)

| Employment Status | Married | Widowed | Separated/ Divorced | Never Married |
|---|---|---|---|---|
| Retired (N = 114) | 6 | 74 | 8 | 12 |
| Homemakers (N 232) | 19 | 78 | 2 | 1 |

$X^2$ = 41.67; 3df; p < .001

one year of high school while the homemakers had slightly over eight years of education. However, perhaps reflecting their husbands' incomes, the family income of the homemakers was somewhat higher than that of the retired.

Although over three-fourths of the women were widows, the home-makers were more likely to be married than the retired (Table 5.1). Indeed, 12 percent of the retired women had never married. Living arrangements reflected marital status, in that 79 percent of the retired lived alone, as compared to only 60 percent of the homemakers. Among the widowed who lived with others, 14 percent of the homemakers lived with children, while only five of the retired made their home with children. The retired more often lived with siblings (6 percent) than did homemakers (less than 1 percent). When marital status was controlled, homemakers had more living children (M = 2.72) than did the retired (M = 1.91). They did not, however, differ in the number of living brothers and sisters.

### INFORMAL SOCIAL TIES

Presumably, intimate friends are important in late life in part because they provide potential buffers against losses associated with aging (Keith, 1979). Neither employment nor full-time homemaking was a barrier to the maintenance of at least one close friendship. Fewer than 10 percent of both groups of women had no intimate friends, but employment status exerted some influence so that more retired women (67 percent) than homemakers (54 percent) had two or more very close friends (Table 5.2).

But these differences in friendship ties were not reflected in social isolation. In their estimates of how often they got together with their closest friend, over 20 percent of both groups of women saw a best friend daily. Although differences in frequency of interaction were small, more

TABLE 5.2     Number of Intimate Friends of the Retired and
Homemakers (percentages)

| | Number of Intimate Friends | | |
|---|---|---|---|
| Employment | None | One | Two or more |
| Retired (N = 114) | 8 | 25 | 67 |
| Homemakers (N = 232) | 7 | 39 | 54 |

$X^2 - 6.16$; 2 df; $p < .05$

TABLE 5.3     Total Number of Friends of the Retired and Homemakers
(percentages)

| | Total Number of Friends | | |
|---|---|---|---|
| Employment Status | None | One or Two | Three or more |
| Retired (N = 114) | 7 | 23 | 60 |
| Homemakers (N = 232) | 7 | 34 | 49 |

$X^2 = 4.96$; 2df; $p < .08$

homemakers (38 percent) than retired women (29 percent) saw their closest friends less often than once a week. Since the widowed may depend more on confidants and friends than the married, differences in marital status might account for some of the variation in friendship patterns of the homemakers and retired. If friendship does mitigate the impact of losses in old age, we would expect that the widowed, retired women, who had experienced two major life changes, might especially establish relationships with friends. Analysis showed that the relationship between marital status and the number of close friends and between marital status and the change in informal contacts over the previous seven years was similar for the two groups of women. Widowhood, then, had not prompted closer contact with a confidant.

Examination of the total number of friends revealed a pattern similar to that of intimate friends, with the retired having somewhat more friends (Table 5.3); however, the women did not differ in the total number of friends who visited them.

But had the retired and homemakers maintained informal contacts over time to the same extent? Although Fox (1977) did not have longitudinal data, she suggested that the retired may step up friendships after retirement to compensate for opportunities lost in withdrawing from work.

TABLE 5.4    Change in Amount of Informal Interaction for the Retired
            and Homemakers (percentages)

|                      | Change in Informal Interaction | |
| Employment Status    | Less | Same or more |
|----------------------|------|--------------|
| Retired (N = 114)    | 57   | 43           |
| Homemakers (N = 232) | 70   | 30           |

$X^2$ = 5.23; 1 df; p < .05

TABLE 5.5    Amount of Yearly Involvement in Formal Organizations of
            the Retired and Homemakers (percentages)

|                      |      | Number of Meetings Attended | |
| Employment Status    | None | One to Sixteen | Sixteen or Over |
|----------------------|------|----------------|-----------------|
| Retired (N = 114)    | 70   | 14             | 16              |
| Homemakers (N = 232) | 78   | 14             | 8               |

$X^2$ = 4.75; 2df; p < .09

These data show that while the women may have had fairly comparable amounts of contact with confidants, they managed their less intimate informal interaction differently, so that compared with seven years earlier, retired women (43 percent) more often than homemakers (30 percent) had either increased or maintained the same amount of contact in informal relationships (Table 5.4).

**FORMAL SOCIAL TIES**

In general, retired women more than homemakers were involved in formal organizations and were more likely either to have increased or maintained contact with church organizations since the first interview (Tables 5.5 and 5.6). While both groups of women participated less in church activities at the second interview than they had earlier, retired women increased their involvement (10 percent) more often than home-makers (2 percent).

**LONELINESS**

Homemakers were somewhat lonelier than retired women at the time of each of the interviews, but both were less lonely at time two (Table 5.7).

TABLE 5.6    Change in Involvement in Religious Organizations of the
Retired and Homemakers (percentages)

| | Change in Involvement | | |
|Employment Status | Less | Same | More |
|---|---|---|---|
| Retired (N = 114) | 55 | 36 | 10 |
| Homemakers (N = 232) | 61 | 37 | 2 |

$x^2 = 9.81; 2df; p < .001$

TABLE 5.7    Change in Frequency of Loneliness among the Retired and
Homemakers (percentages)

| | Employment Status | | | |
| | Retired (N = 114) | | Homemakers (N = 232) | |
| Loneliness | Time 1 | Time 2 | Time 1 | Time 2 |
|---|---|---|---|---|
| Some | 56 | 34 | 66 | 41 |
| Never | 44 | 66 | 34 | 59 |

NOTE:   Since time 1 and time 2 observations were not independent, chi square values
were not calculated.

Over 20 percent of both groups had changed and reported less loneliness
than they had experienced seven years earlier. By the second phase of the
study, over half of both the retired women and homemakers indicated that
they were never lonely.

EVALUATIONS OF LIFE

Homemakers and the retired did not differ significantly in their evaluations of life. To compare the relative importance of factors in determining
appraisals of life, social and personal resources associated with evaluations
of life were examined separately for homemakers and the retired. Nine
variables that were significantly correlated with life satisfaction among the
retired were entered simultaneously in a multiple regression analysis. This
technique indicates the relative influence of a single independent variable
on a dependent variable while controlling for the effects of other variables.

Five variables explained 53 percent of the variance in life evaluations of
the retired. Corresponding to other research, a measure of health was the

**TABLE 5.8    Summary of Multiple Regressions for Evaluations of Life for Retired Women and Homemakers**

| | | | | Evaluations of Life | | | |
| | Retired Women | | | | Homemakers | | |
|---|---|---|---|---|---|---|---|
| | r | b | Beta | | r | b | Beta |
| Change in health | .54 | 2.54* | .32 | Loneliness | −.43 | −3.07* | −.35 |
| Organizational involvement | .43 | .45* | .26 | Education | .27 | .25 | .18 |
| Loneliness | −.41 | −2.34* | −.28 | Current health | .33 | 1.57* | .15 |
| Change in church activity | .42 | 2.00* | .25 | Change in friends | .27 | 1.24 | .13 |
| Total number of visits | .20 | .39* | .19 | | | | |
| R = .728    R² = .529 | | | | R = .564    R² = .318 | | | |

*Denotes coefficients that were twice the size of their standard errors

most important correlate of evaluations of life for retired women (Table 5.8). Women who believed their health had changed for the better during the preceding seven years appraised their lives more positively. Involvement in formal organizations, increased church involvement, as well as a greater amount of informal visiting contributed to the life satisfaction of the retired. Although education, current health, comparison of health, and change in informal interaction were significantly correlated with life satisfaction and were entered in the analysis, they did not have a direct effect on evaluations of life. Age was not significantly related to evaluations of either life or death among the retired.

Eight variables that were significantly correlated with life satisfaction among homemakers were considered simultaneously in a regression analysis (Table 5.8). Loneliness was the only predictor of perceptions of life that was comparable for both retired women and homemakers. Women who were less lonely were more pleased with the way their lives had worked out. Loneliness, along with three other variables, explained 32 percent of the variance in the satisfaction of homemakers. More education and better health were associated with positive evaluations of life. Although they had not increased informal contacts to the degree that retired women had, homemakers who had become more involved in informal relationships during the years since the first interview viewed life more positively. Involvement in formal organizations, change in religious involvement, change in health, and comparison of health were significantly related to evaluations of life, although they did not directly influence life satisfaction. Age was not significantly related to evaluations of either life or death among homemakers.

A major difference in the factors associated with perceptions of life by the two groups of women was the direct importance that involvement in formal organizations had for the retired. Although organizational involvement was related to positive assessments of life by homemakers (r = .29), it did not contribute directly to satisfaction when other variables were controlled.

While loneliness was salient to the well-being of both homemakers and the retired, the context of loneliness was somewhat different for the two groups of women. High organizational involvement by homemakers was associated with reduced loneliness (r = .24), which in turn was linked with life satisfaction. All three measures of health, i.e., evaluation of health (r = -.33), change in health (-.22), and comparison of health with that of others (-.41) were more strongly associated with loneliness among the retired than among homemakers (-.12, -.13, -.09). Poor health probably interferes with maintaining friendship ties, which then influence both loneliness and well-being directly.

**PERCEPTIONS OF DEATH**

The retired and homemakers did not differ significantly in their perceptions of death. Number of closest friends was the most important predictor of perceptions of death among retired women (Table 5.9). More friends seemed to be a buffer against negative views of death. A positive evaluation of one's health compared to that of others was linked with positive observations about death. Persons who were less lonely and who had more overall contact with others also had more positive feelings about death. These four variables accounted for 32 percent of the variance in perceptions of death of the retired. Current health and change in religious involvement were significantly related to perceptions of death among the retired, but these variables had no direct influence when other variables were controlled.

For the most part, the personal and social resources were poor predictors of homemakers' perceptions of death, accounting for 8 percent of the variance (Table 5.9). Only income and number of close friends were

**TABLE 5.9**   Summary of Multiple Regressions for Perceptions of Death
for Retired Women and Homemakers

| | | | *Perceptions of Death* | | | |
|---|---|---|---|---|---|---|
| *Retired Women* | | | | *Homemakers* | | |
| r | b | Beta | | r | b | Beta |
| **Number of**  closest friends .44 | 1.24* | .35 | Income | .24 | 1.02* | .22 |
| **Comparison of**  health .36 | 4.73* | .28 | **Number of**  closest friends .20 | | .49 | .13 |
| Loneliness −.35 | −2.46 | −.17 | | | | |
| **Total number**  of visits .20 | .62 | .17 | | | | |
| R = .570   R² = .325 | | | R = .285   R² = .081 | | | |

*Denotes coefficients that were twice the size of their standard errors

salient in influencing attitudes toward death; women with higher incomes
and more close friends had more positive views of death.

# CONCLUSION

## SUMMARY AND DISCUSSION

This research indicated that sources of satisfaction and correlates of
perceptions of the future of very old retired women and homemakers were
somewhat different. Furthermore, some of the factors associated with
well-being suggested differences in the ways the two groups managed their
lives. For example, involvement in formal organizations (both civic and
religious) was especially important to the well-being of retired women.
Retired women may turn to organizational involvement as an accommodation to withdrawal from work. Skills needed to enter and succeed in
the workplace may also be those that make participation in formal
organizations more beneficial and meaningful. Organizations can provide a
place for continued application of skills that are no longer used in the
workplace.

Informal relationships with others contributed to positive evaluations
of life experiences, especially for retired women and to a lesser extent for

homemakers. Having more close friends as sources of support was linked to positive attitudes toward death for both groups of women. These interpersonal ties may have assisted women as they redefined their lives in very old age and provided anchors as they anticipated death. Retired women especially conceptualized death more positively when they had more contact with others and when they experienced less loneliness.

It was hypothesized that nonfamily contacts would be more central to the well-being of retired women. Clearly, more types of nonhome-centered contacts were important to the evaluations of retired women, but availability of specific family members (e.g., children, siblings) was not very salient to either homemakers or the retired. Once again, the importance of friends in old age was demonstrated. Furthermore, the social support derived from marriage was not related to evaluations of life and death. Other research has shown that marital status may be more important in determining the well-being of men than women (Keith, 1979).

Personal and social resources were better predictors of evaluations of life than of perceptions of death for both the retired and homemakers. But they were substantially better predictors of the perceptions of retired women than of homemakers. Fox (1977) also found that personal and social resources were less adequate to explain the well-being of homemakers. The pattern of relationships between social resources and evaluations of life and death suggests that social ties may have different meanings for the two groups of women.

Factors related to the functioning of the home might have explained more of the variance in the well-being of homemakers. The family setting into which women initially retire is probably very different from that in which only the male retires and the wife has been a full-time homemaker. It may be that homemakers make greater adjustments in order to accommodate the husband's retirement than do retired women. Keating and Cole (1980), for example, observed that the social networks of homemakers were different after their husbands retired. Couple activities rather than individual activities were dominant. In contrast, the retired women in this research and those studied by Fox (1977) continued to pursue and even increased their nonhome involvement.

Of course, the well-being of homemakers and employed women may vary depending on the stage of their respective careers. In addition to some of the obvious differences in demands that accompany homemaking and employment outside the home, it has been suggested that family-centered and career-oriented women are often at very different stages of role development (Birnbaum, 1975). For example, family-centered women may have high self-esteem in their early adult years when they are more involved in motherhood and family obligations. At the same time career-centered individuals may be less well established and have doubts and anxiety about their abilities. A decade or more later, the pattern may reverse, with professional women having achieved career goals while homemakers may experience a reduced sense of self-worth (Birnbaum, 1975).

In the instance of the very old women studied here, some earlier differences may have diminished over time, with their lives becoming more comparable as the influence of employment declined. The longitudinal evidence on loneliness, however, suggested that although the retired and homemakers changed in the same direction, some differences persisted. Only more specific longitudinal analyses over longer periods of time can assist in untangling the effects of initial differences in values and attitudes toward work outside the home as compared to homemaking and the effects of the actual experiences in these two careers.

## IMPLICATIONS FOR PRACTICE

One of the intents of this research was to consider possible long-range effects of employment in later life. In the future, employment may differentiate the lives of women more than this research indicated. As women become more committed to work and are employed in less traditional occupations, the influence it has on their nonwork lives may increase or at least change. The generation of women studied were perhaps more marginal to the occupational structure (Lopata and Steinhart, 1971) than e ployed women may be in the future. Even so, research has suggested that women may experience some difficulty adjusting to retirement (Atchley, 1976b; Jacobson, 1974). Presumably, preretirement programs and counseling could address some of the potential problems in the withdrawal from work. The present research is informative for preretirement planners.

In addition to information on finances and health, planners of preretirement programs and seminars should attend especially to the social aspects of adjustment to retirement. Homemakers may be involved in preretirement programs as spouses of employees, and employed women may be in programs at their own place of work. This research suggests that planners and counselors may want to emphasize somewhat different factors in working with these women. Retirement counseling should encourage continued and, if possible, increased involvement of retired women in formal organizations, including church organizations. The importance of social factors in adjusting to retirement is illustrated in the negative effects that loneliness has for both groups of women. Anticipating the importance of social ties can lead to planning in preretirement to establish an environment in which opportunities for contact are readily available. Formal and informal interaction should be more amenable to intervention before and during retirement than personal characteristics such as income or marital status.

## DIRECTIONS FOR FUTURE RESEARCH

Clearly, different models are needed to describe the well-being of very old homemakers and retired women. While the majority of women who retire do not seem to increase their household activities (Szinovacz, 1980), future research should compare the organization of household roles in families of younger retired women and homemakers. Along with assessment of activities outside the home, comparative sources of satisfaction within the home need to be considered in relation to the well-being of the retired and homemakers.

# II

# PREPARING FOR RETIREMENT: ATTITUDES AND PLANS

**Successful adaptation to role** transitions is contingent on a dual process: anticipatory socialization into the new role and psychological readiness to leave one's old role (Atchley, 1972). Both processes can be furthered by instrumental and emotional preparedness for the transition event.

Owing to their interrupted work histories, women can and often do suffer substantial reductions in income after retirement. To avoid such reductions, or at least alleviate the consequences of income loss, financial planning is necessary well before the retirement transition. It has also been argued that owing to their dual roles in the labor force and at home, married female workers may lack the time to develop hobbies and leisure activities before their retirement (see Szalai, 1972; Walker and Woods, 1976). Furthermore, women have been shown to retire earlier than men (see Palmore, 1965) and may thus be "off-time" (Seltzer, 1976) when entering the retiree role. All of these circumstances would seem to render adequate retirement preparation particularly important for women. However, policies and programs that rely on the stereotype of the male retiree may give women little opportunity to take such preparatory steps.

The present retirement literature provides little information on the retirement preparation of women. Chapters in this part of the book attempt to narrow this information gap by addressing differences in retirement attitudes and plans between men and women, as well as among divergent groups of women.

In Chapter 6, Naomi Kroeger investigates the relative use of formal and informal retirement programs by men and women employed in the private sector, as well as the determinants of retirement planning for both groups. Gender differences in retirement plans and expectations of university employees are the focus of Chapter 7. In their chapter, Evelyn Newman and her associates present information on professional men's and women's attitudes toward retirement, their major concerns for retirement, and their intentions to continue working after retirement from university jobs. Sharon Price-Bonham and Carolyn Kitchings Johnson provide evidence concerning the determinants of women's retirement attitudes in Chapter 8. Using a sample of professional and nonprofessional women, these authors are able to demonstrate the different preretirement circumstances that further or hinder development of positive retirement attitudes among these two groups of women. The final chapter of this part (Chapter 9) is devoted to an analysis of the consequences of retirement planning for women. It centers on the question whether (and if so, which) retirement plans contribute to women's emotional well-being after retirement.

# 6

# PRERETIREMENT PREPARATION: SEX DIFFERENCES IN ACCESS, SOURCES, AND USE

## Naomi Kroeger

**Does planning for retirement ease** the transition to the retirement role? Since retirement is a new life phase, quite different from the style of life that had been followed by most men and many women for two score years or more, one would expect that people who had thought about the implications of retirement would be able to adapt more gracefully to retirement than would those who had ignored the approaching end of their work career. As any major role transition calls for socialization into the differing expectations and demands of the new role, preretirement preparation should function as a kind of anticipatory socialization, permitting the retiring worker to explore the edges of retirement before it comes.

This chapter will explore efforts at preretirement preparation made by a sample of workers now retired from occupations in the retail trade to identify the characteristics of those who do undertake this kind of activity. It will contrast the experiences of people who participated in formal programs and those who worked out their own "self-help" programs with the retirees who reported no effort to learn about the implica-

*AUTHOR'S NOTE: This research was supported by a grant from the National Institute of Mental Health, Center on Aging. Special recognition is given to the project staff: Patricia Chartock, Ph.D., Project Director; Sandra Durmaskin, Research Associate; Dolores Perez, Research Assistant; and Co-Principal Investigator, Rose Dobrof, Ph.D.*

tions of retirement for their lifestyle, and will especially focus on the differential preparation for retirement between men and women, a subject much neglected in the literature.

## SURVEY OF THE LITERATURE

Retirement is increasingly recognized as one of the significant turning points in the life career of an individual, or at least for that majority of adults who have spent all or much of the later part of their lives in the labor force. Whether or not the move into retirement constitutes entry into a new role, "the retirement role," as contrasted with a "work role," has been the subject of much discussion. Many have viewed retirement as a "roleless role" (Blau, 1973; Havighurst et al., 1969; Burgess, 1960; Donahue et al., 1960) because the expectations and norms of the role are not clearly identifiable. Hall's (1980: 203) comment that "retirement is the only role in which contributions to society are not expected," misleading as it is, probably reflects the "roleless role" conception as well as any.

The merits of this debate go beyond the scope of this chapter. For our purposes, let us assert that retirement consists of a movement from one social position—that of permanent labor force participant whose primary activities are exchanged for pay or profit—to another—that of retiree who has withdrawn from the permanent labor force and whose income consists at least in part of a pension based on prior employment (Atchley, 1972). Such a change in social position necessarily entails some changes in the activities and behaviors of the role incumbent. In other words, we can assume that there exists a "retiree role" which is different from a "work role." The retirement role poses difficulty because it both overlaps the aging role and shares core-structured elements of the work role. Starting with the latter, the core characteristics of the work role include the provision (for most people) of a substantial source of their income, the determination of the activities of a significant portion of their waking hours (which may or may not be personally satisfying), and the structuring of a network of relationships that may or may not overflow the work role boundaries. Each of these constitutes an element of the retirement role that must be taken into account. Although the retirement role is conditioned to varying degrees by aspects of the aging role—physical limitations, loss of significant others, and the like—which go on regardless of employment status, the adjustment process must center on those elements of the work life that are changed because of passage into the new role.

Like others of life's roles involving a major transition from one life stage to another (marriage and parenthood come to mind), retirement has spawned a bountiful supply of materials focused on preparing the novice for the joys and traumas of the new life waiting ahead. Books and articles in the popular press, retirement seminars given in continuing education settings, and formal preretirement programs offered through the work setting all provide for anticipatory socialization opportunities.

To what degree are these measures effective in helping someone move successfully into retirement? While "how to" manuals may abound and professional journals piously advocate the need for preretirement preparation, rather little is known about either the long- or short-range effects of such exposure. Glamser and DeJong (1975) found that participants in a preretirement program felt better prepared for retirement than did a control group of potential retirees (all males) who were not exposed to the program. However, a postretirement follow-up six years later revealed no differences between either of the two experimental groups (who had received individual briefing or had participated in a discussion group and the control group) in their answers to the question: "How long did it take you to become used to being retired?" Neither were there any differences in their responses to measures of life satisfaction, retirement attitudes, and job deprivation. Although none of the participants of the discussion groups rated themselves "not well prepared" for retirement, they were no more likely than men in the control group to report that they had been "very well prepared" for retirement (Glamser, 1981). Other studies report different findings. Greene et al. (1969) found that workers who had participated in preretirement programs adjusted better than those who had not; however, this might well be explained by self-selective factors that make those who choose to participate more receptive than those who do not.

While most evaluation studies of preretirement planning concern themselves with the impact of specific programs and/or approaches, Simpson and her associates (1966d) took a more general approach to preretirement preparation as exposure to information through personal contact and discussion, as well as through media sources, such as reading materials or programs which the retiree had seen or heard. They started with the premise that retirement was not an institutionalized role and consequently was enshrouded by much uncertainty. Because this status lacks institutional structure, the individual must depend on his/her own resources to discover what to expect in retirement. However, they argued, there is no clear-cut link between preretirement exposure to knowledge about retirement and consequent planning or adaptation to retirement. An important intervening variable is anticipation. Those who looked forward to retirement would have been more attuned to information available through the media and receptive to seeking information through personal channels. This positive orientation to retirement and consequent exposure to knowledge would encourage preretirement preparation and planning, which would then result in positive adjustment. Their hypothesis was generally supported.

Anticipation of retirement consistently predicted retirement adjustment for all occupational ranks, and among those who looked forward to retirement, persons with high exposure to information were consistently more satisfied with retirement than those with low exposure. A mixed picture emerges among the men who had not looked forward to retirement. Exposure to knowledge did nothing to help the reluctant white-collar worker (who was most likely to be adjusted to the absence of work anyway); exposure to knowledge helped the middle-status worker reach the same level as the higher-status white-collar man, but exposure to knowledge about retirement or the lack thereof made little difference to the semi-skilled worker. If they were reluctant to retire, they missed work, no matter what.

These findings were supported by Streib and Schneider (1971), who found that willingness to retire was more important for predicting adjustment to retirement than was so-called "voluntary" retirement, and that this was more true for women than for men. Unfortunately, this study gives no indication of what preretirement preparation had been undertaken by the respondents. Sheldon et al. (1975) and Peretti and Wilson (1973) have also pointed to the link between anticipation of retirement, the likelihood of doing preretirement planning, and the subsequent probability of good retirement adjustment. Yet, as Mitchell (1972), a retiree himself, has observed, the sine qua non of retirement are health, income, and friends, and he advocates preretirement education to help individuals learn how to attain these essentials.

Much has been said about the importance of anticipatory socialization to ease the passage into new roles, especially when these roles mark the transition into a new life stage where the "old life" passes into memory. Preretirement preparation falls into this category. Atchley (1976a) has identified a "preretirement" phase that consists of two parts: the remote and the near. The remote envisions retirement as something in the far future with little present impact on one's current life plans, although the concern over the stability of the Social Security system and the advertising campaigns touting tax sheltered retirement accounts may make the early

1980s significant as a time that heightened awareness of retirement planning among the young. The near phase recognizes retirement as imminent, within the rapidly approaching future, when the preretiree rehearses retirement through fantasy (see Atchley, 1976a: 67).

While the prudent may have made specific financial provisions for their later years during the remote period, it is most typical that thoughts of retirement do not become real until late in the work career. Of the retirees in this sample, for example, only 8 percent had "always planned" to retire at the age they did; 38 percent had been thinking about retirement from one to five years; 27 percent began to consider retirement seriously in the last year of work; and for an unfortunate 20 percent, retirement was abrupt and unexpected. Men were more likely than women to have thought about retirement for more than a year; this applies to 58 percent of the men and 49 percent of the women. Women were twice as likely as men to have thought of retirement in the last year of work (34 percent to 17 percent), but men were more apt to be hit by an unexpected retirement (25 percent to 16 percent), frequently because of business closing.

Preretirement planning can be approached in a number of ways. Formal preretirement planning programs offered through place of employment, unions, or extended planning programs are usually targeted for the "near retirement" stage—too late for adequate financial planning but presumably useful in focusing attention on the new role to be entered. This is the type of preparation most often alluded to in the articles advocating preretirement planning or in the studies evaluating the effectiveness of preretirement planning. Such programs may be minimal, covering only what benefits and pensions will be forthcoming through the union or employer, or they may extend over many sessions, dealing with everything from retirement homes to coping with the interpersonal adaptation required by "twice the spouse and half the money."

The second approach is the informal, using other individuals or the mass media—books, magazines, television—as sources of information. While the opportunity to participate in formal programs is usually limited by accident of employment, all have access to the media should they be motivated to learn in advance what their new lifestyle might be like. An important part of the informal process is what Atchley (1972) has termed the "unconscious" preparation, so important for socialization, wherein the prospective retiree absorbs the attitudes and images of retirement, as well as the self-perception of someone who would pick up a book on retirement planning and carry it out of the bookstore (albeit in a plain brown wrapper). Role models among retired friends and opinions of employed friends about retirement as a way of life also shape the consciousness of the potential retiree about retirement as a desirable way of life, as do the reactions of spouses and others in the immediate network.

Do most retirees go through this period of anticipatory socialization, and what are the consequences if they do not? Who is less likely to seek out information about retirement? Are formal programs superior to informal preparation for stimulating retirement planning? Do women differ from men in their approach to retirement planning? These are the issues we turn to in our study.

## METHODS

### DATA COLLECTION AND SAMPLE

The data for this study are based on interviews with 264 men and women retired from jobs in the merchandising industries, including major department stores, smaller retail shops, merchandising chain stores, buying offices, and the like. Lists of persons who had just retired were obtained from personnel directors of the participating companies and two store workers unions. Included were all retirees, regardless of their occupational classification (salesperson, buyer, warehouse worker, elevator operator, seamstress) or level in the company (executive, non-executive). Of the sample, 58 percent were women, 79 percent were white, with 1 percent of the remaining 21 percent classified as Asian or Hispanic. Most of the sample (81 percent) were non-executives; 19 percent had retired as executives.

All of the respondents had worked in the New York City area and were interviewed as soon after retirement as possible. For a number, however, there was a large discrepancy between the official date of retirement and the last day of work, so that the interval between final day of work and date of interview ranged from a week or two to two years. Interviews were conducted in person where possible; if an individual had moved out of the area, he or she was interviewed by telephone. Interviews included both closed and open-ended questions to allow for both quantification of the data and for full discussion of the retirement experience. The data being reported here are based on interviews conducted between May 1980 and March 1981, the first wave of a two-wave longitudinal study.

## MEASURES

Several measures of retirement preparation[1] were included in the survey. Participation in formal programs was measured by the two sets of questions: "Did your store or union have a program to help prepare older workers for retirement?" (If yes), "Did you participate in the program?" "Did you receive information about retirement from any other sources? For example, did you go to any discussion group or lecture on pre-retirement planning?" (If yes), "What were these other sources?" Respondents were considered to have participated in a formal preretirement program if they had participated in their store or union program or if they stipulated a formal program in the general source question.

Informal preparation was also measured through two variables: (1) the naming of books, articles, television programs, or personal conversations in the general information question; and (2) the answer "yes" to the question: "Before you retired, did you read any books or magazine articles relating to retirement?" These two measures were then combined to give a fourfold measure of retirement preparation: formal plus informal sources, formal only, informal only, and no preparation.

## HYPOTHESES

Several hypotheses, based on past research, might be posed to predict who will undertake preretirement preparation. The first set of influencing factors is occupational status and education. Simpson et al. (1966d) found that middle-status workers were more likely to discuss retirement with others than were either semi-skilled or higher-status white-collar workers. Furthermore, they were also most likely to have turned to the media for information, with white-collar and semi-skilled workers following in that order—a not surprising finding considering their greater verbal ability than that of lower-status workers and their more positive orientation to retirement than that of upper-level workers.

The sample of workers in the two studies is not completely comparable, since our sample can be conveniently divided only into executive/non-executive categories. Simpson's upper-level workers included (along with executives, college professors, doctors, and lawyers) occupations marked not only by high prestige and compensation but by a high degree of autonomy over use of time. Executives, especially in the retail industries, are not only subject to the constraints of an organizational career, but their industry is also noted for its high volitility and stress. Thus, we would not expect executives to be especially resistant to retirement (as are more autonomous professionals). On the other hand, the middle-status workers in the Simpson study were all quite comparable to the majority of the non-executive workers in this study, many of whom were salespersons or skilled workers employed in this specialized setting. Both groups should be well disposed toward retirement; however, we would expect that the higher educational level and broader world view occasioned by their positions predispose executives toward retirement planning to a greater degree than non-executives, regardless of whether they are men or women. Likewise, we would expect persons with higher educational attainments, especially those who had attended college, to be more given to preparation for the same reasons.

A second major influencer of retirement preparation is readiness to retire. This variable was measured by the question: "If it had been up to you alone, would you have retired at that time (i.e., when you did) or would you have preferred to continue working?" Interestingly, at a time when mandatory retirement laws are virtually inoperative, almost two-thirds (63 percent of the men; 64 percent of the women) of the retirees said they would have preferred to continue on the job. The meaning of this response needs to be qualified, obviously. For many of these individuals, retirement had come as the result of health problems, changes in the workplace, business closings, interpersonal tensions on the job, personal emergencies, and the like. In most cases the situation had become so difficult that the respondent had used retirement as an escape route from an otherwise unpleasant position; in others, the options—for example, moving out of state with the company—were less acceptable than was retirement; for still others, a disability had become so severe that continued work was virtually impossible. The response, "I would have preferred to continue working," really means "I would have continued working if this situation had not happened." While the variable may not measure external coercion, it does seem to measure the lack of psychic readiness to leave the workforce. Thus we would expect it to act as an antecedent variable; that is, those who would have preferred to continue working would be less likely to acquaint themselves with information about retirement, even though they might have known that retirement was inevitable, given the increasingly serious nature of the precipitant situation.

A third major factor in retirement preparation, related in many respects to the voluntary or involuntary nature of retirement, is the length of time individuals had thought about retirement. This is really only an operationalization of the effects of "near time" when retirement ceases to exist only in the abstract future and becomes a point in time which can be dated. We would expect a direct relationship between the length of time spent in anticipation of retirement and the likelihood that the individuals had engaged in some kind of retirement preparation if for no other reason than increased exposure time. Persons who retired "suddenly," of course, are those who retired without plans. Not only would they have had less time to seek out informational sources, but they would probably not have had the same level of information, either.

Still another element in preretirement preparation is the existence of a social network that encourages a positive or negative view of the retiree role. Such support can be given directly, as through a spouse who encourages the individual to do retirement planning and/or who shares in the planning experience; it can be given indirectly through the attitudes of working peers about retirement as a desirable way of life; or it can be given through the living example of people who have already retired. Should all of these communicate retirement as a time of personal dislocation, devoid of positive support from significant others, we might expect a lack of interest in thinking about retirement and certainly in taking such concrete steps as attending formal preretirement courses or consciously reading about retirement.

## FINDINGS

### SEX DIFFERENCES

As shown in Table 6.1, men and women take vastly different approaches to preretirement preparation. Men are more likely to use informal sources (either alone or in combination with formal sources), whereas women rely somewhat more on formal programs and are much more likely than men to have had no retirement preparation.

However, we also see that these men and women had differential access to preretirement planning programs sponsored by their place of employment or union: 53 percent of the men, as compared to 36 percent of the women, were employed in situations where formal preretirement programs

**TABLE 6.1    Type of Preretirement Preparation Used, by Sex**

| Type of Preretirement Preparation Used | Women % | | Men % | |
|---|---|---|---|---|
| Formal & Informal | 13 | | 18 | *** |
| Formal only | 14 | | 10 | |
| Informal only | 32 | | 47 | |
| No preparation | 41 | | 25 | |
| | 100 | (155) | 100 | (106) |
| % Using informal sources | 44 | (155) | 65 | (106)*** |
| % With preretirement programs through work or union | 36 | (156) | 53 | (108)*** |
| % Of respondents who attended available programs | 56 | (84) | 46 | (67) |

$X^2$   *p < .05    **p < .01    ***p < .001

were held. Where women did have the opportunity to attend such programs, they did so at a somewhat higher rate than did men (Table 6.1).

Of even greater interest was the use of informal sources, almost entirely represented by the mass media—books, articles, or television programs—since these are equally available to all, regardless of sex or organizational affiliation. The importance of the media becomes clear when we compare the means used by those people who did not have formal programs available with those who did. While a few hardy individuals had attended formal programs they had located for themselves, most people, men especially, merely substituted informal means for formal programs. Women, on the other hand, most often did nothing to prepare themselves for retirement if formal programs were not available.

Because men and women were differentially located in the occupations represented in this sample, and because their access to preretirement programs was a function of their place of employment, we can evaluate their means of retirement preparation only by looking at the two groups of retirees separately to determine if systematic differences exist that explain who does and does not prepare for retirement.

## OCCUPATIONAL STATUS AND EDUCATION

We predicted that both executives and more highly educated retirees would be more active in preretirement planning than others. Unfortunately, executives and, because there is a great deal of overlap, retirees with higher levels of education were underrepresented among those who had formal programs available to them. Among both executives and college-educated retirees without access to formal programs, men and women prepared at essentially the same rate. Non-executives and men with a high school education or less were as likely to do something whether formal programs were available or not; they simply substituted "self-help" for organized preretirement planning. Women in both categories were quite different from men. If they did not have a formal program at hand, they were much less likely to seek out information on their own. In all, 65 percent of the non-executive women and 70 percent of the women who had not gone beyond high school did nothing, as compared to 32 percent and 39 percent, respectively, of the men, differences that were statistically significant at high levels (Table 6.2).

## ORIENTATION TO RETIREMENT

A number of studies cited earlier have demonstrated that readiness to retire has great impact on both interest in preretirement preparation and on subsequent adjustment to retirement. Two variables were used to measure different aspects of retirement readiness. "How long had you thought about retirement before you finally made the decision?" measures the degree to which retirement was part of a long-term plan in contrast to an unexpected occurrence that precludes adequate psychological preparation. "If it had been up to you alone, would you have retired (when you did) or would you have preferred to continue working?" more directly measures personal readiness to retire regardless of external circumstances.

Both of these variables are related to the kind of preretirement preparation individuals availed themselves of. Having had a fairly long "incubation" period for the idea of retirement resulted in more preretirement preparation, especially for men (Table 6.2). Of those without access to a formal program, over three-quarters of the men, but only about 40 percent of the women who had thought about retirement for more than a year, had done some "homework" on the subject. When formal programs were available, only 11 percent of the men, compared to 31 percent of the women, had made no move toward retirement preparation.

The sex differences are even more drastic in the case of sudden retirement, although the small number of people so affected renders the findings very tentative and statistically not significant. Only 17 percent of the women who had no access to formal programs and did not expect to

**TABLE 6.2**    Type of Preretirement Program Preparation, by Sex, Access, and Selected Variables

| | | Access to formal programs | | | |
|---|---|---|---|---|---|
| | | No | | Yes | |
| | | Women % | Men % | Women % | Men % |
| *Level:* | | | | | |
| Executive | Informal only | 55 | 53 | | |
| | None | 45(20) | 47(15) | (4)[1] | (8) |
| Non-executive | Informal only | 33 | 65*** | 23 | 35 |
| | None | 65(79) | 32(34) | 29(52) | 24(49) |
| *Education:* | | | | | |
| H.S. or less | Informal only | 28 | 58** | 21 | 33 |
| | None | 70(74) | 39(31) | 29(48) | 29(42) |
| College | Informal only | 64 | 67 | | 40 |
| | None | 32(25) | 33(18) | (8)[1] | 0(15) |
| *Readiness:* | | | | | |
| Rather work | Informal only | 31 | 50 | 23 | 35 |
| | None | 66(64) | 50(30) | 26(35) | 22(37) |
| Rather retire | Informal only | 50 | 79* | 19 | 35 |
| | None | 50(34) | 16(19) | 33(21) | 20(20) |
| *How long thought of retirement?:* | | | | | |
| Over 1 year | Informal only | 40 | 76** | 21 | 46* |
| | None | 58(42) | 24(25) | 31(29) | 11(37) |
| Up to 1 year | Informal only | 42 | 50 | 25 | |
| | None | 58(33) | 41(12) | 25(20) | (6)[1] |
| Unexpected | Informal only | 17 | 42 | 0 | |
| | None | 78(18) | 58(12) | (7) | 50(14) |
| *Working friends:* | | | | | |
| Favorable | Informal only | 40 | 68* | 29 | 39 |
| | None | 56(52) | 32(28) | 36(28) | 18(28) |
| Unfavorable, don't know | Informal only | 35 | 52 | 14 | 31 |
| | None | 65(46) | 43(21) | 21(28) | 24(29) |
| *Retired friends:* | | | | | |
| Favorable | Informal only | 41 | 60 | 23 | 27 |
| | None | 58(69) | 37(35) | 23(39) | 20(30) |
| Unfavorable, don't know | Informal only | 31 | 64 | 18 | 44 |
| | None | 66(29) | 36(14) | 41(14) | 22(27) |

$X^2$ (2df)    *p < .05    **p < .01    ***p < .001

1. Base too small to calculate percentages

NOTE:    Percentages do not add to 100 because category "formal and informal" was omitted.

retire still sought out informal programs, but 42 percent of the men took steps toward retirement preparation.

We would expect the lack of preparation that came with sudden retirement to reflect itself also in the behavior of retirees who said that they would rather be working than retired. Such is not the case so long as formal preretirement programs are available. Men and women attended them at about the same rate, regardless of their expressed willingness to retire. The big differences, both between sex and willingness to retire, can again be seen in the "self-help" group. Half of the men who would rather be working had ignored preretirement preparations; only about one in six of the willing male retirees had done the same. Women were less planful in general, and two-thirds of the more reluctant women had done nothing, compared to 50 percent of those who wanted to retire.

## INFLUENCE OF FRIENDS

The opinions of working or retired friends could play an important role in preretirement preparation. As shown in the lower part of Table 6.2, both men and women who lacked the possibility for formal programs were somewhat more likely to make no preparation if their working friends were negative about retirement than if they had favorable attitudes. Essentially the same was true if they had retired friends who were unhappy with retirement or if they had no retired friends at all. Men in particular seek out informal retirement programs if their working friends express positive opinions about retirement. Women whose working or retired friends hold negative attitudes about retirement were the least likely to obtain informal retirement preparation.

Generally, these findings suggest that participation in formal retirement programs is primarily a function of the accessibility of such programs. Among those retirees without access to formal programs, conditions that decrease individuals' likelihood to prepare for their retirement affect women more than men. The highest nonparticipation rates occurred for women without college education and in non-executive positions, as well as for those women whose friends expressed unfavorable opinions about retirement.

## RETIREMENT PREPARATION AND ECONOMIC INFORMATION

The value of preretirement preparation presumably is to ease the transition into the retirement role by giving prior knowledge that will prevent the rude shock that comes when a new reality runs counter to one's expectations. Some of the realities of retirement—what to do with time, how to cope with freedom, and the like—must be experienced before their impact can be realized; however, some prior factual knowledge, especially about the state of one's finances, can be helpful in making realistic plans that will not court disappointment.

Since formal preretirement programs usually place great emphasis on the financial aspects of retirement (and virtually everyone who had gone to a formal preretirement program reported that financial aspects had been covered), we examined the relationship between the kind of exposure to preretirement information and the level of knowledge about both income and expenses in retirement. The questions asked were: "Before you stopped working, how accurate an idea did you have of how much it would be? Did you have a fairly accurate idea, expected more, expected less, or had no idea?" and "Before you stopped working, how much time did you spend in figuring out what your expenses would be in retirement? Would you say that you did not think of it at all; that you had a general idea of what your expenses would be, or that you had a fairly accurate idea of what your expenses would be?"

It would be stretching credibility to assume a simple relationship between the type of preretirement preparation and subsequent accuracy in gauging retirement income and expenses. For if one wanted to be very literal in interpreting direct relationships, it would appear from Table 6.3 that the informal means of retirement preparation are more effective than are formal presentations. In all, 72 percent of the women and 80 percent of the men who had used this method only had accurately calculated their retirement income, in comparison to the 57 percent of the women and 73 percent of the men who attended formal programs. The most probable explanation is that those who are thinking about retirement and who take steps to prepare themselves are also the kind of people who are aware of the importance of knowing about available income.

Lack of retirement preparation is associated with inadequate economic retirement information. Both men and women without preparation were much more likely to have no idea of what income to expect than were those who made some attempt at preparation. Prior preparation is less effective in helping retirees estimate accurately what will be their retirement expenses, but again, both men and women who had done some preparation were better informed than the nonprepared. Women who failed to attend retirement programs appear particularly unsure of their retirement expenses. Almost two-thirds of this group had no idea how much their expenses would be, as compared to only 22 percent of the men.

TABLE 6.3    Relationship Between Preretirement Preparation and
Economic Information, by Sex and Selected Variables

| *Idea of Retirement Income* | | *Women* % | | *Men* % | |
|---|---|---|---|---|---|
| Formal: | Accurate | 57 | *** | 73 | ** |
| | Had no idea | 18 | (28) | 19 | (26) |
| Informal: | Accurate | 72 | | 80 | |
| only | Had no idea | 8 | (39) | 6 | (49) |
| None | Accurate | 50 | | 54 | |
| | Had no idea | 42 | (53) | 39 | (26) |
| *Idea of Retirement Expenses* | | | | | |
| Formal: | Accurate | 29 | *** | 39 | |
| | Had no idea | 25 | (28) | 35 | (26) |
| Informal: | Accurate | 36 | | 37 | |
| only | Had no idea | 40 | (42) | 31 | (49) |
| None: | Accurate | 23 | | 27 | |
| | Had no idea | 64 | (56) | 22 | (26) |

$X^2$  (4df)  *p < .05  **p < .01  ***p < .001

NOTE: Percentages do not add to 100 because the category "fairly accurate" was omitted.

## DISCUSSION

These findings lead to some provocative questions about the differences between men and women in retirement preparation. First, women seem to need more external structure to do retirement preparation. If a formal preretirement program is available, they will go; but if such structured preparation is not available, they are much less likely than men to turn voluntarily to informal sources, for instance, to the literature on retirement that is widely available. On the other hand, if a formal program is available, they are more consistent than men in making use of it. That is, women who had thought of retirement seriously from between a few weeks to a year were as likely to have attended preretirement sessions as someone who had longstanding plans for retirement.

This leads to a second difference. Men seemed to have a longer "incubation" period for the idea of retirement. They typically had been thinking of retirement for one to five years and engaged in a lot of preparatory activity, especially informal, during this period. Women, on the other hand, were most likely to have thought about retirement for less than a year (although they were not as apt as men to be surprised by the "unexpected" retirement—possibly an artifact of this particular sample). Unlike men, women appeared disinclined to do any more or any less preparation during this period when retirement was beginning to take shape as a reality.

Does retirement mean something different to women than it does to men, so that they do not engage in the same kind of casual exploration of the subject that one does on idle Sunday afternoons? It is in the area of informal information-getting that women consistently fall short of men. Does retirement, that leisure role which for so long was assumed to attack the very heart of men's identities, hold for men some fascination of the unknown which passes over women? This could be, for women who have spent virtually all their lives in the labor force and who have thought about retirement for more than a year (the situation parallel to the typical man) are somewhat more likely to read about retirement than are their sisters who have been in the labor force for two-thirds of their life or less. The number of cases, however, is too small to do a definitive analysis. So the question remains unanswered. However, preretirement preparation of this casual sort appears to be as effective for heightening awareness of retirement issues as are formal programs and may be even more important for shaping in fantasy the freedoms of this new life so very different from the world of work known to the men.

Women, especially those who have been housewives, have already tasted of the kind of autonomy found in the occupation of housewife and may not need the same kind of transition to a role that they already know but do not necessarily love. However, we would also suggest that the bridging function is an important one, both in setting up psychological readiness to leave the work role, as well as for stimulating action in more specific areas, such as the evaluation of financial status. As we have seen, those people who do not go through a period of retirement "exploration" are also less likely to think about retirement income and expenses, so essential for making realistic plans for retirement.

Not only are women generally less inclined than men to take a personal initiative in preretirement preparation, they are also more susceptible to adverse effects on retirement planning of selected personal and situational circumstances. Position in the lower social status groups, unwillingness to retire, and negative retirement attitudes on the part of friends were all related to particularly little use of informal information sources by women. At least as far as estimates of retirement expenses are concerned, the lack of preretirement preparation leaves women much worse off than men.

One obvious policy implication of these results is the need to establish formal retirement programs for women employed in the private sector. Since women are less likely than men to obtain retirement information through informal sources, their retirement preparation seems contigent on the provision of retirement programs at the workplace. Women in the lower income groups who are especially vulnerable to financial losses at retirement should be targeted for early preretirement programs providing them with information on how to estimate postretirement incomes and expenses, as well as to plan economically for their retirement.

## NOTE

1. The terms "preparation" and "planning" are used interchangeably in this chapter, primarily for purposes of textual variety. Obviously, reading an article or even attending a series of workshops is not the same as deliberate and systematic planning for finances, housing, activities, and the like. We are positing something more modest—that even this minimal "psychological preparation" affects the transition to the retirement role.

# 7

# RETIREMENT EXPECTATIONS AND PLANS: A COMPARISON OF PROFESSIONAL MEN AND WOMEN

Evelyn S. Newman, Susan R. Sherman,
and Claire E. Higgins

**It has long been assumed that** retirement from paid employment has little significance for women due to their greater involvement in family roles (Blau, 1973; Cumming and Henry, 1961). As the proportion of women in the workforce continues to expand and as they remain in the workforce for longer periods of time, it seems likely that both work roles and the retirement experience will be of significance for women, as well as men.

Sex differences in attitudes and adjustment to retirement have been reported by Atchley (1976b, 1976c), Beutner and Cryns (1979), Coyle and Fuller (1977), Fox (1977), Jacobson (1974), Jaslow (1976), and Thoennes et al. (1978). While some research suggests that females experience less anxiety about or resistance to retirement than males (Sheldon et al., 1975), the opposite trend has also been observed frequently. For instance, Jacobson (1974) found that women were less likely than men to be positively oriented toward retirement, and in Streib and Schneider's (1971) study, women appeared more apprehensive than men about the effects of retirement. Women were also shown to take longer than men to adapt to the retirement transition (Atchley, 1976b, 1976c) and to find adjustment to retirement particularly difficult if their initial attitudes were negative (Levy, 1980).

As far as retirement planning is concerned, evidence in regard to gender differences is inconclusive. While some studies show women to prepare less for retirement than men (see Atchley, 1981), Beutner and Cryns (1979), in a study of university professionals, found women to engage in more planning than their retired male colleagues. Women were also more concerned than men with the practical aspects of retirement (i.e., use of time, skills, financial aspects) and regarded a greater number of issues as important to retirement planning, whereas men attributed primary importance to family relationships after retirement.

This chapter describes plans and expectations concerning the retirement of professional men and women in a university population. The study moves beyond planning for the act of retirement (i.e., timing of retirement) to the attitudes and plans regarding the next stage in the process, namely, the retirement role itself. Questions were asked pertaining to major concerns about retirement, what respondents expected to miss most during retirement, and plans for working after retirement from their university positions. A discussion of plans and expectations concerning retirement among professionals is especially important, since a widely held assumption is that individuals with strong work attachment (which is associated with professional status) will react negatively to retirement (Miller, 1965). For instance, Darnley (1975) points to the continuing emphasis on the work ethic which dictates one's occupation to be a primary source of identification and self-worth. Fillenbaum and Maddox (1974) found that nearly all healthy, retired male faculty work for pay at some time after retiring. This continued work was related to a personal dislike of retirement.

Kimmel (1974) suggests the importance of role models for attitudes toward occupation and retirement. With increasing numbers of women in the workforce, it may well be that for women, as well as for men, work becomes the primary source of identification and self-worth, particularly if they work in high-prestige, professional occupations.

## METHODS

A university population was chosen for the present study because this group has not been extensively studied in the past and also because most women in this group work by choice, rather than from necessity. The sample includes both faculty and nonteaching professionals (NTPs), such as librarians, administrators, and counselors.

A 35-item questionnaire was mailed to all faculty and NTPs at three types of State University of New York campuses: a University Center, a 4-year college, and a community college. Of the 2058 sent, 958 were returned, for an overall rate of return of 45.5 percent. The return rate from the three types of colleges was very close, ranging from 44 percent at the University Center to 49 percent at the 4-year college.

Because of suspected differences in the work climate of the three types of sites, it was anticipated that professionals from the different types of campuses would have different expectations for retirement. In initial analyses of the data this did not turn out to be the case, and therefore combined data are reported.

## SAMPLE CHARACTERISTICS

Of the 958 respondents, 74 percent were men and 26 percent were women. Of the men, 72 percent were faculty and 28 percent were NTPs, while 66 percent of the women held faculty positions and 34 percent were NTPs. Median age was similar for both men and women faculty (43.5 for men, 41.2 for women), but was considerably lower for NTPs, particularly female NTPs (men 38.0, women 31.3). Modal marital status differed for men and women: 86 percent of the men were married, while only 51 percent of the women fell in that category. Modal levels of education also evidenced gender differences—55 percent of the men had Ph.D.s, while 54 percent of the women had only a master's degree. The modal job title for male faculty was full professor (35 percent), while for female faculty it was assistant professor (38 percent).

In summary, males were more frequently married, had higher levels of education, and a higher-status job title than females. There was a wide age gap between male faculty and female NTPs. Variations in these background variables may have an impact on the relationships between sex and attitudes/plans. Especially age and occupational position can be expected to interact with gender effects (see Prentis, 1980). Therefore, controls for these variables were introduced in the tabulations by sex.

## RESULTS

### EXPECTATIONS ABOUT RETIREMENT

Table 7.1 indicates that for the present sample, expectations for retirement are gender-related. While this holds true for the total population, this

**TABLE 7.1**   Gender Differences in Attitudes Toward Retirement, by Occupational Position and Age (percentages)

|  |  | *Attitude* | | |
|---|---|---|---|---|
|  |  | *With pleasure* | *With mixed feelings, fear or dread* | *(N)* |
| Faculty | men | 54 | 46 ** | (367) |
|  | women | 40 | 60 | (121) |
| NTP | men | 61 | 39 | (134) |
|  | women | 51 | 49 | (57) |
| 21–40 | men | 57 | 43 * | (194) |
|  | women | 42 | 58 | (76) |
| 41–60 | men | 57 | 43 | (278) |
|  | women | 49 | 52 | (91) |
| over 60 | men | 46 | 54 | (28) |
|  | women | 27 | 73 | (11) |
| Total | men | 57 | 43 ** | (502) |
|  | women | 44 | 56 | (179) |

\*   $p < .05$
\*\* $p < .01$
NOTE: Excludes respondents who "had not thought about" retirement.

trend is more pronounced for faculty, as well as for the younger (21-40) and oldest (61 and over) age groups. However, owing to the small N for the latter group, the $\chi^2$ value does not reach significance.

Consequently, our data would appear to lend limited support to Coyle and Fuller's (1977) and Atchley's (1976c) contention that women tend to have less positive attitudes toward retirement than men. Possible explanations for these more negative attitudes have been suggested. First, since women tend to live longer than men, they face potentially many more years of retired life than do their male counterparts, which may in some ways contribute to their ambivalence about retirement. Second, it has been suggested that since many women have returned to work after their children are grown, they have less time in the workforce to complete personal career goals. This would not apply, however, to the younger women in this sample.

When respondents were asked how much they had thought about their own retirement, although the differences were not statistically significant,

TABLE 7.2   Gender Differences in Thoughts About Retirement, by
Occupational Position and Age (percentages)

| | | *Thought about retirement* | | | |
|---|---|---|---|---|---|
| | | *Great deal* | *Some passing thought* | *Not at all* | *(N)* |
| Faculty | men | 23 | 63 | 14 | (517) |
| | women | 17 | 71 | 12 | (165) |
| NTP | men | 19 | 64 | 17 | (186) |
| | women | 16 | 56 | 28 | (82) |
| 21–40 | men | 11 | 63 | 26 | (328) |
| | women | 5 | 67 | 27 | (132) |
| 41–60 | men | 29 | 65 | 5 | (341) |
| | women | 28 | 66 | 6 | (103) |
| over 60 | men | 53 | 44 | 3 | (32) |
| | women | 50 | 50 | 0 | (12) |
| Total | men | 22 | 63 | 15 | (704) |
| | women | 17 | 66 | 17 | (248) |

\*   $p < .05$
\*\* $p < .01$

there was a slight tendency, as shown in Table 7.2, for more men than
women to have thought about it a lot. It may be that in keeping with their
more negative attitudes, women simply do not allow themselves to think
about what they regard as an unpleasant topic. Furthermore, more NTPs
than faculty had not thought about it at all. These differences can be
largely explained by age differences, as both male and female faculty were
older on the average than male and female NTPs. Female NTPs were ten
years younger than female faculty, and male NTPs were five years younger
than male faculty. Since they were both younger and female, as might be
expected, the group which had thought about their own concerns for
retirement the least were the female NTPs.

The respondents who indicated that they had given thought to
retirement were then asked to rank their major concerns. In all, 115 (14
percent) respondents replied that all concerns listed in the questionnaire
were of equal importance. More female NTPs selected this response than
any other group, perhaps an indication of their lesser concern with
retirement; that is, with the specifics of what it might really mean for
them. These responses are not shown. Table 7.3 shows the distribution of

TABLE 7.3    Gender Differences in Most Important Concern for Retirement, by Occupational Position and Age (percentages)

| | | Most important concern | | | | |
|---|---|---|---|---|---|---|
| | | Finances | Use of time | Second career | Where to live | (N) |
| Faculty | men | 57 | 19 | 12 | 12 | (326) |
| | women | 56 | 25 | 7 | 12 | (101) |
| NTP | men | 67 | 19 | 10 | 4 | (106) |
| | women | 67 | 15 | 13 | 5 | (39) |
| 21–40 | men | 68 | 18 | 6 | 8 | (177) |
| | women | 73 | 13 | 9 | 5 | (63) |
| 41–60 | men | 52 | 20 | 16 | 12 | (233) |
| | women | 48 | 28 | 9 | 15 | (68) |
| over 60 | men | 62 | 14 | 10 | 14 | (21) |
| | women | 50 | 38 | 0 | 12 | (8) |
| Total | men | 59 | 19 | 12 | 10 | (433) |
| | women | 59 | 22 | 9 | 10 | (140) |

* p < .05
** p < .01

the concerns chosen as the most important. (Ties between two or more concerns are not shown.) No statistically significant gender differences emerged. With regard to the most important concern, although all four groups ranked finances as their greatest concern, NTPs, both men and women, tended to be more concerned with finances than were faculty men and women. Although male faculty and NTPs were about equally concerned with use of time, female faculty were more concerned about this than were female NTPs. Both male and female faculty seemed slightly more concerned than both groups of NTPs with where to live. It appears that type of university position and age were more predictive of type of concern than was gender.

## PLANS FOR RETIREMENT

Respondents were asked whether their plans included work after retirement, and if so, whether this work was to be part time or full time. Results appear in Table 7.4. Only 7 percent of all respondents planned not to work at all, while 68 percent indicated that they planned postretirement

**TABLE 7.4**  Gender Differences in Plans to Work, After Retirement, by Occupational Position and Age (percentages)

|  |  | *Plans to work* | | | |
|  |  | *Full- or part-time* | *Don't know* | *Won't work* | *(N)* |
|---|---|---|---|---|---|
| Faculty | men | 72 | 21 | 7 | (510) |
|  | women | 62 | 30 | 8 | (163) |
| NTP | men | 67 | 28 | 5 | (184) |
|  | women | 58 | 35 | 7 | (82) |
| 21–40 | men | 66 | 28 | 6 * | (321) |
|  | women | 55 | 40 | 5 | (131) |
| 41–60 | men | 74 | 19 | 7 | (339) |
|  | women | 67 | 22 | 11 | (102) |
| over 60 | men | 88 | 10 | 3 | (32) |
|  | women | 73 | 9 | 18 | (11) |
| Total | men | 71 | 23 | 6 * | (695) |
|  | women | 61 | 31 | 8 | (245) |

* $p < .05$
** $p < .01$

work (mostly part time). There was an overall significant gender difference in plans to work versus not to work. When controls for age and occupational position are applied, only gender differences for the 21–40 age group are significant, but the basic trend remains the same for all groups. The female NTPs had the least concrete plans, with 35 percent stating that they didn't know whether they would work—possibly, again, a reflection of their younger age.

Those who thought they might work were asked to what extent their postretirement work would be a continuation of their present type of work. Of those responding, 11 percent indicated that although they desired to work, they either did not know at that time precisely what work they would be doing, or that some work might and some might not be related to their present careers. As seen in Table 7.5, of the remainder, 31 percent indicated that their work would be the same as at present, and 45 percent indicated that it would be related to present work. While planning for postretirement work is not identical with actual work, this finding is consistent with the finding of Fillenbaum and Maddox (1974) that nearly all healthy retired male faculty do work for pay at some time after

TABLE 7.5    Gender Differences in Type of Postretirement work, by
Occupational Position and Age (percentages)

| | | Same as present | Related to present | Unrelated to present | (N) |
|---|---|---|---|---|---|
| | | | *Type of work* | | |
| Faculty | men | 37 | 43 | 20 | (381) |
| | women | 30 | 52 | 18 | (109) |
| NTP | men | 21 | 43 | 36 | (144) |
| | women | 22 | 42 | 36 | (59) |
| 21–40 | men | 37 | 36 | 27 | (244) |
| | women | 28 | 46 | 26 | (87) |
| 41–60 | men | 28 | 49 | 23 | (255) |
| | women | 25 | 53 | 22 | (73) |
| over 60 | men | 34 | 58 | 8 | (26) |
| | women | 38 | 37 | 25 | (8) |
| Total | men | 33 | 43 | 24 | (526) |
| | women | 27 | 49 | 24 | (168) |

* p < .05
** p < .01

NOTE: Excludes respondents who do not plan to work, who do not know what type
of work they will have, or who mentioned more than one work type

retirement, and that this work is closely related to their area of expertise.
Table 7.5 indicates that there are no significant gender differences in
expectations for postretirement work. Young male faculty had the greatest
desire for work that is a continuation of their present work. Female
faculty were next in favor of this, with both groups of NTPs least
favorable. About one-third of the NTPs indicated that the work would be
unrelated to present work, whereas less than one-fifth of the faculty (men
or women) stated this. This may be a realistic appraisal of their possibil-
ities. It may be impossible for those who are engaged in administrative
work to continue such work. Furthermore, faculty who are engaged in
research can anticipate the opportunity for continued research and writing, even after retirement. Consultation work would also be expected to be
more available to faculty than to NTPs. It appears, then, that with regard
to type of work, current occupational position makes more difference
than does gender. It was also found that the larger the institution, the
more likely that postretirement work would be a continuation of present

work. Again, perhaps, a greater opportunity to continue research and writing than to continue classroom teaching is a structural basis for retirement plans.

## SUMMARY

It appears that with regard to expectations and plans for retirement, there are not very large gender differences among professional university or college staff. Since men's and women's work roles are becoming more similar, this would be expected. It was found that men were looking forward to retirement with more pleasure than were women, and that men were more certain of their postretirement work plans.

In addition to these rather meager gender differences, we found differences between faculty and NTPs. These must be viewed against the age difference: Female NTPs were ten years younger than female faculty, and male NTPs were five years younger than male faculty. Faculty had thought about retirement somewhat more and were more likely to desire work that was a continuation of present work. NTPs tended to be more concerned about finances than were faculty, whereas faculty tended to be more concerned than NTPs regarding where to live. Faculty were slightly more likely to want to continue working because they like their work so much they don't want to give it up, whereas NTPs were more likely to be afraid of not keeping occupied. Strauss et al. (1976) reported that job titles that reflect status are retained after retirement; professors did not come to be called "Mister." It may be that NTPs do not sense this kind of continuity.

Despite the fact that the males in this study had higher levels of income and higher-status job titles than the females, gender differences in attitudes and planning were not large. Additionally, since some differences were found between the teaching and nonteaching professionals, this study would seem to lend further weight to arguments that occupational position plays a major role in retirement plans and expectations.

One implication to be drawn from these data is that university professionals in general, and faculty in particular, desire to continue working after their formal retirement. While some work opportunities are obviously available through personal and private initiatives, educational institutions should be encouraged to facilitate participation on the part of their former employees. It is also evident that financial issues constitute a major retirement concern even for persons employed in relatively high-level and well-paid occupations. Older female professionals particularly fear that use of time may become a problem at retirement. Such concerns could be alleviated through adequate preparation for retirement, preferably at an early age. However, most respondents had not given serious thought to retirement until their later years. An important step toward adequate retirement preparation would thus be to sensitize younger workers to retirement issues and to encourage their participation in programs at an early age. The policy of many employers to offer preretirement programs primarily to those approaching retirement age is clearly dysfunctional; it enhances employees' tendency to avoid retirement issues until it is often too late to address potential problems.

# 8

# ATTITUDES TOWARD RETIREMENT: A COMPARISON OF PROFESSIONAL AND NONPROFESSIONAL MARRIED WOMEN

Sharon Price-Bonham
and Carolyn Kitchings Johnson

During the last few decades the increased number and proportion of women in the labor force have precipitated numerous studies on the effects of women's employment on their roles as wives and mothers, their occupational rights and opportunities, as well as on the impact of women within traditional "male" jobs (Hoffman and Nye, 1974; Sweet, 1973). However, there has been a paucity of research on women and retirement, and while it is clear from research on men's retirement that occupational status plays an important role for retirement attitudes and adjustment (see Atchley, 1972, 1976a), investigations on women's retirement often do not differentiate among women working in divergent occupations (Barnett and Baruch, 1978b) or exclude women in high-prestige professions from their analyses owing to relatively small sample sizes for this group (Campbell et al., 1976). The few studies that do include women in higher occupational status groups failed to investigate the relative effect of selected predictor variables on retirement attitudes

*AUTHORS' NOTE: This project was funded in part by the College of Home Economics, University of Georgia.*

(Anderson et al., 1978; Prentis, 1980). Therefore, the major purpose of this study is to compare professional and nonprofessional women's attitudes toward retirement, and to explore characteristics that contribute to positive attitudes among women in both groups.

## REVIEW OF LITERATURE

Research shows links between job attachment (Simpson and McKinney, 1966), occupational status (Epstein and Murray, 1968), income level (Atchley, 1972), or identification with the worker role (Loether, 1967) and individuals' reactions to retirement. Several authors have reported that women in divergent occupational status groups differ in these same characteristics. For example, professional women, when compared to nonprofessional women, have been found to hold a stronger identification with their work role (Fogarty et al., 1971); more often be continuous, full-time workers (Holmstrom, 1972); have had mothers who were employed when they were children; have at least one child but seldom more than two (Bebbington, 1973); have postponed having children until they were well established in their careers; have higher incomes (Fogarty et al., 1971), and be more self-reliant and self-sufficient (Burke and Weir, 1976). Therefore, it could be concluded that professional, as compared to nonprofessional, women would more often have had a same-sex role model in the labor force (as well as one who retired), would have had more money and a longer work history to plan and prepare for retirement, would be less dependent on their spouse for retirement, and would hold a stronger identification with their work role. However, there is conflicting evidence as to how these variables might affect one's attitude toward retirement.

### IMPORTANCE AND IDENTIFICATION WITH THE WORKER ROLE

Historically, it has been accepted (and expected) that men identify with their occupational role. However, work for women has only been viewed as significant prior to marriage and childbirth, and in cases of widowhood or financial reverses (Lopata and Steinhart, 1971). In fact, Lopata (1966) reported that women who were employed full-time still maintained a home-centered identity and held the attitude that every woman should be married, have children, and that family roles should have primary salience. Similarly, Lopata and Steinhart (1971), after studying widows in an urban area, reported that women were only marginally involved in the occupational structure, had taken jobs that were convenient, and had no program of career succession. This lack of involvement was attributed to the fact that women participate in multiple roles resulting in lower commitment to the work role, the American value system's restrictions on women's orientation to work, and to women's being forced into occupations which they would not otherwise choose (Harmon, 1967).

However, there are exceptions to this pattern, particularly among educated, professional women (Lopata, 1966) who have stronger involvement in their work role than do women in lower-level occupations (Lopata and Steinhart, 1971). A married woman's occupational role may not be an economic necessity but may have an expressive, non-economic emphasis; that is, the job may be inherently desirable to the woman (Riley et al., 1963). Research has also indicated that married women who are well-educated and freer to choose their roles may be seeking in the work role a "fair share of social recognition as individuals to augment the limited status derived from their homemaker role" (Arnott and Bengtson, 1970: 505). This differential involvement with the work role was recognized by Fogarty et al. (1971) when they distinguished between the career-oriented woman, who views work as highly important and seeks an organized developmental job sequence, and the job-oriented woman, who works only for reasons such as economic security, without an organized sequence.

The importance of work in an individual's life could influence his or her attitude toward retirement. It has been suggested that strong attachment to their occupation prevents people from developing a positive reaction to retirement, whereas persons with low attachment to their work role look forward to retirement (Palmore, 1965; Atchley, 1972; Fillenbaum, 1971). Also, people who view their occupation as the central organizing factor in their lives tend to regard retirement as disrupting and threatening to their primary role identification (Fillenbaum, 1971). In contrast, persons who view their occupation primarily as a source of income and not as intrinsically satisfying may perceive retirement as an opportunity to pursue other activities (Shanas, 1972).

Contrasting evidence is reported by Atchley (1972), who after studying social workers with high job commitment concluded that it was possible for people to be both highly committed to their work and to develop a positive orientation toward retirement. Lowenthal (1972) viewed this ability to adapt as developing early in one's life and as being positively related to adjustment to retirement. For example, persons who were involved in both work and nonwork activities often had both instrumental and expressive life goals, and this flexibility rendered retirement less disruptive (Thurnher, 1974). It may be that persons who have cultivated role flexibility and who have participated in several roles throughout their life experience fewer adjustment problems in retirement (King and Howell, 1965). Professional women who are strongly attached to their jobs can therefore be expected to express relatively negative attitudes toward retirement, particularly if they lack role flexibility.

## INCOME

The professional woman, as compared to the nonprofessional woman, has a higher income, and this fact may increase her options during retirement. Owing to her advantageous financial situation, she may find it relatively easy to satisfy her needs and achieve her personal goals during this stage of life (Sussman, 1972). For the woman employed at the lower echelons of the occupational ladder, on the other hand, retirement often signifies the end of a much-needed source of income, resulting in a negative attitude toward retirement. Consequently, retirement appears to be attractive only if there is an adequate income (Atchley, 1972), for it is only women in professional occupations who can look forward to a satisfactory retirement income.

## WOMEN AND RETIREMENT

Retirement has not been viewed as holding equal significance for women and men (Lowenthal et al., 1975). Some findings support this assumption. For instance, Palmore (1965) concluded that women, regardless of income, voluntarily retire more frequently than men. One reason postulated for this finding is that many women experience several roles (wife, mother, homemaker) throughout their life cycle which they perceive to be equally significant as the worker role. This phenomenon affords women the opportunity to "practice" role transitions, thereby making the transition to retirement easier and resulting in feminine resilience in old age:

> Women are not as devastated as men are likely to be when old age, another impermanence, separates them from the productive, involved, financially independent world of middle age [Kline, 1975: 490].

However, several investigators fail to corroborate these findings. Atchley (1976c) reports that retired female school teachers and employees of a telephone company, compared to men, took longer to get used to retirement, and were lonelier and more depressed. Fox (1977) found that retired women had a lower level of social contacts than employed women, resulting in a less positive affect balance on the part of the retirees. She concluded that social contacts constitute a stronger determinant of the psychological well-being of female retirees than of working women or housewives.

Jacobson (1974) studied industrial workers and found that women were more reluctant to retire than men. Specifically, the women's attitude toward retirement was related to the social aspects of the job, i.e., women whose principal social contacts (friends) were at the job were more reluctant to retire than women with other social contacts. She concluded that retirement may be a more stressful experience for women than previously suggested.

When Laurence (1961) asked business and professional women to list the areas that would present the greatest difficulty in the next five years, the preretirement subjects listed problems with health and keeping constructively busy. This result seemed to imply that women were concerned about leaving their jobs and about their retirement. In a longitudinal study of higher-educated and -income persons, Streib and Schneider (1971) also found retired women, as compared to men, to report a sharper increase in feelings of uselessness.

In summary, it appears that many women consider retirement as a significant and in some cases problematic life transition. Their attitudes toward retirement appear to vary according to occupational status, identification with the work role, opportunity to practice role transitions, role flexibility, social contacts, and resources available for retirement, including income. Interrelationships among these variables may account for the inconsistent findings of previous research.

## METHODS

### SAMPLE AND MEASURES

This study was an expansion of an earlier study by Johnson and Price-Bonham (1980). In the earlier study, 59 women were interviewed. However, one of the concerns in that study was the occupational homogeneity of the respondents. Therefore, the sample was expanded to 100 women for this study, including 52 who were classified as professional (professors, lawyers, executives, managers) and 48 who were classified as nonprofessional (clerical and sales). The subjects were presently employed and ranged in age from 55 to 63 years. The sample was restricted to married women in order to examine the relevancy of the work role as compared to other roles. Respondents were located through places of employment, alumni associations, womens' clubs and organizations, and community leaders in the Athens-Atlanta, Georgia, area. Women were initially contacted by phone, the study was explained, and a request for their participation was made. The data were collected by a combination of interviewing (by the authors) and a self-administered questionnaire.

Data were collected for the following variables:

*Demographic Variables.* Data were collected regarding how many hours the respondent worked per week, level of education and/or special training for job, employment history, wife's salary, family income, duration of present job, number of children, husband's occupation, and husband's income.

*Job attachment* was defined as work motivation, job commitment, and attitudes toward the company, supervisor, job, and work. Scales were adapted from the Oregon University study on preretirement counseling and retirement adjustment (College of Business Administration, 1969) and from Simpson and McKinney (1966).

*Primary role perception* was defined as the role a woman considered most important. It was attempted to determine if the respondents identified stronger with family role(s) or occupational role(s) by using questions adapted from Ginzberg (1966). In addition, each subject ranked the importance of the roles of daughter, wife, mother, worker, homemaker, and friend (Lopata, 1973).

*Attitude toward health* was measured by the subject's perception of their present health status. The scale for this variable was adapted from the University of Oregon study, and the higher the score the more positive subjects' attitude toward their own health.

*Life satisfaction* was defined as the subject's general feelings of well-being and contentment and was measured with a scale adapted from the University of Oregon study. The higher the score, the more satisfied the subject was with her life.

*Financial Plans for Retirement.* Each woman was asked how much financial planning had been done for retirement, expected sources of retirement income, and the amount of expected retirement income.

*Plans for Postretirement Activities.* Questions (adapted from the University of Oregon study) were asked in order to determine how much planning and what type of plans had been made for activities after retirement.

*Reasons for Retirement.* Using questions (adapted from the University of Oregon study) on mandatory retirement, one's own desires, and others' expectations, reasons for retirement were obtained.

*Sex role attitudes* were measured using a Likert Scale (Osmond and Martin, 1975) that contained items clustered into four categories: familial roles, extrafamilial roles, stereotypes of male/female nature and behavior, and social change related to sex roles. Each item was scored along a five-point continuum, with a higher score indicating more "modern" sex role attitudes and a lower score a more "traditional" sex role attitude.

*Attitude toward retirement* was measured using a scale adapted from the University of Oregon study. This scale measured subjects' perception of the effect retirement would have on their lives. The scores ranged from 9 to 36, with higher scores indicating a more favorable attitude toward retirement.

## SAMPLE CHARACTERISTICS

The sample consisted of 48 nonprofessional women and 52 professional women. Similar to other studies comparing professional and nonprofessional women, the data presented in Table 8.1 indicate that the professional women were significantly different in salaries, family income, husband's educational and occupational level, hours worked per week, time spent in leisure activities, length of time they had been in their present position, and number of jobs held. There were no significant differences in other demographic variables, including number of children (professional women had a mean of 2.3 children, nonprofessional women 2.4 children), years in the labor force (professional women had been in the labor force for an average of 21.2 years, nonprofessional women 20.2 years), and time out from working for such events as childbirth and childrearing (professional women had been out of the labor force M = 8.6 years; nonprofessional women M = 8.9 years).

Attitudinal differences between the two groups of women were in the expected direction, indicating stronger work commitment and less identification with home-centered roles on the part of professionals. Specifically, professional women expressed more positive attitudes toward work (t = 4.41, p < .01; eta$^2$ = .23), expressed a higher job commitment (t = 3.20; p < .01, eta$^2$ = .15), viewed the role of homemaker as less important (t = 3.32; p < .01, eta$^2$ = .19), and expressed more modern sex role attitudes (t = 4.87, p < .01; eta$^2$ = .26) than nonprofessional women.

There were no significant differences in the women's attitude toward retirement. Specifically, the nonprofessional women held slightly more

**TABLE 8.1    Attitude Toward Retirement and Selected Variables for Professional and Nonprofessional Women (correlation coefficient values)**

| | Attitude Toward Retirement | |
|---|---|---|
| Variable | Professional Women | Nonprofessional Women |
| Length of time at present job | −.34* | .26 |
| Hours worked/week | −.29* | .17 |
| Level of education | −.31* | −.23 |
| Salary | −.20 | −.16 |
| Number of jobs held | −.17 | −.12 |
| Family income | .29* | .19 |
| Husband's occupational status | .20 | .24 |
| Attachment to present job | .19 | .10 |
| Commitment to work | −.55** | −.23 |
| Primary role perception | | |
| a. importance of wife role | .12 | .19 |
| b. importance of worker role | .14 | .16 |
| c. importance of mother role | .16 | .21 |
| d. importance of homemeker role | .21 | .20 |
| e. importance of friend role | .22 | .12 |
| Attitude toward health | .26 | .24 |
| Life satisfaction | .12 | −.44** |
| Financial plans for retirement | | |
| a. Degree of planning | .18 | .28* |
| b. Sources of planned retirement income | .16 | −.36* |
| c. Degree husband's pension was viewed as source of income after retirement | .30* | .28* |
| Plans for postretirement activities | | |
| a. Continue work activities | .36** | −.18 |
| b. Number of leisure activities planned | −.34* | .26 |
| Reasons for retirement | | |
| a. Mandatory | −.20 | −.08 |
| b. Other expectations | −.25 | −.14 |
| Sex role attitudes | .03 | .30* |

NOTE: A negative relation indicates a more negative attitude toward retirement.
* $p < .05$; ** $p < .01$

positive attitudes toward retirement (M = 24.58; S.D. = 4.2) than the professional women (M = 22.48, S.D. = 3.9), but in general, both groups expressed positive attitudes toward retirement.

## RESULTS

Correlation coefficient values were computed in order to determine possible relations between selected predictor variables and the attitudes toward retirement held by professional and nonprofessional women. As indicated by the data presented in Table 8.2, eight variables were significantly related to the professional women's attitudes toward retirement, and only five variables were significantly related to the nonprofessional women's attitudes toward retirement. In only one case (degree to which husband's pension was viewed as a source of retirement income) were the same variables significantly related to attitudes toward retirement for both professional and nonprofessional women. Variables related to the work role were more often significantly related to the retirement attitudes of professional women, while economic and personal variables played a more important role in the retirement attitudes of nonprofessional women.

According to the zero-order correlations, professional women were significantly less likely to express positive retirement attitudes if they had a lengthy employment history and currently spent a considerable amount of time with work activities. The higher their education, the more negative their retirement attitudes. High family income, but not the women's own wages, seemed to enhance positive retirement attitudes, as did reliance on the husband's pension as retirement income. Professional women who were strongly committed to their work reported particularly negative retirement attitudes.

Except for reliance on the husband's retirement benefits, none of these variables significantly related to the retirement attitudes of nonprofessional women. For the nonprofessionals, we found a negative relationship between current life satisfaction and retirement attitudes, as well as a positive association between egalitarian sex role norms and positive retirement attitudes.

Some interesting patterns emerge in regard to relations between retirement planning and attitudes. For nonprofessional women, financial retirement plans seemed to further the development of positive retirement attitudes. Professional women, on the other hand, appeared more favorably oriented toward retirement if they anticipated some continuation of

**TABLE 8.2   Analysis of Demographic Data for Professional and Nonprofessional Women**

| Variable | Mean Value | | t value | eta$^2$ |
| --- | --- | --- | --- | --- |
| | Professional Women | Nonprofessional women | | |
| Respondent's salary | $14,200 | $8,700 | 4.47** | .26 |
| Family income | $32,100 | $22,200 | 4.17** | .23 |
| Respondent's level of education | 17+ years[1] | 13-14 years[2] | 7.67** | .51 |
| Husband's level of education | 17+ years | 15-16 years | 2.77** | .11 |
| Husband's occupational status | Professional Rank | Middle Range | 3.14** | .15 |
| Hours respondents worked per week | 47.7 hours | 30.2 hours | 3.30** | .16 |
| Hours respondents spend in leisure time per week | 2.5 hours | 6.2 hours | 4.41** | .22 |
| Years in present position | 13.8 years | 8.2 years | 5.21** | .41 |
| Number of jobs held in work career | 5.9 jobs | 3.2 jobs | 2.61* | .13 |

1. 17+ years of education indicates some graduate work or professional education beyond a bachelor's degree.
2. 13-14 years of education between one and two years of college

* p < .05; ** p < .01

their current work activities beyond the retirement transition. Correspondingly, those women indicating extensive leisure plans for retirement were inclined to view this life stage in a more negative light.

A stepwise regression technique was used in order to determine the relative magnitude and possible differential influence of these variables on professional and nonprofessional women's attitudes toward retirement. The $R^2$ values for both groups of women were quite high, accounting for 54.4 percent and 49.8 percent, respectively, of the variance in the dependent variable (see Table 8.3). Only one variable, husband's pension as a source of retirement income, was entered for both groups of women. It is noteworthy that the more that both groups of women depended on their husband's pension as a source of retirement income, the more positive were their attitudes toward retirement. This finding could be indicative of a basic belief that the men would "provide" for their wives, or that the husband's benefits should be the major basis for the couple's economic security after retirement. For example, further analysis revealed that 47 (90.4 percent) of the professional women and 43 (89.5 percent) of the nonprofessional women were depending on their husband's pension as the major source of retirement income.

Even more surprising was the finding that only 29 (55.7 percent) professional women and 21 (43.8 percent) of the nonprofessional women had paid into any retirement fund of their own. In fact, over 50 percent of the women who had not paid into a retirement fund had actually opted not to do so. The second major source of expected retirement income was, as might be expected, Social Security. In all, 48 (92.3 percent) of the professional women and 40 (83.3 percent) of the nonprofessional women had paid into Social Security throughout the major portion (or all) of their work careers. However, due to interrupted work histories and lower salaries resulting in lower Social Security benefits, they rely on their husband's Social Security to a greater extent than their own. The economic security expected to ensue from the husband's benefits tended to enhance both professional and nonprofessional women's attitudes toward retirement.

Three variables that were entered into the regression analysis for the professional women had to do with their occupational roles, namely, commitment to work, time at their present job (both negatively related to attitude toward retirement), and work-related activities planned for after retirement. The first two relationships suggest that women who are strongly involved in their current work roles are rather reluctant to give up

**TABLE 8.3  Results of Stepwise Regression Analysis on Attitude Toward Retirement**

| Variables entered for Professional Women | $R^2$ Values | $r'$ Value | Variables entered for Nonprofessional Women | $R^2$ Values | $r'$ Value |
|---|---|---|---|---|---|
| Commitment to work | .302 | -.55** | Life satisfaction | .194 | -.44** |
| Work relative activities planned for after retirement | .386 | .36** | Sources of planned retirement income | .333 | -.36* |
| Time at present job | .448 | -.34* | Sex role attitudes | .399 | .30* |
| Leisure activities planned for after retirement | .509 | -.34* | Husband's pension as source of retirement income | .450 | .28* |
| Husband's pension as source of retirement | .544 | .30* | Degree of financial planning for retirement | .498 | .28* |

1. A negative relation indicates a more negative attitude toward retirement.

* $p < .05$; ** $p < .01$

work for retirement. This interpretation is also supported by the positive relation between work activities planned and the professional women's attitude toward retirement. Professional women who plan to continue work-related activities after retirement will undergo less change during the retirement transition and may thus view retirement as a less disruptive event than women without work intentions. The negative relationship between number of planned leisure activities and retirement attitudes which shows for the professional, but not for the nonprofessional women must be regarded within this context. Planning for many postretirement leisure activities could be less a sign of advance preparation than of a rather desperate attempt to maintain an active life after retirement outside the work role.

The variables entered into the regression analysis for the nonprofessional women were more financially and personally oriented. Three of the five variables dealt with financial issues after retirement. Both reliance on husband's pension and financial planning positively contributed to retirement attitudes, whereas expected use of various retirement income sources (including savings and investments) was negatively related to the nonprofessional women's attitude toward retirement. Women who count on their husband's benefits and who have made financial retirement plans may anticipate less economic problems and thus view retirement in a relatively positive light, whereas women who have to rely on several income sources after retirement might perceive their retirement incomes as relatively unstable and also fear exhausting their economic resources.

Those women who indicated high satisfaction with their present life expressed less positive attitudes toward retirement. Given the lower family income of nonprofessional women, they may be more concerned about the financial aspects of retirement and view their work income as essential for the maintenance of their present living standard. The positive relation between egalitarian sex-role attitudes and attitude toward retirement might indicate that a nontraditional sex-role ideology serves women as an adaptive coping resource, a trend which was previously shown for adjustment to divorce (Brown et al., 1977). Also, women who are satisfied with their current role as working wife could view retirement as depriving them of a valued life interest. Women who work despite adherence to traditional sex role norms may do so primarily for economic reasons. Loss of income at retirement could signify a decrease in financial well-being for this group.

## IMPLICATIONS

In spite of the increasing emphasis on women and employment, the issue of women's retirement has been widely neglected, and few attempts have been made to investigate the impact of women's occupational status on their attitudes and reactions to retirement. It was the purpose of this modest study to investigate the attitudes of preretirement professional and nonprofessional women toward retirement. The findings indicate several significant demographic and attitudinal differences between the two groups of women. It could also be shown that different variables affect the two groups' attitudes toward retirement, but both professional and nonprofessional women depended on their husband's retirement income.

It is obvious that the work role is not of equal importance to all women. Professional women develop a strong commitment to their work, whereas nonprofessional women seem to view work more in terms of extrinsic gratifications, i.e., as a source of income. Consequently, future research on women's employment and retirement should control for occupational status.

Both groups of women in this study expressed relatively positive attitudes toward retirement, although such attitudes were slightly more common among the nonprofessional women. The different regression results obtained for professional and nonprofessional women further confirm the divergent meaning of work and retirement in their lives.

Professional women tend toward a more negative retirement view if they are strongly committed to their work and do not envision any continuation of work activities after retirement. These women may profit from retirement programs that help them develop meaningful leisure pursuits (rather than a vast number of vague retirement plans), as well as from opportunities for professional activities after retirement. Slow phasing-out of their professional roles, such as in partial retirement plans now offered by some universities, could also ease these women's retirement transition. Furthermore, employers and various agencies could engage retired professional women for the provision of limited services in their areas of expertise. Since these women seem to suffer primarily from the loss of intrinsic job gratifications and usually have adequate retirement incomes, they may be willing to deliver such services for little or no pay. Nonprofessional women, on the other hand, seem particularly concerned about their economic situation after retirement. These women's financial worries could be alleviated by careful financial planning and enrollment in adequate pension plans.

The positive relationship between retirement attitudes and reliance on husband's benefits for both groups of women highlights the inadequacy of current benefit policies for women. A change in this trend requires reorientation of policies at the governmental, industrial, and private levels.

At the governmental level, most policies regarding the family and work imply that in intact marriages there is one wage earner—the man. With this underlying assumption, laws that "keep working women in this (secondary) place" have been developed. For example, Social Security is predicated on the one-earner breadwinner family. Social Security is paid on an individual basis, but benefits are allotted on a family basis. In addition, there is no mechanism by which women might contribute to this system during the time they might be out of the labor force for child bearing and rearing. Due to lower salaries and interrupted work histories, women's Social Security benefits will be lower. Consequently, retiring women are being punished for fulfilling society's expectations.

There is a lack of policies at the governmental level regarding pension benefits. Many occupations that women are involved in often do not include a pension system (domestic, sales, small businesses). Because of the job mobility of many women (they are expected and reinforced by law to follow their husbands), as well as their interrupted work histories, women are not in a pension system long enough to qualify for benefits, and often lose the contributions they made to various systems. In addition, it is becoming increasingly apparent that husbands and wives often naively assume that the wife will receive the husband's pension benefits should he precede her in death. However, in many systems benefits go only to the husband, and if he dies, the wife does not receive them. Also, with increasing divorce rates, wives can no longer count on economic security in old age. Middle-aged and older divorcees may suddenly find they are no longer entitled to their husband's pensions. Government needs to address these issues (among others) for all women and to develop policies to assure that women, in all roles, have access to an earned pension system.

At the industrial level there are few written policies. Since women seem to depend on formal retirement programs (see chapter 6, this volume), corporations and educational institutions should offer preretirement programs specifically designed for women. In addition to offering relevant information about Social Security benefits, employers should also encourage women's participation in private pension plans.

Policies at the personal level are almost always unwritten and often unspoken but have tremendous impact on lives. In contrast to policies at the governmental or industrial levels, the internalized policies can be changed by the individual. This is relevant, as many women have been socialized to believe a man will "take care of them" throughout their lifetime. Consequently, women are less apt to prepare for their own retirement. However, because of different life expectancies, the high divorce rate, and women's low benefits, it is important that women plan and assume responsibility for their own retirement incomes.

In summary, it is evident that retirement experiences vary by the occupational status of women. Retirement programs need to take these differences into consideration. Special efforts are also necessary to overcome current inequities in the retirement benefits of men and women that render wives dependent on their husbands' retirement benefits.

# 9

# RETIREMENT PLANS AND RETIREMENT ADJUSTMENT

## Maximiliane Szinovacz

**Are retirement plans essential** for adaptation to this life transition? Which plans are the most salient? To what extent are retirement plans carried out, and how does nonrealization of retirement plans impact on adjustment? None of these questions can be adequately answered on the basis of current research. However, the provision of efficient retirement preparation programs would seem to be one important means in aiding individuals adjust to this life transition. The present study constitutes an attempt to find at least preliminary answers to these questions. Specifically, data are presented on women's retirement plans, the extent to which plans are implemented, and the relative importance of specific retirement plans for adjustment.

## PREVIOUS RESEARCH

Studies concerned with the effect of preretirement conditions on women's retirement adjustment have centered on selected demographic and personal characteristics, retirement timing, and retirement attitudes (Atchley, 1971; Barfield and Morgan, 1978a; Coyle and Fuller, 1977;

*AUTHOR'S NOTE: This project was funded by the NRTA-AARP Andrus Foundation, Washington, D.C.*

Fillenbaum, 1971b; Levy, 1980; Pruchno, 1981), but neglected women's own retirement plans. The general trend suggested by these investigations is that negative retirement attitudes and/or psychological unpreparedness for the retirement transition can have long-lasting effects on adaptation.

As far as preretirement planning among women is concerned, it has been established that they are less likely than men to be covered by private pension plans (Benner et al., 1981) and also seem to have less access to retirement programs offered by employers (Atchley, 1981; see also chapter 6, this volume). Prentis (1980) further notes a general lack of preretirement preparation for his sample of middle-aged white-collar working women. His findings also indicate that women may become more inclined to plan for retirement when they approach retirement age rather than developing such plans well ahead of the transition process. Preparations centered on economic issues and leisure activities, as well as a variety of other life spheres.

While it is generally assumed that retirement plans constitute an important part of the anticipatory socialization process and further retirement adjustment, even the literature on men's retirement offers inconsistent evidence in this regard. For instance, it is unclear whether retirement programs have long-lasting effects on the participants and which plans or programs are the most effective (Bynum et al., 1978; Glamser, 1981; Manion et al., 1969; McPherson and Guppy, 1979; Monk, 1971).

Given the lack of pertinent research and the inconsistency of previous findings, exploratory investigations are necessary to develop guidelines for large-scale investigations on this important issue. The present study takes a first step in this direction.

## METHODS

### DATA COLLECTION AND SAMPLE

Data collection for this study was based on extensive face-to-face interviews with recent women retirees. Subjects were identified through retirement records of universities and high schools, state and city files, as well as through private employers and community programs for the elderly. Respondents were initially contacted through mailed questionnaires. Those who returned the questionnaires, qualified for the study, and agreed to participate were then interviewed in their homes by trained female interviewers. The interviews contained both open-ended and closed questions and lasted between 1 and 3 1/2 hours, with an average of 104 minutes. All interviews were tape-recorded and subsequently transcribed.

The final sample consists of 115 women, most of whom (95 percent) had retired within five years prior to the interview. They had been employed for an average of 19 years in their last job and had worked over 30 years throughout their lifetime. Since the study was conducted in a middle-sized city in Florida, it is also worthwhile to note that the subjects were Florida residents before their retirement and had resided in North Florida for an average of 35 years. The majority of the subjects had worked in lower- (29 percent) and middle-level (25 percent) white-collar jobs, but the sample also included blue-collar and service workers (13 percent), as well as medium-level (27 percent) and higher-level (6 percent) administrative and professional workers. Of the respondents, 77 percent were white, the remainder were black. The average educational level achieved by the women was 14 years, and their average personal retirement income was slightly above $9000. Some of the women were still under 60 years of age, yet none of the respondents indicated that they were considering becoming employed in the future. Of the subjects, 42 percent were married, 30 percent widowed, 18 percent divorced, and 10 percent had never married. Apart from the 42 percent of married women who lived with their spouses, 40 percent lived alone and 18 percent with other persons.

**MEASUREMENT**

Data concerning retirement plans are based on respondents' answers to the following questions: Did you make any plans for retirement? Before you retired, did you plan to start some new hobbies or to become involved in some new activities once you quit work? Did you make any financial plans for your retirement? Each of these questions was followed by probes concerning types of plans, and for the last two questions, probes on whether plans were followed through. Since subjects were currently retired, the reports on retirement plans were retrospective and thus subject to some bias owing to recall errors or postretirement events. However, the general figures obtained for this sample are similar to those shown in earlier research on preretirement samples.

Several scales were used to measure women's postretirement adjustment. Specifically, the instruments included an extended and modified version of Thompson's (1958) job deprivation scale, the Kutner et al. (1969) morale scale, and Bradburn's measures of positive and negative

**TABLE 9.1**   Mean, Median, Standard Deviation, and Reliability of
Adjustment Scales

|                  | M    | Md   | s.d. | alpha |
|------------------|------|------|------|-------|
| Job deprivation  | 2.87 | 2.88 | 0.33 | .89   |
| Morale           | 3.26 | 3.19 | 0.44 | .84   |
| Positive feelings| 2.91 | 3.00 | 0.56 | .67   |
| Negative feelings| 3.54 | 3.68 | 0.53 | .72   |

feelings of happiness. The scale scores were derived through Likert scaling procedures and had a potential range of 1 to 4 (M = 2.5). Higher scores indicate higher adjustment, or less negative feelings of happiness. The mean, standard deviation, median, and reliability (Cronbach's alpha) of these scales are shown in Table 9.1. These data indicate that subjects generally adjusted quite well to retirement; for each scale, average scores were above the scale mean of 2.5.

## RESULTS

### RETIREMENT PLANS OF WOMEN RETIREES

Descriptive data on the women's retirement plans are presented in Tables 9.2 to 9.5. Of the respondents, 57 percent answered in the affirmative the general question as to whether any retirement plans had been made. Their descriptions of these plans suggest that financial plans were most common, followed by plans to travel, hobbies, community activities, and increased interaction with children and relatives. Some women also purchased new homes or property and camping vehicles (Table 9.2).

Financial plans were made by 63 percent of the subjects, and they were practically always carried through. Since a good proportion of this sample was obtained from state employee files, most of the women were covered by state pension plans, a condition that is not quite typical for the total population of female retirees (see Beller, 1980). In addition to the pension plans, women prepared for retirement by saving, creating additional income sources, and paying off debts before retirement. Those women who failed to make financial plans for their retirement were also asked why no plans had been made. In answering this question, the majority

**TABLE 9.2    General Retirement Plans**

|  | *Percentage* |
|---|---|
| General plans: | |
| pension | 17 |
| other financial | 32 |
| relation to children, relatives | 10 |
| new home, property | 9 |
| travel | 19 |
| camping vehicle | 5 |
| religious activities | 3 |
| community activities | 10 |
| work-related acitvities | 5 |
| hobbies | 12 |
| other | 11 |
| Total | 57 |

indicated that they had benefit plans or that financial plans weren't necessary for them. Other reasons given included lack of financial flexibility, support from others, and sudden retirement that didn't give them the chance to make retirement preparations (see Table 9.3).

Two-fifths of the respondents reported that they had some assistance with their financial retirement plans (e.g., short courses offered by employers). Those who would have liked additional assistance most frequently mentioned more information on benefits, help with investments, and help with their budgeting. A few women also complained that the information on benefits they had received was unclear and not accurate. Some of the case study materials further suggest that some of the courses offered by employers were held as small workshops and offered only once, so that women who missed one session or the workshop as a whole failed to receive some or all of the information.

The final question on retirement preparation concerned plans for activities and hobbies. Of the retirees, 59 percent said that they had made such plans, but these plans were not always carried through. Only 37 percent of the subjects actually started some new activity after their retirement, and 30 percent did not engage in at least some of the activities they planned to become involved in. Among the activities planned, travel and volunteer work were most frequently mentioned, followed by needlework, community activities, social contacts, and religious activities. Failure to engage in planned activities was most often explained by the fact that other

TABLE 9.3    Financial Plans

|  | *Percent* |
|---|---|
| Financial plans: |  |
| savings | 42 |
| insurance | 6 |
| additional income | 33 |
| benefit plans | 20 |
| tighter budget | 5 |
| pay off debts | 15 |
| replacement purchases before retirement | 9 |
| other | 8 |
| Total | 63 |
| Reasons for no financial plans: |  |
| not necessary | 19 |
| retirement too sudden | 17 |
| no financial flexibility | 14 |
| support by others | 11 |
| had benefit plan | 42 |
| other | 6 |
| (N = 36) |  |
| Financial assistance needed: |  |
| more information on benefits | 18 |
| help with budgeting | 15 |
| help with investments | 18 |
| information on taxes | 3 |
| information on health benefits | 5 |
| information on housing | 3 |
| more exact information | 5 |
| other | 18 |
| had assistance | 41 |
| (N = 39) |  |

activities kept them too busy to start new ones. Illness, family responsibilities, and diverse situational and external circumstances also prevented some women from realizing their retirement plans (see Table 9.4).

## RETIREMENT PLANS AND ADJUSTMENT

In order to establish whether retirement plans affect women's adaptation to this life transition, correlations between retirement plans and the

**TABLE 9.4   Plans Regarding Activities**

| | Activities | |
| | planned | started |
| | % | % |
| --- | --- | --- |
| Activities: | | |
| nothing | 43 | 63 |
| sport, exercise | 5 | 4 |
| yard work | 1 | 0 |
| needlework | 8 | 4 |
| arts and crafts | 6 | 1 |
| music | 3 | 2 |
| read | 2 | 3 |
| household and family | 4 | 4 |
| community | 8 | 7 |
| volunteer | 11 | 4 |
| educational | 1 | 0 |
| social | 7 | 4 |
| religious | 8 | 7 |
| travel | 17 | 9 |
| work-related | 2 | 2 |
| letter writing | 2 | 1 |
| other hobbies | 5 | 4 |
| other | 3 | 1 |

| | Percent |
| --- | --- |
| Reasons for not starting: | |
| lazy | 3 |
| health | 13 |
| financial | 8 |
| no time, busy with | 5 |
| other activities | 40 |
| family responsibilities | 11 |
| outside circumstances | 11 |
| no planning | 24 |
| other | 8 |
| (N = 75) | |

four adjustment indicators were computed. Since demographic and other relevant variables may affect the direct relations between plans and adjustment, several control variables were introduced, namely, retirement age, marital status, income, race, and retirement for health reasons. Both the zero-order and partial correlation coefficients between plans and adjustment are shown in Table 9.5.

**TABLE 9.5   Retirement Plans and Selected Adjustment Indicators (zero-order and partial correlation coefficients)**

|                     | Job deprivation | | Morale | | Positive feelings | | Negative feelings | |
|---------------------|------|---------|------|---------|-------|---------|-------|---------|
|                     | zero | parital | zero | partial | zero  | partial | zero  | partial |
| General plans       | .13  | .11     | −.02 | −.05    | .19*  | .20*    | .19*  | .16     |
| Plans for activities| .05  | .06     | .05  | .07     | .26** | .36**   | −.04  | −.02    |
| Financial plans     | .04  | .06     | −.02 | −.03    | .01   | .07     | −.01  | .02     |

* p < .05;  ** p < .01

NOTE:  Control variables were:  early retirement (before age 59), income, marital status (married), race, and retirement for health reasons. All nominal variables were coded as dummy variables. Ns for the zero-sum and partial correlation coefficients differed slightly owing to missing values (115 and 107, respectively).

The results obtained from the zero-order correlations suggest that neither job deprivation nor morale are affected by retirement plans. Positive feelings of happiness after retirement seem to be furthered both by general retirement plans and by plans for activities. The former relationship is slightly reduced when the controls are introduced, whereas the relationship between positive feelings and plans for activities increases notably after the controls are entered. The zero-order correlations also indicate a significant positive relationship between general plans and lack of negative feelings, but this relationship is reduced to a nonsignificant level when the control variables are held constant. Overall, these results suggest that general retirement plans, and especially plans for activities, are associated with positive feelings of happiness after the retirement transition.

**REALIZATION OF LEISURE PLANS**

One reason why previous studies concerning the effect of retirement planning on later adjustment may have led to divergent results is that the implementation of plans was usually not considered. It is likely that adjustment to retirement depends not only on the extent of planning but is also contingent on whether or not plans were actually carried out. Since most women followed through with their financial retirement plans, many of which required preretirement action, only the implementation of leisure plans is examined here. As indicated above, quite a few women failed to engage in the activities they had planned to start after retirement. Specifically, 43 percent of the subjects had no plans, 19 percent had made plans but implemented none of them, 10 percent realized only some of their plans, and 28 percent followed through with all of their plans.

In order to test the effect that differential planning and implementation of leisure activities have on women's adjustment, analyses of variance and multiple classification analyses were performed. These analyses again included controls for retirement age, marital status, income, race, and retirement for health reasons. The results are presented in Table 9.6. The adjustment scores for each planning category are expressed in terms of their deviation from the scale mean score. Both original values and those adjusted for the control variables are shown for each adjustment measure. In each case, negative values indicate less adjustment for that group than for the total population, and positive values suggest higher than average adjustment.

We again find no significant relationship between planning and the job deprivation and morale scores, although the former main effect approaches statistical significance ($p < .10$). In both cases, the combined effect of the control variables is significant at the $p < .01$ level. For the happiness measures (positive and negative feelings), significant effects show for the planning variable, but not for the covariates. Positive feelings of happiness prevailed, particularly among those women who planned postretirement activities and who implemented all of their plans, whereas the nonplanners especially scored relatively low on positive feelings. Negative feelings were also least pronounced among those who planned and realized all of their plans, but in this case it was particularly women who only followed through with some of their plans who tended toward negative feelings.

## DISCUSSION

The present study provides evidence that both retirement planning and plan implementation contribute to positive feelings of happiness after the retirement transition. This trend is restricted to plans for activities; financial plans did not significantly differentiate between the satisfied and dissatisfied retirees. The lack of significant relationships between financial plans and adjustment in this sample could be a consequence of data collection procedures. Most women included in this sample were covered by state pension plans, a condition that is atypical for the majority of

**TABLE 9.6  Multiple Classification Analysis of Selected Adjustment Indicators, by Realization of Activity Plans**

| Deviation from mean: | Job deprivation | | Morale | | Positive feelings | | Negative feelings | |
|---|---|---|---|---|---|---|---|---|
| | not adjusted | adjusted | not adjusted | adjusted | not adjusted | adjusted | not adjusted | adjusted |
| No plans (46) | -.01 | -.02 | -.03 | -.03 | -.13 | -.17 | +.03 | +.01 |
| Plans, none started (21) | -.07 | -.02 | +.05 | +.11 | -.07 | -.01 | -.11 | -.06 |
| Plans, some started (11) | -.08 | -.18 | -.03 | -.15 | +.07 | +.03 | -.32 | -.39 |
| Plans, all started (30) | +.09 | +.11 | +.02 | +.03 | +.22 | +.26 | +.15 | +.17 |
| Eta/Beta | .18 | .24 | .07 | .17 | .26 | .31 | .26 | .29 |
| $R^2$ | | .28 | | .20 | | .16 | | .13 |
| F (main effect) | | 2.50[a] | | 1.05 | | 3.66* | | 3.15* |
| F (covariates) | | 6.08** | | 4.23** | | 1.65 | | 1.11 |
| F (total) | | 4.74** | | 3.04** | | 2.40* | | 1.88[a] |

a. $p < .10$; * $p < .05$; ** $p < .01$

NOTE: Control variables were: early retirement, income, marital status, race, and retirement for health reasons.

women retirees (Benner et al., 1981). It may be particularly women who have to rely on Social Security benefits for whom financial planning would be especially relevant. Also, other materials from this project suggest that women who expected financial problems after retirement were particularly anxious to prepare for the anticipated income loss. For these women, financial planning may have prevented serious economic problems after retirement, but this does not necessarily lead to increased positive feelings of happiness.

Since the data on retirement plans were retrospective, the causality of associations cannot be determined. It might very well be that women with high positive affect perceive themselves as planners, or the relationships could also indicate that women with high positive feelings (even before retirement) are also more likely to engage in plans for activities and to implement such plans than the more depressed retirees.

It is not entirely clear why planning was related to feelings of happiness but not to the other adjustment indicators. Obviously, the different scales tap divergent dimensions of adjustment. The job deprivation scale expresses the extent to which women miss various aspects of their former work lives, and such feelings may persist even if leisure plans were made and seem to be only slightly reduced if such plans were implemented. The morale scale centers on perceived changes in life satisfaction with age and is strongly related to the women's economic condition (Szinovacz, 1982a). The happiness scales, on the other hand, focus specifically on feelings of usefulness and self-worth, and such feelings may be more directly affected by leisure activities than women's life satisfaction or job deprivation.

The present data certainly confirm that preparation for leisure activities constitutes an important element in women's adjustment to the retirement transition. It is also evident that such plans will only have the desired result if they are actually implemented. Retirement preparation programs, therefore, should include information on leisure activities in general and community as well as social activities in particular. It would seem that activities which provide women retirees with a sense of accomplishment and usefulness and which facilitate social contacts might be most effective in ensuring emotional well-being after the retirement transition. Hospitals, community groups, and service agencies certainly should take advantage of women retirees' expressed interest in volunteer work and community activities. However, the responsibilities assigned to retired volunteers or community workers should correspond to women's personal needs and physical capabilities. Case study materials from this investigation indicate that several women interested in volunteer work were discouraged from enrolling or left the programs because of rigid time schedules and physically exhausting assignments.

Another frequently mentioned leisure interest of women retirees is travel. Realization of this interest is often made impossible by the women's restricted financial means. Indeed, of those women who reported "things they would like to do but could not afford," 78 percent mentioned travel. Senior citizen agencies, churches, or travel agencies could arrange cheap trips for retired women. These trips may not only satisfy women's interest in travel, but would also provide them with opportunities to make new friends. Again, travel arrangements for retired women will have to take their special needs and capacities into consideration. Lengthy trips which involve a lot of walking, for instance, are hardly appropriate for older women.

In summary, women retirees definitely could profit from preretirement programs providing information on leisure activities in general and diverse volunteer and group programs in their communities. Since such information is usually not available to employers, agency personnel or program representatives may be invited to present special sessions as part of employers' preretirement programs, or to speak before groups and organizations frequented by older women (e.g., churches, library, urban league). Indeed, some of the more active retirees may themselves be quite willing to offer such information sessions and may have more impact on their retired sisters than young agency representatives. As one of our respondents complained about agency personnel:

> They should listen to retirees themselves instead of some younger person saying this would be nice, something my grandmother would enjoy or want to do. Because you have no idea until you're there . . .

# III

## ADJUSTING TO RETIREMENT: THE FEMALE EXPERIENCE

**It is quite unrealistic** to assume (as some textbook authors have done) that every older woman who retires from the labor force will just resume her full-time household role and live happily ever after. Quite apart from the fact that many women retirees are not married or will become widows soon after their retirement, even married women who worked for a considerable time during their later years will experience major life changes upon retirement. At the least, gainful employment provides a clear-cut structure to the timing of daily activities, and it implies that much of one's time is occupied with work-related tasks. Removal of this daily schedule after retirement clearly produces major life changes. Whether or not these changes are viewed in a positive or negative light depends on a variety of personal and situational circumstances.

The chapters in the final part of this book address the question as to which specific pre- and postretirement conditions enhance or hinder women's adjustment to the retirement transition, and they also demonstrate variations in adjustment and its determinants between the sexes, as well as among various groups of women. In Chapter 10, Robert Atchley uses longitudinal data to investigate gender differences in the retirement transition process. He presents evidence on men's and women's concerns at the preretirement stage, on changes in life circumstances during the retirement transition process, as well as on determinants of life and retirement satisfaction among postretirement subjects. The subsequent two chapters explore retirement adaptation processes among professional women. Ruth Jewson's case materials, though based on a small and nonrepresentative sample, offer in-depth and lively accounts of the various life changes experienced by retiring professional women. Marilyn Block examines the effect of work pattern and other influence factors on the retirement satisfaction of a larger group of college-educated retirees. Chapter 13 is devoted to an analysis of the various problems experienced by lower- and middle-class retirees and investigates the relative impact of these problems on various adjustment indicators. In the final chapter of this section, Timothy Brubaker and Charles Hennon address the widely neglected issue of the effects of women's retirement on the marital relationship. Specifically, the authors compare currently employed and retired women's expectations for and perceptions of the division of household responsibilities between spouses.

# 10

# THE PROCESS OF RETIREMENT: COMPARING WOMEN AND MEN

## Robert C. Atchley

**The retirement process involves** three major periods: preretirement, the retirement transition, and postretirement. The preretirement period involves looking ahead to retirement—to what life in retirement will be like. Decisions about whether one will retire, and if so, when, are made during this period.

The retirement transition involves leaving one's job and taking up the role of retired person. Because retirement has often been assumed to have a negative effect, it is important to have measures for each individual on such factors as physical health, mental health, and activity level both before retirement and after.

The postretirement period obviously involves life without a job, but there are numerous other factors such as health, activity level, or having to live alone that can also occur during this period. The most important thing to learn about the postretirement period is what conditions are most essential to a high degree of satisfaction with one's life in retirement (for an expanded discussion of the retirement process, see Atchley, 1976a).

The ideal way to study the retirement process would be to follow several samples of people who began the process at different times until all had either died or lived perhaps 20 years past retirement. This way we

*AUTHOR'S NOTE: This research was supported by grant R01 MH 26121 from the National Institute of Mental Health.*

would have information on the entire process for numerous individuals and, by comparing people who began the process at different times, we could get a picture of the process that was somewhat independent of the times in which various phases of retirement took place. For example, it is conceivable that people who went through the retirement transition in 1970 found it easier than those who did so in 1980 because economic uncertainties were greater in 1980. By comparing the two samples, we could get an idea of the range of effects the transition might have under varying economic circumstances. Unfortunately, such a study would take about 50 years to do properly.

In the meantime, there are other ways to look at the retirement process—not as adequate as the way described above, but far better than nothing. The first thing we can do is look at a sample of people in the preretirement period who are various distances from retirement. Then we can look at a sample of people for whom we have before-and-after data on the retirement transition. Then we can look at a sample of people in the postretirement period who have been retired for various lengths of time. Table 10.1 shows the relationship between our general view of the retirement process and the various samples in our study that we use to approximate it. It also shows some of the issues we might want information about. The purpose of this chapter is to use data from a longitudinal study designed to address these issues in order to compare the process of retirement for women and men.

Earlier chapters have clearly documented the need for more research on women's retirement, but it is important for such research to compare women's retirement with that of men, for if there is no gender difference in the process, then it makes little sense to address "women's retirement" as if it were a separate issue. In addition, we need to control for the effects of factors such as age, living arrangements, socioeconomic status, and health in order to avoid attributing influence to gender that actually results from something else. It is also important to use recent data in order to see how retirement has changed since earlier studies.

# METHODS

## THE STUDY

The results reported here are taken from a study designed specifically to examine retirement as a process that can occur over many years. The

**TABLE 10.1  Studying the Retirement Process**

| Period | Preretirement | Retirement Transition | Postretirement |
|---|---|---|---|
| Samples | persons in the preretirement period in 1975 (N = 356) | persons who retired between 1975 and 1977 or 1977 and 1979 (N = 168) | persons who were retired in 1975 (N = 296) |
| Questions of Interest | —attitude toward work<br>—attitude toward retirement<br>—planned age of retirement<br>—availability of pensions<br>—health<br>—occupation<br>—mandatory retirement rules | Measures before & after retirement on:<br>—attitude toward retirement<br>—health<br>—activity level<br>—self-confidence<br>—life satisfaction | —attitude toward retirement<br>—life satisfaction<br>—activity level<br>—income adequacy<br>—number & importance of goals<br>—health |

NOTE: For all periods it is important to control for various sociodemographic factors when looking at the results. The ones used here include: sex, age, socioeconomic status, and living alone.

155

study design involves identifying all persons aged 50 or over in a small town community and studying them every two years. We chose to do a community study for several reasons. First, if all of the people in the sample live in the same community, then differences in activity level or organizational involvement cannot be due to variations in community facilities, transportation, and the like. Second, if the entire population is studied, then bias in sample selection is not an issue. Third, by taking the entire population, we include people who have had irregular work histories and people who work for small business. Both of these types of people are underrepresented in the retirement literature. Fourth, an entire community population provides a fuller range of occupations than the occupationally based samples of many earlier studies (Atchley, 1976b, 1976c; Streib and Schneider, 1971; Levy, 1980; Szinovacz, 1980). Finally, the cost of the study was reduced substantially by concentrating the effort in a single geographic area.

The community selected was a small town of 25,000 located in a large metropolitan region. It is typical of many small towns in that it is geographically close enough to be socially and economically influenced by a major metropolis but distant enough to remain independent of major urban problems. As an environment, it is large enough to offer numerous opportunities for participation and small enough to allow genuine community supports to develop.

In 1975, questionnaires were mailed to 1515 persons who were 50 or over and lived in the community selected. These people represented the complete population as identified by: (1) a postcard census of all mailing addresses, (2) voter registration records, and (3) reports of long-time community residents. 1106 usable responses were received. The response rate of 73 percent was a good return for a social survey. The panel was resurveyed again in 1977, 1979, and 1981 with 852, 678, and 656 returns, respectively. Considering the number of deaths, the panel retention has been good.

The samples we will use to approximate the retirement process were taken from the 1975 through 1979 waves of data. The preretirement sample was defined as everyone who was employed full-time in 1975. There were 356 people who met this criterion. The retirement transition sample was defined as those who changed from full-time employment to full retirement or retirement with part-time employment over the 1975-77 period or the 1977-79 period. There were 168 people who experienced retirement over the first four years of our study. The postretirement sample was defined as everyone who was fully retired in 1975—a total of 296 respondents.

## MEASURES

The instrument used consisted of an 18-page, self-administered questionnaire. In addition to the usual demographic data on age, sex, marital status, occupation, education, race, religion, number of children, and so on, we included several scales designed to measure important concepts. Attitude toward the job was measured by a single-item, 5-point scale. We used such a simple measure because earlier research had shown that attitude toward work was not a powerful factor in the retirement process (Cottrell and Atchley, 1969; Atchley, 1976a; Powers and Goudy, 1971).

Attitude toward retirement was measured by a semantic differential that required respondents to rate "your life in retirement" on a series of 16 bipolar adjective pairs such as good/bad, full/empty, busy/idle, happy/ sad, and so on. This measure had been used in earlier research with good success (Atchley, 1974). The reliability of this scale was .92 (Cronbach's alpha).

Functional health was measured by a 6-item checklist of functions developed by the National Center for Health Statistics. Items included such things as walking up and down stairs, doing light work around the house, work at a full-time job, and heavy work around the house. It was designed to measure the level of physical functioning in a behavioral sense rather than a medical sense. Reliability was .78.

Self-reported health was measured by a single item asking the respondent to rate his or her health as very good, good, fair, poor, or very poor. This sort of scale, while simple, has been found to correlate highly with physicians' assessments (Maddox and Douglass, 1974).

Activity level was measured by summing the respondents' frequency ratings on 18 types of activities, such as watching television, visiting with friends, being with children or grandchildren, gardening, going for walks, attending church, and so on.

Goal directedness is the extent to which the person has goals he or she feels are important. It was measured by asking the respondents to rate 16 goals in terms of their importance to them personally. Items included such things as having a satisfying job, being dependable and reliable, having close ties with family, being accepted by prominent people in the community, and so on. Responses could range on a 5-point scale from very important to very unimportant. Reliability of the scale was .81.

Self-confidence is a person's perception of himself or herself as capable of taking appropriate action when needed. It was measured by a 6-item scale that included such items as "I can do pretty much anything I put my mind to" and "I am afraid to talk to people in authority about myself." Reliability was .81.

Life satisfaction is the person's feelings about life in general. Lawton (1972) devised a 16-item scale to measure life satisfaction or morale that had three major dimensions: emotionality or agitation, loneliness/dissatisfaction, and reactions to the person's own aging. Items included: "I get mad more than I used to," "How often do you feel lonely?" (Sometimes, a lot), and "I have as much energy as I did this time last year." Reliability of the scale was .89.

## RESULTS

### THE PRERETIREMENT PERIOD

In 1975, there were in our sample 214 men and 142 women in the preretirement period. All were employed full-time. About half of them said they were within five years of retirement; the other half saw retirement as more than five years away. In comparison with national norms, the men in the sample were overrepresented in the top two occupational categories (professionals and administrators) by about 13 percent and in the bottom two categories (unskilled service workers and laborers) by about 5 percent. This means that there was a more even distribution across occupational categories in the sample than in the nation as a whole. The occupational distribution for women in the sample was quite similar to that for women throughout the nation. The sample was 95 percent white.

Of the preretirement sample, 27 men and 33 women said they did not plan to retire. This represents 12.6 and 23 percent, respectively, and is a statistically significant difference. In addition, the types of people who did not plan to retire differed significantly from those who did plan to. Men who did not plan to retire were nearly all self-employed and in good health. Women who did not plan to retire were generally unmarried, in average health, and in lower-status occupations.

Presumably, a very positive attitude toward one's work could lead to a negative attitude toward retirement, but attitudes toward work and retirement are uncorrelated. Only 10 percent of either men or women had a negative attitude toward their work in the preretirement stage. Yet less than 1 percent of either sex had a negative attitude toward retirement.

Of those who gave a planned age at retirement (187 men and 109 women), the mean for both sexes was 64. But when we looked at detailed subgroups in terms of planned retirement age, some interesting sex differences occurred. Women were much more likely to plan to retire before age 60 (22 percent, compared to 14 percent for men). These women tended to have high social status, to be married, and to be in good health. On the other hand, women were also more likely to plan retirement at age 70 or later (11 percent, compared to 6 percent for men). These women tended to have low social status and to be unmarried. These findings reinforce earlier notions of important class differences with respect to women's retirement (Kerckhoff, 1966; Heyman and Jeffers, 1968). They should also serve as a caution against relying too heavily on very general statements about women's retirement.

While attitudes toward work and retirement are uncorrelated, they each influence the planned age at retirement, but in a different way for women than for men. Among women, the lower the occupational status, the larger the number of expected pensions, and the less positive the attitude toward retirement, the higher the planned age at retirement. Among men, a high planned age of retirement was related to a positive attitude toward work, a less positive attitude toward retirement, and a low number of expected pensions (see Table 10.2).

Among women, the economic aspects of retirement seem to dominate the decision to retire later. Those who plan to retire late are in lower-status occupations. They also expect a higher number of pensions. It could be that they *must* work longer in order to qualify for additional pensions. Their later planned retirement is not based on a more positive attitude toward work but rather a less positive attitude toward retirement.

Note also that planned retirement age is not related to coverage by mandatory retirement (even in 1975, before the mandatory retirement age was raised) or self-rated health for either sex. This latter finding is due to the fact that very few in our preretired samples were in less than good or very good health.

**THE RETIREMENT TRANSITION**

In our longitudinal study, 61 men and 28 women retired between 1975 and 1977, and 49 men and 30 women retired between 1977 and 1979. For

TABLE 10.2    Predictors of Planned Age of Retirement Among Those
in the Preretirement Stage

| Predictor | Regression Analysis[1] Beta Coefficients | |
| --- | --- | --- |
| | Men | Women |
| Covered by Mandatory Retirement | −.08 | −.07 |
| Occupational Status | −.05 | −.43* |
| Health | −.09 | .18 |
| Number of Pensions Expected | −.21* | .32* |
| Attitude Toward Retirement | −.23* | −.29* |
| Attitude Toward Work | .24* | .12 |
| Total $R^2$ | .13 | .27 |
| N | (214) | (142) |

*Significant at the .05 level or less

1. Regression analysis is a statistical procedure that begins with a matrix of correlations and identifies the combination of independent variables (causes) that best predicts the dependent variable (effect). The beta coefficients do not reflect an absolute magnitude, but they can be used to show the *relative* predictive power of the various independent variables. The total $R^2$ is the percentage of the variation in the dependent variable that was predicted by the given combination of independent variables. Thus, in the above example, the independent variables predicted better for women than they did for men ($R^2$ of .13 versus .27).

these 168 people, it is possible to look at how the actual event of retirement (as opposed to being *in* retirement) influenced their attitudes toward retirement, life satisfaction, self-confidence, and activity level.

Before retirement, 17 percent of the women and 11 percent of the men had negative attitudes toward retirement, but after retirement *none* of these people had a negative attitude. Having a negative attitude just before retirement was related to being in fair to poor health, having low social status, and seeing one's income as inadequate. Thus, people who saw retirement negatively in advance tended to be those with fewer health, social, and financial resources. But retirement turned out to be better than they had expected. The mean attitude scores went up slightly for women and tended to remain about the same for men. The means for both sexes were quite high. Scale scores ranged from 21 to 98, with a score of 48 or less representing a negative orientation toward retirement. The means were in the 82 to 85 range both before and after retirement for both sexes, for both two-year intervals.

The only control variable that changed this picture was living arrangements. Going into retirement living alone produced a significant increase in attitude toward retirement for both men and women, but living with a spouse did not increase positive orientation toward retirement. In fact, living with a spouse was related to a significant *decrease* in attitude toward retirement for the 30 women who retired between 1977 and 1979. These findings support the earlier literature which, taken as a whole, suggests that retirement does not have a predictable impact for married women (Szinovacz, 1980; Fengler, 1975; Maas and Kuypers, 1975; Kerckhoff, 1966; Heyman and Jeffers, 1968). Of course, it is important to note that a decrease need not result in a negative attitude. Indeed, the women who retired between 1977 and 1979 had a 1979 mean score of 82.6, not far off the overall mean. The reason they experienced a significant drop in retirement orientation was due to a much higher than average expectation of retirement in 1977 (88.3).

Retirement tended to improve life satisfaction slightly for both men and women. There were no variations in this pattern when controls for marital status, health, income adequacy, social status, or living arrangements were introduced. Retirement had no effect whatever on self-confidence for either sex.

Retirement reduced activity level significantly for both sexes among those who retired between 1975 and 1977. Activity scores could range from 27 to 98. A score of 36 or less indicated low activity. Just before retirement, the mean scores were 67.4 and 70.9 for men and women, respectively. After retirement, the means were 61.3 and 61.2. Even though both sexes were still quite active after retirement, the reduction in activity was much greater for women than for men. Thus, while women were much more active than men before retirement, after retirement the sexes were practically identical in terms of mean activity level. The greatest reductions in activity level occurred for women in fair to poor health who dropped from a mean activity level of 68.3 in 1975 to 50.0 in 1977.

On the other hand, for those who retired between 1977 and 1979, the effect of retirement on activity level was not significant for either men or women. The main reason for this variation between the samples is that the 1975-77 sample was much more active before retirement than was the 1977-79 sample. Postretirement activity scores were similar for both samples for both sexes. This result illustrates the value of using multiple time periods. Using only the 1975-77 retirees, we might have erroneously concluded that retirement tends to reduce activity level. Using both samples, however, we see the 1975-77 data in a less negative light.

TABLE 10.3   Subgroups Departing Significantly* from the Total in
             Terms of Mean Attitude Toward Retirement

| | |
|---|---|
| Overall Mean | 79.0 |
| Those with Inadequate Income | |
| Men | 74.6 |
| Women | 70.8 |
| Married Women | 81.5 |
| Those in Poor Health | |
| Men | 75.3 |
| Women | 71.4 |
| Women in Very Good Health | 87.7 |
| Women with High School Status | 82.4 |

*Differences significant at .05 or less, by analysis of variance

### THE POSTRETIREMENT PERIOD

In 1975, there were in our sample 121 men and 154 women who were
retired. Our concern was with the subjective well-being of these people,
and how it might vary by sex. The measures we looked at were attitude
toward retirement, activity level, and overall life satisfaction.

Attitudes toward retirement were very positive among our retired
respondents. The mean scores were 79.8 for retired women and 78.0 for
retired men, a significant difference. Table 10.3 shows that inadequate
income and poor health depressed attitudes toward retirement for both
men and women in retirement, but the adverse effects were greater for
women than for men. On the other hand, being in very good health was a
tremendous advantage for women but made no difference for men.
Women also benefited from high social status and being married, while
these factors made no difference for men. The picture we get here is that
retired women's attitudes are influenced more by both adverse *and* advantageous circumstances compared to retired men.

Activity levels were relatively high among both men and women in
retirement, and there was no significant sex difference. The overall mean
was 63.9, a figure only slightly lower than that for the preretirement group
(67.5). (Recall that 36 or lower represents low activity.) Activity level in
retirement was influenced mainly by health and income. Those in poor

Robert C. Atchley

163

**TABLE 10.4   Predictors of Attitudes Toward Retirement**

| Predictor | Regression Analysis Beta Coefficients | |
| --- | --- | --- |
| | Retired Men | Retired Women |
| Goal Directedness | .01 | .13 |
| Age | −.02 | .24* |
| Functional Health | .00 | .42* |
| Activity Level | .37* | .35* |
| Income Adequacy | .09 | .16* |
| Social Status | −.01 | −.08 |
| Living Alone | −.01 | −.03 |
| Total $R^2$ | .16 | .56 |
| N | (121) | (154) |

*Significant at .05 or less

health were significantly less active than the norm, and those with very good health were significantly more active. Income adequacy operates in the same way. Marital status and social status made no difference. Thus, the sex differences that appeared with regard to attitude toward retirement have no correlary with regard to activity level.

Life satisfaction was high for both men and women in retirement. On a scale ranging from 19 to 36, the overall mean for the retired was 31.4. There was no sex difference. Controls for income adequacy, marital status, and social status uncovered no significant variations. Poor health depressed life satisfaction, and very good health increased it for retired women but not for retired men.

Finally, we wanted to see how various factors influenced attitude toward retirement and life satisfaction. Table 10.4 shows the results of a regression analysis using goal directedness, age, functional health, activity level, income adequacy, social status, and living alone as independent variables, with attitude toward retirement as the dependent variable. Separate regressions were done by sex. Activity level was the only factor that influenced attitude toward retirement consistently for both sexes, but even this variable behaved very differently for men than for women. Activity level was the only strong predictor of morale among retired men.

**TABLE 10.5    Predictors of Life Satisfaction**

| Predictors | Regression Analysis Beta Coefficients | |
| | Retired Men | Retired Women |
|---|---|---|
| Goal Directedness | .17* | .08 |
| Age | .05 | .16* |
| Functional Health | .07 | .25* |
| Activity Level | .31* | .43* |
| Income Adequacy | .22* | .08 |
| Social Status | −.06 | .04 |
| Living Alone | −.02 | .05 |
| Total R$^2$ | .24 | .30 |
| N | (121) | (154) |

*Significant at .05 or less

Among retired women, health was more important than activity level, and age was more important than income adequacy. Interestingly, the older the retired woman, the more positive her attitude toward retirement was likely to be.

The two sexes differed substantially in terms of how well the combination of demographic, social, and situational variables predicted variations in attitude toward retirement. The attitudes of men were not very predictable. For retired women, the independent variables achieved more than a modest degree of prediction. This relates back to our earlier point that retired women seem to be more influenced by various negative situational factors than are men. Given the fact that retirement attitudes were generally quite high, the room for variation was mainly in a downward direction. Goal directedness (the extent to which a person had numerous important personal goals), social status, and living alone had no significant predictive value.

Table 10.5 shows the results of a similar regression analysis with life satisfaction as the dependent variable. Activity level again came through as a consistently influential factor, being the top-ranked independent variable for both subgroups. But here the resemblance stops. For men, the other predictors are goal directedness and income adequacy, while for women the other predictors of high life satisfaction are older age and better health.

Retired men and women were quite different, both in terms of the predictability of life satisfaction and the specific set of factors significantly involved. For retired men, life satisfaction was a little more predictable than retirement attitude because a larger number of predictors were significant for life satisfaction. For example, although activity level was still the best predictor, both goal directedness and income adequacy were significant predictors of life satisfaction but not of retirement attitude. Life satisfaction of retired women was much less predictable than their attitude toward retirement. Health was a less important predictor of life satisfaction than of retirement attitude, and while income adequacy predicted retirement attitude, it did not predict life satisfaction significantly.

One important implication of these comparisons is that neither retirement attitude nor life satisfaction can be inferred from the other. While some of their causes are similar for both men and women, this is not consistently so, and many of their causes are quite different.

Another important point is the dissimilarity between retired men and women. What they think is not very predictable in terms of a generally applicable set of factors. The factors associated with their attitudes toward retirement and their life satisfaction are neither the same set of factors, nor do they operate in the same way for the subgroups. This means, of course, that women's retirement is indeed a separate issue compared to men's.

## SUMMARY

We examined the process of retirement for women and men by looking at 356 people who were in the preretirement stage (over 50 and employed full-time), 168 persons who retired between 1975 and 1977 or 1977 and 1979, and 296 persons in the postretirement stage (see Table 10.1).

For those in the preretirement stage, we were interested in attitude toward retirement, attitude toward work, whether they planned to retire, and their planned retirement age. We wanted to know how these factors related to one another and whether there were significant differences between men and women.

Women were more likely than men to say that they did not plan to retire. Men and women were quite similar in terms of their attitudes toward work and retirement and the average age at which they planned to retire. But the dynamics of planned retirement age were quite different for women compared to men. Among women, those who planned to retire early were upper-status married women in good health who very much looked forward to retirement. Those who planned to retire late had lower status, tended to be unmarried, and had a less positive view of retirement. Negative economic factors seemed to play a strong part in the decision to retire later for women. Among men, retirement was much more likely to occur at or near the traditional age of 65 rather than earlier or later. Those who planned to retire later (only about 6 percent) were motivated by more positive attitudes toward the job and less positive attitudes toward retirement rather than by negative economic factors.

For those who went through the retirement transition, we found that retirement generally had no negative effects on attitude toward retirement, life satisfaction, or self-confidence. If anything, retirement tended to improve them. Retirement did reduce activity level, but only in one of our two samples, and postretirement activity level was still high. Activity levels dropped more for women than for men, especially for women in fair to poor health.

For those already in retirement, women were significantly more positive in their attitude toward retirement than men, although both sexes were quite positive. Women's attitudes were more sensitive than men's to both advantageous and adverse circumstances.

Both sexes were quite active in retirement, and there was no significant difference between them in this regard. Health was the major determinant of activity level. Life satisfaction was also high and showed no gender difference. Life satisfaction was influenced by activity level for both sexes. In addition, women's having high life satisfaction was related to good health and older age, while men's depended more on income adequacy and having many goals.

In terms of factors influencing attitude toward retirement and life satisfaction in retirement, the results were quite diverse. Activity level showed up as an important factor for both sexes. These results support the notion that more active people have a higher sense of well-being compared to those who are less active.

Otherwise, the retired men and women represented quite distinctive subgroups in terms of the factors that related to retirement attitude and life satisfaction. Functional health and income adequacy were significant predictors, while other factors such as age, goal directedness, social status, or living alone were much less important.

Retirement was very positive for the vast majority of the people in this study, no less so for women than for men. Factors such as lower activity level, poorer health, or inadequate incomes tended to make attitudes toward retirement less positive, but not negative.

## IMPLICATIONS

These findings have several implications for various ideologies about how to adjust best to aging. The three most commonly used models for "successful" aging are disengagement, consolidation, and substitution (also called "activity theory"). The disengagement model (Cumming and Henry, 1961) held that because society really didn't want the participation of older people and because older people were preoccupied with their own inner concerns, the best strategy for a satisfying late life was to drop out. Our findings show absolutely no support for this idea. Our retired respondents were not dropouts and were highly satisfied with their lives.

The substitution approach (Havighurst et al., 1963) held that the best way to adjust to aging was to find substitutes for lost roles in order to preserve earlier levels of activity (this is why it has been called activity theory). But our findings show that compared to the preretirement sample, the postretirement sample showed a lower level of activities, even though they presumably had more time for them since they were retired. In the retirement transition sample, activity levels sometimes went down, but they never went up for any subgroup (and remember that life satisfaction was high).

The consolidation approach (also called "selective disengagement" by Streib and Schneider, 1971) held that lost roles could be compensated for by redistributing effort among remaining roles and perhaps lowering overall activity (Atchley, 1972). But our findings showed no significant increase in nonjob activities following retirement, and life satisfaction was high.

All of these ideologies were centered around activity, and our findings support its importance. In what way is it important? Why is a moderately high activity level associated with high life satisfaction? In my opinion, the association between activity level and life satisfaction exists because they are both promoted by the same set of factors. I do not believe that a high activity level of itself can change low life satisfaction, any more than high life satisfaction can cause people to be highly active. I think the early theorists, myself included, did not go far enough beneath the surface to look for enabling conditions. For people to be either satisfied or highly active, they generally have to be able to participate in what *they* define as a meaningful life. Participation requires two things above all: a sound body/mind and opportunities. People continue in their preretirement activity patterns because they already know that both capacity and opportunity are there. They don't have to guess about it. This is most likely to be true in a small town of the type we studied.

What do our findings imply for those interested in women's issues? First, women are more likely than men to plan never to retire, and if they do plan to retire, to retire late. These women tend to have low-status occupations and to be unmarried. Economic issues were more important in the retirement decisions of the women in our preretirement sample than of the men. This implies that retirement financial planning and resources for women are important issues. Indeed, elsewhere I have argued that given the concentration of women in small business, only a national effort will succeed in reaching them (Atchley, 1979).

The retirement transition is not a problem for either men or women. However, our findings show that sometimes married women can expect too much of retirement. This is another area where retirement planning can help by encouraging people to be more realistic.

Women's attitudes in retirement respond more than men's to ups and downs in circumstances. This is a common finding. However, even those in what most of us would call adverse circumstances appear to be coping well.

Keep in mind that the findings reported here occurred under optimum conditions. Our respondents were generally healthy people who lived in a relatively safe community with plenty of opportunities for participation. In these circumstances people generally look forward to retirement, go through the transition smoothly, and find life in retirement satisfying. The most important sex differences we found appeared to result from the economic problems of unmarried women.

# 11

# AFTER RETIREMENT:
# AN EXPLORATORY STUDY OF THE
# PROFESSIONAL WOMAN

## Ruth Hathaway Jewson

The retiree's perception of herself determines the attitudes of others. There is a unique quality to each person's retirement. I think it is especially difficult for individuals whose personhood has depended upon recognition/status/administrative power, and relatively easy for persons people-oriented or tuned to the arts. Everyone must cope with energy loss, failing faculties, and the intensity born of a sense that time is running out.

So commented a woman who was interviewed for this study of the stage in a professional woman's life when she leaves gainful employment and adjusts to retirement. Retirement is a critical transition point in a person's life, whether it is viewed positively or negatively. The structure required by work has been removed. Established patterns are disrupted as one leaves the work world and as reorganization occurs. The life sectors of work, family, friends, and leisure are all affected as a different set of preoccupations becomes prominent (Rapoport and Rapoport, 1975a, 1975b). There is variation in how the process of moving into the relatively undefined—and in many cases undervalued—social role of being retired is perceived, and there are differences in satisfaction with retirement.

*AUTHOR'S NOTE: This chapter is a summary of the author's dissertation.*

The study of the retirement stage is important for at least three reasons. As traditional sex roles have changed, with professional employment becoming culturally accepted for women, many more females are employed today in professional positions than in earlier times. In addition, the number of older people, especially older females, in the population has increased, and improving survival rates mean that employed women usually retire well before death occurs. Also, with the advent of the Social Security system and somewhat better pensions, some income security has made retirement easier. In a sense, the present generation of retiring persons may be looked upon as pioneers.

According to Sussman (1972), the task for the retiring person is to determine his or her options, to enter into new "careers" (the term "career" is used to mean a new or rearranged series of role sequences an individual pursues in a life sector with which he or she is involved in areas such as leisure, work, education, religion, or politics), and to keep from sinking into a group social identity. He reminds us that retired persons are not a homogeneous group, though many seem to hold this view. There are wide individual and group differences.

As Sussman (1972) expresses it, the central variable in the retirement process is the number of options a person can exercise. His central hypothesis is that options maintenance is directly related to one's self-esteem and social responsibility in retirement. Situational and structural variables that give incentive or provide constraints in relation to the availability and choice of options for new careers in available life sectors include whether or not the person retires from choice, social class, level of retirement income, linkage systems (friendship groups; kinship network; marital, inheritance, and work systems; and voluntary organizations), and preretirement preparation.

A woman's retirement options may differ from a man's because of societal, institutional, social-psychological, and personality variables. The female may have had more anticipatory socialization for retirement than the male, because whether married or not she has had a homemaker role which continues in retirement.

The objective in this study was to obtain a picture of the general characteristics of the retired professional woman and her options through examining her relationships to such central components of her life at this stage as work, family, leisure, friendship, housing, health, and socialization for retirement. In addition, feelings about being retired—the inner experience of it—were sought.

The relevant variables relating to the critical transition of retirement will be discussed separately. However, whatever their feelings about retirement, for most of those in this sample it was not considered a crisis. The majority said that they had enjoyed their work and were enjoying retirement, even though if given their choice they might have preferred to continue working. Most said they were finding life pleasant in retirement, though not more pleasant than when they were employed.

> Really, retirement is a much bigger step in life than I anticipated. It's not a crisis, but a very big change. Something to go through. I had thought before, well, everyone retires, and that's that, but it proved to be a bigger change than I had anticipated. I didn't look forward to it as some say they do. It was not just wonderful at the start, as some people say, but it is becoming so.

## METHODS

### SAMPLE

This study was based on semistructured interviews with a sample of 32 retired professional women, and for comparison, 30 other retired persons—16 retired professional males and 14 retired nonprofessional females —living in many parts of the country. Retirement was seen as a part of the continuous life cycle, with new situations and problems to which to adapt.

Because, as several researchers remind us (Neugarten, 1974; Thompson and Streib, 1969), experiences in the early retirement stage and the late retirement stage may be very different, this investigation was limited to a study of persons in their first six years of retirement. The majority in all three groups retired between 61 and 70 years of age; a few worked until they were in their early seventies.

Although retirement of the professional woman is an increasingly common experience, there are not yet large numbers of women retired from professional positions from whom to choose for a study. The present sample was a nonrandom one. To select the professional groups, the writer started with a nucleus of 22 male and female members and former members of the National Council on Family Relations known to be retired from their primary employment. As interviewing progressed, other names were suggested, and this supplied a pool of additional interviewees. The group of nonprofessional retired women was obtained with the help of the director of a high-rise for the elderly in Minneapolis and through church workers in Minneapolis and Rochester, Minnesota.

The population had occupations that were multidisciplinary in character. Most of the professional females interviewed in the present study had had long working careers in such fields as education, social work, and medicine. Although a few had interrupted their careers when their children were small, the majority had been employed for most of their adult years, the longest for 52 years. The professional males were from similar fields as the professional females, with the addition of the ministry.

Several of the professional females and professional males had had distinguished careers which had included writing, receiving awards, and serving as presidents of national professional organizations. The nonprofessional females had been secretaries, laboratory technicians, telephone operators, practical nurses, housemothers, and cooks.

## MEASUREMENT

The questions in the interview guide were based on what the literature suggests are concerns and experiences of persons in retirement, especially in the sectors of work, family, friends, and leisure. In addition, before interviewing began, the writer discussed retirement with several persons in that stage of the life cycle. Before finalizing the interview guide, five persons working professionally in the family field examined the questions. Their agreement on the relevance of the questions to retirement was high and gave the guide judgment validity.

Such information as age at retirement, income level, health, housing, and marital status was relatively factual material. However, a large part of the data was obtained from open-ended questions and discussion, yielding rich descriptive narrative material.

One of the writer's concerns was to account for satisfaction in retirement. Therefore, a Satisfaction in Retirement scale was constructed, using variables from the interview guide that related to the retirees' use of a variety of creative opportunities or options, satisfying use of leisure, sense of fulfillment in retirement, feelings that the main purpose of life had not been taken away with retirement, feelings of having retained a sense of self-esteem, pleasure in retirement, feelings of usefulness, lack of fear of the future, and relief at being retired.

Sets of relationships among variables were investigated using cross-tabulation analysis. Examined by cross-tabulation were the three groups of retirees and their scores on selected variables: personal characteristics and situational variables versus satisfaction in retirement variables, and contingent condition variables versus satisfaction in retirement variables. The joint frequency distributions shown in the cross-tabulation tables were summarized with Kendall's tau. In addition, the narrative material gathered from open-ended questions was analyzed descriptively.[1]

# RESULTS

### FEELINGS ABOUT RETIREMENT

In this sample, 59.4 percent of the professional females, 71.4 percent of the nonprofessional females, and 37.5 percent of the professional males were finding life more pleasurable in retirement. Factors relating to pleasure in retirement included involvement with family, a close family network, a general attitude of satisfaction with life (including having enjoyed one's work), the ability to find and use a wide variety of options, not having waited too long to retire, good health, adequate income, and preretirement preparation.

Most retirees (75.8 percent) still felt useful. Though there was a tendency for females to feel more useful than males, in this sample the difference was not statistically significant. The professional and nonprofessional females appeared to refer most often to home, family, and volunteer activities when discussing feelings of usefulness in retirement, although the professional females were more involved in volunteer activities than were the nonprofessional females. The positive comments made by professional males referred most often to keeping busy in their fields—possibly an artifact of how the sexes react to the term "usefulness," with men thinking more in terms of work. Factors relating to feelings of usefulness in retirement included a close family network, use of a wide variety of options, satisfaction with retirement, and good health.

For most retirees (87.5 percent of the professional females, 92.9 percent of the nonprofessional females, and 75 percent of the professional males), a feeling of purpose in retirement remained high. Factors contributing to a sense of purpose in retirement included good education, retiring in one's sixties rather than in one's fifties or seventies, a close family network, good health, and using a wide variety of options.

The Satisfaction in Retirement scale showed that a majority of those interviewed were quite satisfied with retirement. The results are in line with a statement made by Neugarten, who pointed out that in a recent

national study, 3 out of 4 of the older persons interviewed were satisfied
or very satisfied with their lives in retirement (reported by Casady, 1976).
In addition, Maddox (1977) states that for 95 percent of the people
beyond retirement age, life is very much worth living.

## THE WORK SYSTEM IN RETIREMENT

A similarity was noted when comparing the reasons the professional
females and the nonprofessional females gave for retiring—a majority of
both groups said they had retired from personal choice. The majority of
males retired because of institutional policy. In each group, some retired
because of family reasons, and some because they were tired of rigid
schedules and job pressures or didn't like their work. Only professional
females spoke of any financial advantages to retiring, of letting younger
persons take over, of retiring to avoid having to update one's skills, or
because the timing seemed just right. Only a male spoke of his problems
with a job that was absorptive of his whole family.

Professional males and females had similar broad-based sources of
retirement income (pensions, Social Security, real estate, insurance, savings
and investments, and the like); there was less variety in income sources for
the nonprofessional females.

Most of the retirees in this sample perceived their incomes as adequate,
and several of the professional males and females, but no nonprofessional
females, perceived their incomes as more than adequate. We may note that
for retirees of this period in time, retirement income for females is less
than for males because of poorer salaries when they were employed—a fact
which may be resented by females. We know that by every economic
measure, women are more deprived in their later years than are men. In
1978, among the aged, women (probably nonprofessional women)
accounted for 70 percent of those living in poverty, and the incidence of
poverty is especially high among black aged women and all unmarried
women.

Several professionals of both sexes had part-time jobs. For example, a
female physician after retiring became a consultant to the local county
health department and a part-time instructor in health at a local community college. Two other professional females also taught part-time in
community colleges. One woman led groups at the YWCA and another
substituted in a high school and taught in an adult evening program.
Several were writing, acting as consultants, leading workshops, developing
teaching materials, and giving speeches. One was helping her husband farm.
In general, a profession appears to give one more earning power in
retirement than does a nonprofessional occupation.

Work had been an important source of social contacts and friendships for those in the present sample. One professional female, who could have been speaking for many, commented:

> I regret having less contacts with men now. Retirement for a single woman means that she runs around with women's groups.

Frequently, professional retirees stay in contact with their former positions by extending those careers into related volunteer activities. As one professional woman said: "There's a feeling of former usefulness in work in continuation in community service." Another commented: "In retirement you are through working and are putting into practice what you wanted to do."

Several of the professional retirees felt that they had utilized their capabilities well while they had worked.

> I have real satisfaction that there was a time to serve, the sense of a job well finished. . . . I had a great life of work and love.

## THE FRIENDSHIP SYSTEM

Long-term friendships continued to be maintained by most retirees in this sample. Females, but not usually males, stayed in touch with former colleagues through social events, at least in the first six years of retirement, with which this study was concerned. Contacts ranged from lunch and visiting to more organized, regular gatherings. Several still attended office parties, especially retirement and holiday events. Professionals of both sexes kept in touch with friends by letter-writing. There was little mention of writing letters on the part of the nonprofessional females.

Retirees still had friends who were working, giving them a bridge to their former work world. Professionals still attended conferences. Some occasionally commented that before retirement they had been concerned that in retirement they would have no one with whom they could talk about their continued interest in their former work. This did not seem to turn out to be a problem for most professional females in this sample, although one woman physician who had gone back to work part time expected that it would become a problem to her later.

Professional females and professional males found new friends in retirement more frequently than nonprofessional females, probably because they had found more opportunities than the nonprofessionals to meet people. Since few of the nonprofessional females had moved, perhaps they felt little need for new friends. Perhaps too there is a difference between professional and nonprofessional retirees in their reaching out for new friends. Some professional females expressed surprise that they had developed friendships in retirement with women who had never worked outside their homes.

Church was a common source of new friendships for all three groups. Professional females in particular found new friends through working in political and voluntary organizations. Friendships were usually same-sex or couple friendships.

Neighborhood contacts were enjoyed by women but were seldom mentioned by men.

> I've discovered the joys of neighbors, and do things with them. I help them with repairs, help them water their lawns, we walk, and go to the store together. I'm free to help people any time, day or night—I can have better connections with friends and neighbors.

In early retirement, the majority in all three groups reported increased social contacts, mostly because of that magic ingredient—time.

## THE LEISURE SYSTEM

The retirees as a group appeared resourceful in involving themselves in activities meaningful and pleasing to them. Options were still available, and most retirees found and used them. The use of a wide variety of options was found significant in relation to feelings of fulfillment, pleasure, usefulness, relief at being retired, and a sense of purpose, as well as in relation to creativity and a satisfying use of leisure time.

The leisure activities of the retirees fell into the following groups: creative activities, reading, and organizational activities—professional women were involved with innumerable groups, travel, sports, social contacts, cultural activities, and educational experiences. Both groups of females enjoyed to a greater extent than the males activities that involved using their hands. Professionals of both sexes were more likely than nonprofessionals to consider that creative activities included relationships with people and intellectual activities such as reading, thinking, and writing. Males spoke of somewhat fewer options than females. There was little interest expressed by any group for organized senior citizen activities.

In retirement, a need for separateness from the spouse was apparent. Although recreation often involved both spouses, persons spoke of having individual activities that did not involve the other. In addition, separate spaces were allowed for in many homes. A professional female, for example, used the amusement room for sewing and crafts, whereas her husband had a separate shop in the basement. A professional male had a large darkroom and shop in the basement, plus a separate study, while his wife had a hobby area combined with her first floor utility room. Some men pursued hobbies in their garages, while their wives used spare bedrooms.

## THE FAMILY SYSTEM

Family life was valued in this sample, and self-perceived marital satisfaction tended to be high. The majority felt that their marital relationship had improved since retirement, partly because of having more time. Time was mentioned again and again, and for some there was a sense that it was running out.

> I think that we are more aware of the precious gift of time, and that adds a new dimension to our relationship. . . . It improves all the time. We are learning to live in the present—we have resources, new horizons, gifts we can use at any time of life.

The new consciousness of time extended to relationships with the kin network, with whom a substantial portion of the retirees were very much involved. There was frequent mention on the part of both groups of females of their siblings, and of their nieces and nephews, but little mention of them by males. Again the feeling was expressed that families can become closer in retirement because there is more time.

> Families mean much to us. We are much more involved with our family since retirement, because we have more time, for instance, for helping out with family needs in times of illness in the extended family. Most families have need for help from someone with free time in crises—illness, death, new babies, etc. My husband and I have found this new role to be a worthwhile investment of time and love.

Most retirees in this sample who had children were in close contact with them and were enjoying them as adults. Some retirees were providing emotional and/or financial support to their very old parents and to their adult children, sometimes by helping their grandchildren.

Even though 11 of the professional females and males in the sample were members of retired dual-career families, husbands were more apt to help with the housework than to share in it; for most, it was still mainly the responsibility of the wife. Although there was cooperation, the division of labor in retirement remained quite traditional for this generation of people. Some of the nonprofessional females lost help from their husbands when the females retired and assistance was deemed no longer necessary.

## MOVING IN RETIREMENT

In this sample, 64.5 percent did not move upon retiring. Finding a more desirable climate (preferably with recreational opportunities) and/or being nearer family members were the main reasons for moving. The females who had moved into government-subsidized housing were very satisfied with it, and they were now greatly involved with their new friends there, who had become "family" to them. Occasionally, crime in a deteriorating neighborhood was a reason for a change of residence.

## FINDING MEANING IN THE RETIREMENT YEARS

The professional females and males were more articulate than the nonprofessional females in discussing philosophical issues. They spoke of seeking enjoyment and satisfaction with life in retirement, of finding meaning through helping others, of being realistic about retirement, of accepting life as it is.

> To me, life is a series of "letting go," and now I am letting go of (the former job) so that I can continue to grow with new and exciting experiences. I plan to continue my writing, and look forward to the extra time I have to do so. There is, of course, the never-ending search for Self, a search I have always enjoyed despite the anxieties that invariably accompany such a search. Now I will have more time for self-evaluation and introspection.

## RETIREMENT PREPARATION

Few in this sample had any preretirement preparation. Those who did felt it was valuable, and others regretted the lack of it. There is increasing evidence that persons who plan ahead for retirement make a more satisfactory transition than those who don't.

# SUMMARY AND CONCLUSION

The purpose of this study was to explore what retirement is like for professional women in their first six years of retirement. The sample was a nonrandom one. The nucleus of persons participating in the research were members or former members of the National Council on Family Relations and had worked in some aspect of the interdisciplinary family field. Perhaps because of this, and because persons in the early retirement years are relatively healthy and independent, the findings were quite positive. If the study were to be repeated ten years from now, with the same group, the results might be less optimistic.

Among those interviewed, the majority of women, though not men, were finding life more pleasant in retirement than it had been in their working years. Most retirees of both sexes still felt useful, had a sense of purpose, and were quite satisfied with being retired.

The satisfactions found in retirement by those in this sample were related positively to their ability to identify and use a wide variety of options, their ability to enter into new "careers," their friendship networks, their linkage systems to family members, financial security, good health, satisfactory use of leisure time, and preretirement preparation for a transition period that may seem hazardous even if one has anticipated it.

After discussing retirement with the 62 persons who were in their first six years of that stage, the following recommendations are suggested:

(1) that preretirement education, counseling, and planning be offered in the workplace, schools, churches, and community agencies well before one reaches that period of life, and that information about the psychological, emotional, physiological, social, and environmental aspects of retirement be included. Illustrative concerns might be marital health; relationships with grown children, grandchildren, and/or aging parents; use of leisure time; housing; health; friendships; bereavement, grief, and adjustment to loss; and remarriage;

(2) that this education emphasize involvement in a balance of play and education and work during the entire life cycle, including the retirement years (Gardner, 1981), and that the advantages of a flexible lifestyle be promoted so that one may meet new demands and take advantage of new opportunities in retirement;

(3) that support networks of friends and neighbors, voluntary groups, and church organizations be activated to reinforce the individual and family in retirement. For successful retirement one needs to continue to interact with others, to have needs met for love, affection, emotional support, and physical contact;

(4) that since the need to be involved in satisfying leisure activities continues in retirement, training and research agencies, including universities that offer programs relating to leisure should consider the needs of the retired;

(5) that adequate supportive social services be made available to retirees who need them, and that research needed to make these services effective be undertaken;

(6) that retirees be available to help other retirees in areas such as peer counseling, outreach, advocacy, information, and referral. The Senior Power movement, which organized older people "to do our thing—for ourselves" is an example of a self-help endeavor;

(7) that programs at local, state, and federal levels that offer opportunities for community service by the retired be strengthened and expanded. The persons in this sample, especially the retired professionals, were frequently involved in volunteer activities. They had the time, enjoyed doing something significant, and appreciated the social contacts and friendships obtained from such endeavors. Of the professional females, 63 percent reported finding new friends through working in political and voluntary organizations;

(8) that there be additional research focusing on women and retirement, and that there be research on the retirement of dual career couples, since many retired professional females have been members of such families. Dual-career lifestyle satisfactions that might carry over into retirement include the likelihood of financial security, possible sharing of household responsibilities, higher status, enhanced self-concept, probable increased communication and colleagueship, and shared pleasures;

(9) that the retired themselves be involved in any research about their needs and ways of meeting them; and that they be used as consultants in planning and developing programs concerning them;

(10) that information media be encouraged to give special attention to enhancing the image of the retired and to promoting retirement as an opportunity;

(11) that flexible part-time positions for those in the retirement years who need or want to work be more widely available, with employers encouraged to develop age-neutral appraisal systems to decide about the quality of a person's work;

(12) that the Rapoports' (1975a, 1975b) suggestions of ways that can lead to an increase in happiness in the retirement stage be encouraged: recovering one's capacity for joy by achieving a better understanding of one's inner life motivations, inhibitions, and conflicts; organizing one's life in retirement with "purposeful, enjoyable activity"; and constructing new communities where lifestyles can be created that foster happiness and enjoyment in the retirement years.

Retirement is a critical transition point in a person's life, whether it is viewed positively or negatively. The structure required by work has been removed. Established patterns are disrupted as one leaves the work world, and reorganization occurs. The life sectors of work, family, friends, and leisure are all affected as a different set of concerns is activated. The writer suggests that if the above recommendations are put into effect, the process of moving into the relatively undefined—and in many cases undervalued—social role of being retired may be a more satisfying one.

## NOTE

1. Owing to the large number of tables on which this chapter is based, only a narrative account of results could be presented here. Interested readers are advised to consult the author's dissertation.

# 12

# PROFESSIONAL WOMEN: WORK PATTERN AS A CORRELATE OF RETIREMENT SATISFACTION

## Marilyn R. Block

As retirement becomes increasingly widespread and of longer duration, adjustment to retirement has occupied a large portion of gerontological research in recent years. However, sex differences in work and retirement are seldom examined, possibly because of the assumption that work is not a primary role for women even when they are employed.

Where sex differences in adjustment to retirement have been empirically investigated, women's adjustment patterns have been compared to men's adaptation patterns. Adjustment to retirement has been shown to differ substantially for men and women. The women in sex-comparative retirement studies consistently exhibit poorer adjustment to retirement than the men. However, men tend to retire after 40 or more years of gainful employment. Because women's work roles have historically been of shorter duration and lesser economic and social status, it is difficult to determine whether their comparatively poorer adjustment to retirement is due to alleged sex differences or to their distinct work histories.

Differences in male and female satisfaction with retirement might be accounted for by the number of years devoted to gainful employment and the continuity or discontinuity of that employment. As increasing numbers of women enter the labor force, it seems likely that there will be more women preparing for careers and working continuously until retirement just as men do. Little is known about the impact of retirement on women who have had the satisfaction of a career as opposed to those who have worked sporadically at different jobs.

The purpose of this study was to determine whether work pattern has an effect on professional women's satisfaction with retirement. The research focus was based on the supposition that male and female differences in work pattern, rather than sex, may explain the differences in male and female orientation toward retirement. The most obvious difference between male and female work patterns is the regular career pattern of men and the more irregular career patterns of women (Quadagno, 1978). A related difference involves the typically lengthy total work time of men in contrast to the shorter commitments of women, who traditionally drop out of the labor force to raise families.

It would seem that differences in adjustment to retirement might be attributable to the lengthy and continuous work history experienced by most men and uncommon to most women. It appears likely that as women more closely approximate the regular (continuous) and lengthy career patterns of men, their satisfaction with retirement should also be similar to the male experience.

Since professional women have work patterns that are more continuous and more similar to those of men than other groups of women workers, the impact of work history on these women's retirement satisfaction could provide some insights into possible reasons for the previously observed gender differences in retirement satisfaction. The present study attempts to determine the absolute and relative effect of work pattern on professional women's satisfaction with retirement.


## METHODS


Participation in the study was purely voluntary and involved responding to a mail questionnaire. The purpose of the mail questionnaire was to assess satisfaction with retirement.

Data were collected on a number of variables in order to determine to what extent they contribute to satisfaction with retirement and whether, after their effects were partialed out, work pattern was a meaningful determinant of satisfaction in retirement.

While social resources, health, preretirement planning, and other demographic and economic factors all impinge to some degree on male satisfaction with retirement, there are no data to indicate how well these variables predict satisfaction with retirement for women. Moreover, there are no data to indicate how well work pattern predicts satisfaction with retirement when compared to these other variables.

Questionnaire responses had to meet several criteria in order to be considered usable for this study:

(1) response to the item "Are you retired from full-time work in your life-time occupation?" had to be affirmative;
(2) respondents had to be women;
(3) questionnaire items specific to satisfaction with retirement and work pattern had to be completely filled out.

## SAMPLE

The individual respondents were contacted through the alumni listing for the classes of 1920-1938 of the University of Maryland.

The age range of the respondents was 59-81 years; mean age was 68 years. Year of birth ranged from 1897-1919; mean year of birth was 1910. Age at retirement ranged from 46-78 years; mean retirement age was 61. Length of retirement ranged from 6 months to 19 years; mean length of retirement was 7 years.

No claim is offered that the retirees in the study constitute a sample necessarily representative of the population of retired women. Because most subjects were working in 1970 (the average year of retirement was 1971), comparisons on a variety of dimensions can be made against female labor force participation data for 1970. The respondents differ from similarly aged women in the general U.S. population with regard to marital status, occupational status, education level, and financial status.

*Marital Status.* Compared with general female participation in the labor force, married women with spouse present and never-married women were underrepresented in the sample of retirees, while women who were divorced, widowed, or separated were overrepresented. The retirees in the sample had a median age of 29 at the birth of their first child, in contrast to age 25 for the cohort (1910) in general. Thus, they experienced a longer span of time early in adulthood when they were free from the responsibilities of child rearing.

*Occupational Status.* The occupations of the retirees were higher status than those of the general population of working women. In all, 98 percent were white-collar workers, both during most of their adult lives and at retirement. Only 60 percent of all working women were employed in the white-collar professions in 1970, and two-thirds of these were employed as sales workers and clerical and kindred workers. Within the white-collar professions, the retirees were overrepresented in the professional-technical and managerial-administrative areas, as compared to all working women, and underrepresented in the sales and clerical areas.

The majority of retirees participated in the same occupation through-out their adult life. Of the 20 percent who shifted jobs, the majority (57 percent) remained in the same field but had been promoted to a higher level (e.g., a shift from teaching to school administration or from nurse to nursing supervisor). Thus, 91 percent of the retirees displayed occupa-tional continuity.

*Education Level.* The more education a woman has had, the more likely she is to have pursued a career. The retirees in the sample are nonrepresen-tative of the general population of women in terms of educational achieve-ment. All of the retirees were college graduates, and a great many of them had advanced training beyond the baccalaureate degree. This level of attainment is in distinct contrast to women over age 65 in 1975 (cohort 1910), few of whom (6.3 percent) had completed college.

*Financial Status.* The retirees in this sample appear to be in a desirable financial position when compared to the general population. Not surpris-ingly, the married women in the sample were the most well-off, since these tended to be dual-income families. More than 75 percent of the retirees had three or more sources of income. Again, this is in sharp contrast to the general population; nearly 80 percent of retired Americans rely solely on Social Security benefits for a retirement income (Atchley, 1976c).

## MEASURES

At the outset of the study, two questions concerning women's satisfac-tion with retirement were posed: (1) Is there a relationship between work pattern and women's satisfaction with retirement? and (2) Do variables other than work pattern contribute to women's satisfaction with retirement?

The dependent variable, *satisfaction with retirement,* was assessed by use of the Retirement Descriptive Index (RDI) (Smith et al., 1969). The schedule consists of 63 items, broken down into four scales: activities and work (18 items); financial situation (18 items); health (9 items); and people one associates with (18 items).

The RDI is a descriptive rather than evaluative instrument. It does not ask the respondent directly how satisfied he or she is with retirement; rather, it asks for a description of retirement. In describing retirement, the respondent provides information which may be used to infer satisfaction.

Some of the description involves the use of words that are evaluative (e.g., good, challenging), as well as those that are objective (e.g., self-supporting). In addition, the respondent's attitudes toward her retirement influence her responses even to the more objective words. Finally, some of the words describe actual objective features of the retirement situation that influence satisfaction directly (e.g., need help from children). The descriptive format is used because describing some specific aspect of retirement is easier than trying to describe internal states of feeling (Smith et al., 1969).

The independent variable in the first research question, *work pattern,* consisted of two dimensions: continuity and total work time. Thus, retirement satisfaction of women retirees was examined according to the length of their work history and continuous or intermittent work pattern. A continuous work history was characterized by work without interruption for a minimum of 20 percent of the entire potential working life. Intermittent work was characterized by entry to and departure from the labor force a number of times, where no single span of work equaled or exceeded 20 percent of the entire potential working life.

The amount of 20 percent (9 years) was selected as the criterion for continuous employment for two reasons. First, it implies a moderate degree of commitment to labor force participation, since women who are willing to relinquish work in favor of family or other interests are likely to do so prior to this length of time. Second, it is a short enough span of time that women who enter the labor force after children are grown (age 50-55) and who are mandatorily retired at age 65 or 70 are not excluded from demonstrating a commitment to their employment.

Because each graduating class represented within the sample had a different total possible number of years in the labor force between graduation and the date of this study, the percentage of work periods (calculated in five-year increments) between the ages of 21 and 65 equaled the assigned individual score of total work time. Only 23.18 percent of the continuous workers worked for fewer than 50 percent of the total years of potential labor force activity. Another 37.09 percent were employed for 80 percent of their potential 45 years in the labor force (Table 12.1). By contrast, exactly half of the intermittent workers were employed less than 50 percent of their potential employable years, and only 10.71 percent worked for more than 80 percent of that time.

The independent variables in the second research question are discussed in some detail.

*Health.* Health is a particularly important variable in coping with the changes inherent in the retirement role, since poor health is one of the

TABLE 12.1    Gainful Employment of Continous Workers, by Percentage
of Potential Years in the Labor Force

| Potential Labor Force Involvement | | Continous Workers | | |
| Years | % of Total | N | % | Cumulative Percentage |
|---|---|---|---|---|
| 1-4 | 1-10 | - | - | - |
| 5-9 | 11-20 | 1 | .66 | .66 |
| 10-13 | 21-30 | 6 | 3.97 | 4.63 |
| 14-18 | 31-40 | 15 | 9.93 | 14.56 |
| 19-22 | 41-50 | 13 | 8.62 | 23.18 |
| 23-27 | 51-60 | 14 | 9.27 | 32.45 |
| 28-31 | 61-70 | 20 | 13.24 | 45.69 |
| 32-36 | 71-80 | 26 | 17.22 | 62.91 |
| 37-40 | 81-90 | 33 | 21.85 | 84.76 |
| 41-45 | 91-100 | 23 | 15.23 | 99.99* |

*Does not add to 100 due to rounding

most commonly stated reasons by men for retiring from work (Barfield and Morgan, 1978a). Two objective measures of mental health status and physical health status were administered. The Langner Scale of Mental Symptomatology is the most widely used index of mental health symptomatology in community-dwelling populations. It has been shown to significantly discriminate between individuals independently described as psychiatrically sick or psychiatrically well (Langner, 1962). Physical health was assessed by seven questions concerning physician visits, medication use, and diagnosed illnesses (Guttmann et al., 1977).

*Preretirement Planning.* One factor which has been found to have a positive correlation with successful retirement adjustment is preretirement planning (Bell, 1975; Eteng, 1973). In accordance with role theory, when one is able to undergo anticipatory socialization, one is better able to adjust to one's new role. Planning in advance for retirement constitutes a process of anticipatory socialization. Glamser (1976) finds that a knowledge of retirement issues is positively correlated with attitude toward retirement, as is the respondent's subjective perception of how well prepared he is for retirement. The availability of preretirement planning, the kinds of information obtained through preretirement programs, and the degree of preparation for retirement provided by preretirement programs were all examined.

*Social Resources.* An examination of women's adaptation in old age (Fox, 1977) reveals that retirement has real consequences for women in terms of general level of social contact. Fox asserts that women for whom the occupational role was an integral part of their lives have different interpersonal needs than others. The presence of social supports in the form of friends and kin is known to be related to adaptation in retirement (Streib and Schneider, 1971). Glamser (1976) also finds that a respondent's level of social activity is positively related to attitude toward retirement.

Thus, it would seem that a measure of those social resources considered to facilitate adaptation in old age must be administered in any effort focused on satisfaction with retirement. Eight items were used to measure social resources; four questions probed the existence of social resources, and four more indexed the utilization of these resources (Fox, 1977).

*Demographic/SES Factors.* A number of demographic, social, and economic factors are used as controlling variables in most retirement studies. These include educational level, marital status, and annual family income before and after retirement. Data regarding these variables, as well as information concerning occupational level, age at retirement, length of retirement, and reason for retirement were obtained.

## RESULTS

### WORK PATTERN AND RETIREMENT SATISFACTION

In order to determine whether work pattern related to retirement satisfaction, a one-way analysis of variance was performed. The data (Table 12.2) indicate a significant relationship between work pattern and retirement satisfaction, with continuous workers expressing more satisfaction than intermittent workers.

### DEMOGRAPHIC VARIABLES AND WORK PATTERN

Since women's work histories have been shown to relate to a variety of background factors, which also account for retirement satisfaction (e.g., income), the initial bivariate relationship between work pattern and retirement satisfaction could be spurious. Results shown in Table 12.3 suggest

**TABLE 12.2    RDI Scores of Continuous and Intermittent Workers**

| Type of Worker | N | Mean | Standard Deviation | df | f value |
|---|---|---|---|---|---|
| Continuous | 150 | 149.23 | 27.24 | | |
| Intermittent | 29 | 137.14 | 29.31 | 1,177 | 4.67* |

\* p < .05

that continuous workers differ in several demographic characteristics from intermittent workers. Specifically, continuous as compared to intermittent workers have been employed for a longer time, have engaged in more retirement planning, retired most often in order to pursue leisure interests, are more likely single or widowed, and are less likely to have either very high or very low incomes. No significant differences between the two groups showed in regard to social networks, health, education, and pre-retirement income. These findings suggest that the relationship between work pattern and retirement satisfaction may be affected by other divergencies between the two groups of women. Therefore, further analyses were carried out to determine the relative effect of work pattern on retirement satisfaction.

### DETERMINANTS OF RETIREMENT SATISFACTION

In order to ascertain how much variance in satisfaction with retirement is explained by work pattern, a two-step multiple regression analysis was run. Social resources, health, preretirement planning, income before retirement, and income after retirement were combined to determine how much variance in satisfaction with retirement these variables explained together. Type of employment history and total work time were combined and forced in at step two in order to determine how much additional variance in satisfaction with retirement could be explained by work pattern. The initial five variables, in combination, explained 37.22 percent of the variance, while work pattern explained less than an additional 1 percent of the variance—not a significant increment.

Additionally, a stepwise multiple regression analysis was run in order to determine which individual factors were the best predictors of satisfaction with retirement. Only three factors were significant predictors of satisfaction with retirement: health, preretirement planning, and income after

**TABLE 12.3   Similarities and Differences Between Continuous and
Intermittent Workers**

| Dimension | Continuous | Intermittent |
|---|---|---|
| Daily contact with social network: | | |
| 1-6 people | 30% | 35% |
| 7-15 people | 65 | 55 |
| 16+ people | 5 | 10 |
| Health: | | |
| no or few physical symptoms/ailments | 89% | 93% |
| moderate or many physical symptoms/ailments | 11 | 7 |
| Educational attainment: | | |
| baccalaureate degree | 44% | 58% |
| master's degree | 29 | 18 |
| doctorate | 3 | 0 |
| law/medical school | 4 | 0 |
| other professional school | 20 | 24 |
| Income before retirement: | | |
| less than $10,000 | 13% | 13% |
| $10,000-$19,999 | 36 | 42 |
| $20,000-$29,999 | 31 | 17 |
| $30,000+ | 20 | 27 |
| Length of employment: | | |
| less than 9 years | 0% | 7%** |
| 10-17 years | 10 | 17 |
| 18-26 years | 21 | 45 |
| 27-35 years | 27 | 17 |
| 36-45 years | 42 | 14 |
| Preretirement planning: | | |
| excellent | 57% | 36%* |
| good | 39 | 54 |
| poor | 4 | 4 |
| none | 1 | 7 |
| Reason for retirement: | | |
| failing health | 9% | 14%** |
| mandatory retirement age | 9 | 7 |
| lack of interest in job | 7 | 4 |
| desire for 2nd career | 1 | 11 |
| more leisure time | 51 | 32 |
| other | 23 | 32 |

*(continued)*

TABLE 12.3 (Continued)

| Dimension | Continuous | Intermittent |
|---|---|---|
| Marital status: | | |
| married | 46% | 79%** |
| never married | 25 | 0 |
| separated/divorced | 3 | 7 |
| widowed | 26 | 14 |
| Income after retirement: | | |
| less than $10,000 | 25% | 32%** |
| $10,000-$19,999 | 37 | 32 |
| $20,000-$29,999 | 25 | 4 |
| $30,000 | 12 | 32 |

\* p < .05
\*\* p < .01

retirement (Table 12.4). Neither work pattern nor social resources were significant predictors of satisfaction with retirement.

## DISCUSSION

While the present study supports the assumption that continuous work is associated with high retirement satisfaction, this relationship could be attributed to demographic differences between intermittent and continuous workers. After controlling for these factors, work pattern did not significantly contribute to retirement satisfaction.

The regression on retirement satisfaction showed three variables to be of major importance, namely, health, postretirement income, and retirement planning. Previous research has provided ample evidence that resources such as health and income are prerequisites for successful adaptation to retirement (Atchley, 1972). The present study clearly supports this trend. It is also evident that for these professional women, retirement planning plays an important role in subsequent adjustment to the retirement transition.

The finding that preretirement planning was a significant predictor of satisfaction with retirement suggests that the development of retirement programs for direct use by working women with the guidance of a professional is warranted. Preretirement programs have not focused specifi-

**TABLE 12.4   Predictors of Satisfaction With Retirement**

| Variable | $R$ | Explained Variance: $R^2$ | $R^2$ Change | $F$ |
|---|---|---|---|---|
| Health | .41012 | .16820 | .16820 | 29.08* |
| Preretirement Planning | .52140 | .27186 | .10366 | 24.79* |
| Income After Retirement | .60351 | .36422 | .09237 | 5.65* |

* $p < .05$

cally on the needs and abilities of older women. Retirement planning offers a framework that can encourage women to examine their lives and to discover areas of strength and weakness. In addition, it provides a structure directed toward information gathering and action.

Older women today are heavily concentrated in occupations where pensions are non-existent or inadequate and where their low wages and intermittent work histories mean low Social Security benefits. Their occupations are often physically demanding. Many older women are widowed, divorced, or married to men with low incomes, and these factors are not usually conducive to satisfaction in retirement.

Preretirement planning programs need to emphasize decision-making and goal-setting skills, as well as knowledge in a number of areas, particularly financial issues, since this is an area in which women have traditionally had less experience and have relied upon men or "the system" to manage. Such programs should be available during the middle years in order that building financial assets, establishing involvement in activities that can be carried into retirement, and building proper health habits can be initiated while there is still time to conserve or expand resources for the later years.

Although there appears to be growing national interest in preretirement planning programs, particularly development of programs directed toward subgroups that have been previously overlooked, preretirement planning programs are doomed to ineffectiveness and even failure unless several conditions accompany their development.

First, decision makers need better sources of information about older women and their views about retirement. Developers of preretirement planning programs are not necessarily cognizant as to whether or not retirement represents a crisis for women, nor do they always understand the reasons why women retire.

Second, decision makers need to find means whereby preretirement planning programs for older women can be supported. Government support for such programs through tax incentives or subsidies to employers is one method of overcoming financial barriers.

Finally, preretirement programs must be structured to address the needs and interests of the women they are designed to serve. Of particular importance, although seldom addressed in such programs, is a focus on singleness instead of the usual assumption that wives will enjoy leisure pursuits with a husband.

# 13

# PERSONAL PROBLEMS AND ADJUSTMENT TO RETIREMENT

## Maximiliane Szinovacz

**A good deal of the** retirement literature in general and the research on women's retirement in particular has been devoted to tracing predictors of retirement adjustment. The typical approach taken in these investigations is to select a number of potentially relevant predictor variables and to assess their relative importance for various adjustment dimensions, usually through regression or other multivariate techniques. In the majority of cases, the selected predictor variables consist of demographic variables (e.g., income, age), and specific personal and social characteristics (e.g., health, social contacts, activities). The chosen predictors also tend to be relatively objective characteristics (e.g., income, number of leisure activities, number of specific ailments and disabilities, number of social contacts). Among the variables which have been so identified to impact on women's retirement adjustment are income, health, social and leisure activities, and attitudes toward retirement (for a review of this literature, see Szinovacz, 1982b).

Even though such studies provide important and policy-relevant information, they often neglect the respondents' personal assessments of their problems and of the reasons for retirement problems. Symbolic interactionists have long emphasized the importance of individuals' per-

*AUTHOR'S NOTE: This project was funded by a grant from the NRTA-AARP Andrus Foundation, Washington, D.C.*

sonal perspective for their attitudes and behaviors. The approach to retirement adjustment taken in this chapter builds on this theoretical viewpoint. While it is acknowledged that various objective situational and personal characteristics impinge on a person's adaptation to retirement, the present chapter attempts to identify relationships between subjects' problem perceptions and various indicators of retirement adjustment, when more objective situational factors are controlled. It is thus assumed that women's perceptions of problems—regardless of their objective circumstances—play some role in retirement adjustment. For instance, women with the same income may consider their economic resources to be adequate or inadequate, depending on their personal expectations and needs. Or, women with similar health problems may either give in to their illness and adopt a self-definition of being unable to do many things, or they may attempt to lead an active life despite their disabilities.

To assess the impact of such perceptional and attitudinal factors on retirement adjustment is useful for praxis, particularly in the realms of counseling and information provision. In many cases, adverse retirement circumstances such as low income or poor health cannot be easily altered through intervention. Certainly, long-term policies are necessary to overcome such problems, but in the short term, the functions of some agencies and counselors will be restricted to helping retirees deal with and make the best of problematic circumstances. Such help has to address women's personal perceptions of problems and their attitudes toward the retirement situation. Indeed, in the study reported on below, a good many women felt a "positive attitude" to be a major prerequisite for successful adaptation to retirement. The present chapter follows these women's lead and examines the extent to which personal problem perceptions relate to retirement adjustment.

## METHODS

The sample and adjustment indicators used in this study were already described in Chapter 9 and need not be repeated here. Problems of women retirees were assessed through a series of single item questions on the following issues: use of time, health, friends, expenses, and activities. Specifically, the following questions were asked: How often would you say you have time on your hands you don't know what to do with? Would you say you are able to do almost anything you wish to do, just certain things, or do you have some health problems that keep you from doing a lot of things you wish you could do? Would you say you have enough good friends you can count on if you had any sort of trouble, not quite enough, or none at all? Do you ever worry that your income will not be enough to meet your expenses and bills? The final problem area, activities, was derived from an open questions on negative retirement aspects. Subjects reporting that they were bored, lacked challenging activities, or felt useless were scored as experiencing a problem in this area. In addition to these questions, respondents were also presented with a list of potential problem areas (derived from pretest materials) and asked to indicate whether they experienced any of the listed problems.

## RESULTS

### OCCURRENCE AND DISTRIBUTION OF PROBLEMS

Descriptive data on the single item questions are shown in Table 13.1. It is obvious that most women in this sample do not suffer from serious problems, but still reported having some difficulties in various life areas. About one-third of the women at least sometimes don't know what to do with their time, and 21 percent of the respondents lack meaningful activities. About one-quarter of the subjects experience health problems which prevent them from engaging in some activities, and close to one-fifth feel that they do not have enough friends they can count on. Only a few women indicate serious financial difficulties, but slightly over one-half mention at least occasional worries over their expenses.

The women's answers to the list of potential problems are presented in Table 13.2. It is clear that while each of the listed problems were experienced by a few women, only two major areas of concern were identifiable. The first and most often mentioned problem area concerns home maintenance and heavy household work. The other relatively frequently indicated problem is meeting new people. Overall, however, relatively few of these women experience major problems in their current lives. At least two reasons may account for this trend. First, the retirees in this sample are still relatively young, and in most cases healthy and financially well off and thus unlikely to have serious economic or medical problems. Also, some women may have felt reluctant to admit to problems or may only have responded in the affirmative if they faced serious difficulties in an area.

Additional materials from this project which cannot be presented in detail here suggest that all problems except home maintenance occurred

TABLE 13.1    Selected Problems Experienced by Women Retirees
              (percentages)

| | |
|---|---|
| Don't know what to do with time | |
| quite often | 9 |
| now and then | 26 |
| never | 65 |
| Health stops activities | |
| can do anything | 76 |
| just certain things | 18 |
| a lot of things | 6 |
| Number of friends I can count on | |
| enough | 81 |
| not quite enough | 18 |
| none | 1 |
| Worry about expenses | |
| all the time | 3 |
| most of the time | 1 |
| now and then | 48 |
| never | 49 |
| Lack meaningful activities | |
| mentioned | 21 |
| not mentioned | 79 |

(N = 115)

more often among subjects in the lower socioeconomic status groups
(Szinovacz, 1982a). Problems with home maintenance and heavy household work predominated among white subjects, single and widowed
women, as well as subjects from the middle and higher social strata.

## RETIREMENT PROBLEMS AND ADJUSTMENT

The major objective of this chapter is to investigate the relative effect
of women's personal perceptions of problems on retirement adjustment.
Since the problem variables are nominal data, an analysis of variance
design was used to estimate the absolute and relative effect of five
problems (use of time, health, friends, activities, and expenses) on
women's retirement adjustment. Since demographic and other background
characteristics may affect these relationships, controls for income, retirement age, marital status (married), race (white), and retirement attitude

**TABLE 13.2  Problems Mentioned by Women Retirees**

| | *Percentage with problem* |
|---|---|
| Medical care | 7 |
| Finding a comfortable place to live | 1 |
| Home maintenance | 23 |
| Nutritious food | 1 |
| Getting to places | 3 |
| Meeting new people | 12 |
| Finding out about activities | 5 |
| Heavy household work | 17 |
| Shopping | 2 |
| Financial | 5 |
| Public services | 3 |
| Legal assistance | 3 |
| Help with taxes | 5 |
| Other | 3 |
| (N = 115) | |

(preference for later retirement) were introduced in the analysis. Other results from this study indicate that each of these variables relates significantly to some problems and/or adjustment indicators.

The data shown in Tables 13.3 to 13.5 present the impact of selected problems on the adjustment indicators as deviations from the grand mean. Thus, positive signs indicate higher than average and negative signs lower than average adjustment. The eta values are equivalent to bivariate Pearson correlation coefficients, and the beta values indicate the relative effect of each problem area, controlling for the covariates. The F values represent the combined main effect of all problems, as well as the combined effect of all covariates. Interaction effects among problems were ignored in these analyses.[1]

Relationships between problems and job deprivation scores are demonstrated in Table 13.3. It is evident that use of time and activities have the strongest effects on job deprivation, and these effects remained significant when the controls were introduced. Eta values for health, friends, and expenses were also significant, but their effect on job deprivation was reduced to a nonsignificant level once the covariates were entered. Both the combined main effect of problems and the combined covariate effect were significant. The most important covariates proved to be income (F = 16.30, p < .01), retirement attitude (F = 17.00, p < .01), and race (F =

TABLE 13.3    Multiple Classification Analysis of Job Deprivation, by
              Selected Problems and Covariates

| Problems | | Deviation from mean | | Eta | Beta |
| | | not ad-justed | ad-justed | | |
| --- | --- | --- | --- | --- | --- |
| Use of time | | | | | |
| no | (72) | +.11 | +.07 | .44** | .30** |
| yes | (37) | −.21 | −.14 | | |
| Health | | | | | |
| no | (82) | +.04 | +.02 | .20* | .11 |
| yes | (27) | −.12 | −.06 | | |
| Friends | | | | | |
| no | (88) | +.04 | +.01 | .26** | .05 |
| yes | (21) | −.18 | −.04 | | |
| Activities | | | | | |
| no | (87) | +.08 | +.05 | .49** | .27** |
| yes | (22) | −.33 | −.18 | | |
| Expenses | | | | | |
| no | (51) | +.11 | +.05 | .31** | .14[a] |
| yes | (58) | −.10 | −.04 | | |

$R^2 = .50$

F (main effects) = 8.32**
F (covariates = 11.07**
F (total) = 9.70**

a. $p < .10$; * $p < .05$; ** $p < .01$
NOTE: Controls were income, retirement age, marital status, race and preferred
      retirement timing (later).

3.92, $p < .05$). Thus, women with low incomes, a preference for later
retirement, and black subjects scored relatively low on job deprivation.

A slightly modified picture emerges from the relationships between
problems and morale (Table 13.4). Again, all eta values were significant,
but only the effects of health and activities remained significant after
controls were introduced. Both the combined main and covariate effects
were statistically significant. In this case, income proved to be the single
most important determinant of morale among the covariates (F = 13.31,
$p < .01$).

Neither covariate nor problems significantly contributed to the explanation of women's positive feelings of happiness. Since the overall explained
variance was also very low ($R^2 = .14$), it must be concluded that positive

**TABLE 13.4** Multiple Classification Analysis of Morale, by Selected Problems and Covariates

| Problems | | *Deviation from mean* | | *Eta* | *Beta* |
|---|---|---|---|---|---|
| | | *not ad-justed* | *ad-justed* | | |
| Use of time | | | | | |
| no | (72) | +.09 | +.05 | .30** | .17[a] |
| yes | (37) | −.18 | −.10 | | |
| Health | | | | | |
| no | (82) | +.07 | +.06 | .28** | .23** |
| yes | (27) | −.21 | −.18 | | |
| Friends | | | | | |
| no | (88) | +.05 | +.02 | .24* | .09 |
| yes | (21) | −.22 | −.08 | | |
| Activities | | | | | |
| no | (87) | +.09 | +.05 | .39** | .24* |
| yes | (22) | −.34 | −.21 | | |
| Expenses | | | | | |
| no | (51) | +.13 | +.05 | .28** | .12 |
| yes | (58) | −.11 | −.05 | | |

$R^2 = .36$

F (main effects) = 5.71**
F (covariates) = 5.27**
F (total) = 5.49**

a. $p < .10$; * $p < .05$; ** $p < .01$

NOTE: Controls were retirement age, marital status, race , income, and retirement timing (later).

feelings are subject to other influences than those considered here. These results are not shown.

Negative feelings of happiness, on the other hand, did relate significantly to problems with the use of time, activities, and friends (Table 13.5). The former two effects remained significant after controls were entered into the analysis. And we find again a significant F value for both combined main and covariate effects. Among the covariates, only the effect of retirement attitude was significant ($F = 9.70$, $p < .01$).

## CONCLUSION

These results provide clear evidence that women's perceptions of problems play an important role in their adjustment to the retirement situa-

TABLE 13.5   Multiple Classification Analyses of Negative Feelings by
             Selected Problems and Covariates

| Problems | | Deviation from mean | | Eta | Beta |
|---|---|---|---|---|---|
| | | not ad-<br>justed | ad-<br>justed | | |
| Use of time | | | | | |
| no | (72) | +.15 | +.13 | .40** | .33** |
| yes | (37) | −.30 | −.24 | | |
| Health | | | | | |
| no | (82) | +.04 | +.04 | .12 | .12 |
| yes | (27) | −.11 | −.11 | | |
| Friends | | | | | |
| no | (88) | +.05 | +.01 | .18* | .03 |
| yes | (21) | −.20 | −.04 | | |
| Activities | | | | | |
| no | (87) | +.09 | +.06 | .34** | .23* |
| yes | (22) | −.36 | −.24 | | |
| Expenses | | | | | |
| no | (51) | +.05 | −.04 | .08 | .07 |
| yes | (58) | −.04 | +.03 | | |

$R^2 = .28$

F   (main effects) = 4.59**
F   (covariates) = 2.99*
F   (total) = 3.79**

* $p < .05$; ** $p < .01$
NOTE:  Controls were retirement age, marital status, race, income, and retirement
       timing (later).

tion. Especially inadequate use of time and lack of meaningful activities
were consistently related to relatively poor adjustment, regardless of
income, marital status, retirement age, race, or retirement attitude. As
several of the respondents indicated to another question, a positive attitude and keeping active indeed appear to be prerequisites for a satisfactory
postretirement life.

The data further suggest that it is particularly women in the lower
socioeconomic status groups who experience retirement problems and
have difficulty adjusting to the retirement transition. Many of these
women retired for health reasons and are therefore often not well prepared
psychologically and economically to retire. They are also apt to be
restricted in their activities owing to continuing health problems. Clearly,

these women are "at risk" and in need of various services to overcome their retirement problems. Such programs should not only deal with the economic problems experienced by these women, but should also attempt to break the link between low income and satisfactory use of time and involvement in activities.

Obviously, low-income retirees lack the means to attend expensive entertainments, but lack of economic resources and skills also prevents them from pursuing less costly leisure activities. Other materials from this study indicate, for instance, that transportation and health problems, as well as fear to leave their homes at night, restrict these women's mobility. Lack of educational skills also hinders these women's ability to develop meaningful hobbies at home. For example, some of the low-income respondents were at least functionally illiterate and thus unable to read. They spent a lot of time watching TV or what they call "resting." These women consistently felt that they were much better off when they still worked, even though some of their jobs (e.g., cook, hospital aide) were physically demanding and stressful. Special programs are clearly necessary to help these women develop meaningful postretirement activities.

The other problem area deserving some attention concerns the household and home maintenance problems experienced primarily by middle-income and nonmarried women. Even though homemaker and home maintenance services are available for older persons, eligibility requirements usually restrict their use to the lower-income population. Since demand for such programs seems relatively high among the economically better-situated women (who are nevertheless still unable to afford private services), these programs should be offered to a wider population group, probably with sliding scale fees.

## NOTE

1. Although some problems were significantly related, correlation coefficients were not large enough to indicate a multicollinearity problem. All $r$'s were smaller than .30.

# 14

# RESPONSIBILITY FOR HOUSEHOLD TASKS: COMPARING DUAL-EARNER AND DUAL-RETIRED MARRIAGES

Timothy H. Brubaker and Charles B. Hennon

**The number and proportion** of dual-earner families has increased within the past two decades. Masnick and Bane (1980) report that in 1960, 23 percent of U.S. households consisted of married couples in which both the husband and wife were employed. By 1975, some 30 percent were dual-earner households, and little change is predicted for the next decade. The increase in dual-earner marriages results to a large extent from the higher employment rates of middle-aged, married women. Nearly twice as many women aged 45-59 were employed in 1979 as compared to 1950 (Yearbook of Labor Statistics, 1979). The sharpest increase in labor force participation occurred among married women with children, and this trend is expected to continue (Masnick and Bane, 1980). As these women become older, they are expected to retire from employment. Since their husbands have also retired, an increased number of dual-retired couples are

AUTHORS' NOTE: This research was supported by Family Living Education, University of Wisconsin-Extension, The College of Family Resources and Consumer Sciences, University of Wisconsin-Madison, and the Child and Family Studies Center and School of Education and Allied Professions Research Professorship Award, Miami University. The order of authorship is solely alphabetical.

expected (from marriages in which both spouses have retired from gainful employment). Although there are no data on the number of dual-retired couples at present, it is clear that some older couples have experienced the retirement of both the husband and wife. Without a doubt, dual retirement will increase in the future.

As the proportion of dual-earner households expanded, research was directed toward the effects of female employment on marital relations. Effects of wives' employment on children (Gordon and Kammeyer, 1980; Thompson, 1980), marital quality (Hornung and McCullough, 1981; Locksley, 1980; Richardson, 1979), marital solidarity (Simpson and England, 1981), and husband's career (Ferber and Huber, 1979) have been considered. Some studies (Beckman and Houser, 1979; Model, 1981; Pleck, 1977; Powers, 1971; Yogev, 1981) have examined the division of household tasks in dual-earner marriages, and generally it is found that employed wives have the major responsibility for household activities. For example, a study of 106 faculty women at Northwestern University found that "they assumed most of the responsibility for housework and child care and did not expect or want their husbands to have an equal share in these matters" (Yogev, 1981: 869). However, little is known about employed wives' expectations for household activities in retirement. How do they expect to divide the responsibility for household tasks after they retire? Are employed wives' expectations for household tasks during retirement different from what they were when employed?

There is also a lack of information about women involved in dual-retired marriages. Since dual-earner couples are expected to become dual-retired couples, a number of questions arise. How is the responsibility for household tasks divided in dual-retired marriages? Is the division of responsibility congruent with retired wives' expectations? For the most part, research focusing on women and retirement is one-sided. As noted by Kline (1975), women are usually examined in terms of their reactions as wives to their husbands' retirement. Little is known about the effects of female retirement on marital relationships.

This study examines dual-earner and dual-retired wives' perceived actual and expected division of household responsibilities. As an exploratory study, this analysis provides information about retirement and marriage from the female perspective. The findings have policy implications for preretirement programs, community education, marriage and family counseling, family life education, and family research.

## LITERATURE REVIEW

Ambiguity characterizes the research on the relationship between female employment and household tasks. Wives' employment has been related to the amount of time they spend in household tasks (Blood and Hamblin, 1958; Goebel and Hennon, 1981; Hoffman, 1963; Powers, 1971; Robinson, 1977; Walker and Woods, 1976). For some women, the amount of time spent on housework decreases with employment, and husbands share in these activities (Bahr, 1974; Szinovacz, 1977, 1978). For most, they continue to be primarily responsible for household chores (Beckman and Hauser, 1979; Model, 1981; Oakley, 1974; Yogev, 1981). In general, research suggests that: (1) dual-earner women spend less time in household tasks than homemakers, (2) their husbands complete some of the household tasks but do not increase the amount of time they spend in housework, and (3) dual-earner wives are primarily responsible for traditional female tasks (Araji, 1977; Fogarty et al., 1971; Szinovacz, 1977).

It is important to distinguish between role expectations and performance in regard to household tasks. The person responsible for a household task may not perform the task and vice versa. For example, Araji (1977) found that husbands and wives alike express egalitarian expectations for family roles; however, this egalitarianism is not found in their behaviors. Differences between expectations and perceived behavior are expected in the study of household tasks.

When dual-earner couples retire, do they share responsibility for household tasks more equally? Or is the female primarily responsible for these activities? Little research has focused on household division of labor in dual-retired couples. Although housewives may view the husband's retirement as potential interference in household tasks (Darnley, 1975; Fengler, 1975), the retired wife's perception has not been considered. There is some evidence that retired men are expected to (and do) increase their participation in the household (Ballweg, 1967; Keith and Brubaker, 1979; Keith et al., 1981b; Lipman, 1961; Model, 1981). For example, Keith et al. (1981a) found that retired men were more involved in "feminine" household tasks than employed men. Indeed, Lipman (1961) suggested that such involvement by men may be positively related to their adjustment to retirement. In another analysis, Keith et al. (1981b) found marginal support for this positive relationship. But most of men's increased household activity is in traditionally "masculine" tasks such as yard work, home repairs, or taking out the garbage (Ballweg, 1967; Jackson, 1972). This pattern may vary by social class. Some research suggests that middle-class older couples accept male participation in household activities (Keating and Cole, 1980; Kerckhoff, 1966) more easily than lower-class couples.

All these studies focus on the effects of men's retirement on household tasks. How do female retirees view the division of responsibility for household tasks? Only one researcher (Szinovacz, 1980, 1982a) has focused on the effects of female retirement on marriage and household tasks. Her findings provide evidence for the continuation of a gender-differentiated division of household tasks after the wife's retirement. Most retired women reported little change in the division of household tasks after they retired, and most adhered to a traditional division of labor. For the few couples in which the husband increased his participation in household tasks, the wife was often unable to do housework due to illness. Another study provides additional support for the continuation of gender-differentiated household patterns. Keating and Cole (1980) queried a sample of 400 retired teachers and their wives. Most of these couples continued their preretirement patterns of household activities. Little increase in household activity by the men was found.

The research on employment status and household division of labor suggests that there may be some sharing of household tasks between spouses, but that wives remain primarily responsible. Therefore, dual-earner and dual-retired women should be expected to share some responsibility for household tasks with their husbands. Furthermore, both groups should be expected to share more in the dual-retired than in the dual-earner situation, especially owing to their increased free time.

A number of factors have been found related to women's involvement in household tasks. There is some indication that younger women may expect more involvement from their husbands (Albrecht et al., 1979). Also, education is related to household division of labor (Farkas, 1976). The higher the education of the wife, the more sharing of household tasks is reported (Ericksen et al., 1979). The presence of children in the dual-earner family is also important. Indeed, Poloma et al. (1981) suggest that the career of the female partner in a dual-career marriage is influenced by marriage, and more significantly, by children. Wives have major responsibility for child care in many dual-earner families (Bryson et al., 1978; Model, 1981; Yogev, 1981). Age, education, and number of children at home will therefore be considered in our analysis.

# METHODOLOGY

## SAMPLE

Data for this analysis were collected from a sample of 207 women in dual-earner and dual-retired marriages. These data are a subset of a random sample of women belonging to a national women's organization. A questionnaire approved by the organization was mailed to a sample of the membership in ten counties in a Midwestern state. A return rate of 512 questionnaires (52 percent) was obtained from the 978 mailed.

Categorization of women into dual-earner (145) and dual-retired (62) couples was based on responses to an item concerning current living situation. Dual-earner women are those who stated that they *and* their husbands were employed, and dual-retired are those who reported that they *and* their husbands were retired.

Table 14.1 presents a comparison of selected characteristics of dual-earner and retired women. With the exception of age, education, and number of children living at home, there is little difference between the two groups. Dual-earner women are younger, better educated, and have more children at home than dual-retired women. For both groups, most are in their first marriage and most live in nonurban settings.

## MEASURES

*Measure of Household Tasks.* To determine the current division of responsibility in a household, respondents were asked: "*In your own marriage,* who has the major responsibility for seeing that the following activities are done? Husband, wife, or equal responsibility?" Ten household tasks were presented: cooking meals, washing dishes, mowing the lawn, washing clothes, car maintenance, writing letters, arranging family social events, getting or earning money, cleaning the house, and shopping. This was a measure of the women's perceptions of how responsibility for household tasks is divided in their marriages.

To ascertain the division of household tasks expected in retirement, respondents were asked: "Think of a *retired couple in their seventies.* Who should have the major responsibility to see that the following activities are done?" The same response categories and household tasks were presented. For previous use of this measure, see Keith and Brubaker (1977, 1980).

In both instances, respondents were asked about *responsibility* for completion of activity, not who completes the task. Therefore, our findings do not represent actual behavior within a marriage.

**TABLE 14.1    Comparison of Selected Characteristics of Women in
Dual-Earner and Dual-Retired Marriages**

|  | Dual Earner (N = 145) | Dual Retired (N = 62) |
|---|---|---|
| *Individual Factors* | | |
| Age (Average in Years) | 42.1 | 62.5* |
| Education (percentage) | | |
| —Less than high school graduation | 5.6 | 27.4* |
| —High school graduation | 38.0 | 30.6 |
| —Business/technical school | 12.0 | 8.1 |
| —Some college | 21.8 | 24.2 |
| —College graduate | 17.6 | 4.8 |
| —Graduate degree | 4.9 | 1.5 |
| Residence (percentage) | | |
| —Farm | 38.6 | 28.8 |
| —Rural non-farm | 42.9 | 50.8 |
| —Urban | 18.6 | 20.3 |
| *Family Factors* | | |
| Current Marital Situation (percentage) | | |
| —First marriage | 93.6 | 85.5 |
| —Second marriage | 6.4 | 14.5 |
| Number of children at home (average) | 2.04 | .19* |

* p < .05

*Household Responsibility Index.* To determine which selected characteristics are associated with a traditional or nontraditional division of responsibility, the household tasks were grouped into an index. Traditional orientation includes assignment of major responsibility to the wife for cooking, washing dishes, washing clothes, writing letters, arranging family social events, cleaning house, and shopping, as well as the assignment of major responsibility to the husband for mowing the lawn, car maintenance, and earning money. Nontraditional orientation includes sharing responsibility or assigning responsibility to the male when the female is traditionally responsible, or assigning the female when the male is traditionally responsible. In most instances, "nontraditional" refers to equal responsibility, since few women indicated a role-reversal allocation. Scores for the dual-employed and dual-retired groups were developed. A higher score (2) on the index indicates a nontraditional division of responsibility, and a lower score (1) represents a traditional orientation.

## RESULTS

### DIVISION OF RESPONSIBILITY FOR HOUSEHOLD TASKS

The dual-earner women reported a traditional division of responsibility for household tasks (see Table 14.2). Only two activities—family social events and earning money—were equally shared within these households. Men are responsible for car maintenance and lawn work. Women have responsibility for all other tasks. For these wives, household tasks are their responsibility, and few are shared with their husbands. Dual-earner wives expect the responsibilities for household tasks in dual-retired marriages to differ from their current division of responsibility (see Table 14.2). Specifically, retired husbands and wives are expected to share responsibility for all activities except two. Men should be responsible for car maintenance, and women for washing the clothes. All other tasks should be equally shared. Either these employed women think the division of responsibility changes with retirement, or they believe that most retired persons shared household tasks before they retired. In other words, they either think (or hope) that the division of responsibility will change when they retire, or they think older people have different types of marriages than they have. How do dual-retired couples divide responsibilities for household tasks?

The dual-retired women reported less sharing of responsibility than dual-employed women expect (see Table 14.3). Responsibility is shared in family social events and shopping. Husbands have primary responsibility for lawn work, car maintenance, and earning money. Wives are responsible for cooking, washing clothes and dishes, writing letters, and cleaning house. In short, the women in dual-retired marriages reported a traditional division of responsibility.

Comparison of the current patterns of household activities reported by dual-earner and dual-retired women yields few differences. The only differences in task allocation were in shopping (retired couples are more likely to share) and earning money (retired couples are more likely to assign

**TABLE 14.2   Current and Expected Division of Responsibility for
Household Tasks Reported by Women in Dual-Earner
Marriages (Percentages)**

|  | Current Division for Dual-Earner Couples | | |
| --- | --- | --- | --- |
| Task | Husband | Wife | Equal |
| Cooking | 0.0 | 91.7 | 8.3 |
| Washing dishes | 0.0 | 86.2 | 12.4 |
| Mowing lawn | 44.8 | 29.0 | 26.2 |
| Washing clothes | .7 | 89.7 | 6.9 |
| Car maintenance | 76.6 | 4.1 | 19.3 |
| Writing letters | .7 | 78.6 | 20.0 |
| Family social events | 2.1 | 40.7 | 57.2 |
| Earning money | 42.8 | 2.1 | 52.4 |
| Cleaning house | .7 | 85.5 | 13.8 |
| Shopping | 1.4 | 71.7 | 26.9 |
|  | Expected Division for Dual-Retired Couples by Dual-Earner Women | | |
| Cooking | 0.0 | 43.4 | 53.8 |
| Washing dishes | .7 | 12.4 | 84.1 |
| Mowing lawn | 45.5 | 0.0 | 51.0 |
| Washing clothes | 0.0 | 55.2 | 40.7 |
| Car maintenance | 67.7 | 0.0 | 29.0 |
| Writing letters | 1.4 | 24.1 | 71.0 |
| Family social events | 0.0 | 3.4 | 93.8 |
| Earning money | 14.5 | 0.0 | 81.4 |
| Cleaning house | 0.0 | 20.0 | 77.2 |
| Shopping | 0.0 | 6.2 | 91.2 |

responsibility to the husband). Do retired women expect these patterns in
dual-retired couples?

Retired women expect more sharing of responsibility than actually
occurs in their marriages (see Table 14.3). They claim that dual-retired
couples should share six tasks (washing dishes, writing letters, arranging
family social events, earning money, cleaning house, and shopping). The
retired wife should be responsible for cooking meals and washing clothes,

**TABLE 14.3**    Current and Expected Division of Responsibility for Household Tasks Reported by Women in Dual-Retired Marriages (Percentages)

| | *Current Division for Dual-Retired Women* | | |
| --- | --- | --- | --- |
| *Task* | *Husband* | *Wife* | *Equal* |
| Cooking | 0.0 | 91.9 | 6.5 |
| Washing dishes | 1.6 | 80.6 | 16.1 |
| Mowing lawn | 75.8 | 8.1 | 11.3 |
| Washing clothes | 1.6 | 85.5 | 9.7 |
| Car maintenance | 90.3 | 3.2 | 4.8 |
| Writing letters | 3.2 | 71.0 | 24.2 |
| Family social events | 0.0 | 38.7 | 58.1 |
| Earning money | 53.2 | 1.6 | 41.9 |
| Cleaning house | 0.0 | 79.0 | 19.9 |
| Shopping | 1.6 | 40.3 | 56.5 |

| | *Expected Division for Dual-Retired Couples by Dual-Retired Women* | | |
| --- | --- | --- | --- |
| Cooking | 0.0 | 74.2 | 22.6 |
| Washing dishes | 0.0 | 33.9 | 62.9 |
| Mowing lawn | 79.0 | 0.0 | 17.7 |
| Washing clothes | 0.0 | 75.8 | 21.0 |
| Car maintenance | 83.9 | 0.0 | 8.1 |
| Writing letters | 3.2 | 27.4 | 64.8 |
| Family social events | 3.2 | 4.8 | 87.1 |
| Earning money | 32.0 | 0.0 | 61.3 |
| Cleaning house | 0.0 | 38.7 | 56.6 |
| Shopping | 0.0 | 11.3 | 83.9 |

and her husband should be in charge of the yard work and car maintenance. There is therefore a difference in the expectations for retired couples and their current division of labor. The retired women expect dual-retired marriages to have more equal sharing of household tasks than they perceive to be the case in their own marriages.

A t-test of the Household Responsibility Index scores (degree of traditionalism in role structure) indicates no significant difference between

TABLE 14.4    t-test of Own and Expected Household Responsibility
              Index for Dual-Earner and Dual-Retired Women

|                                      | $N^1$ | $X$  | t value |
|--------------------------------------|-------|------|---------|
| *Own Marriage*                       |       |      |         |
| Dual-Earner                          | 134   | 1.28 | .26     |
| Dual-Retired                         | 57    | 1.28 |         |
| *Expected for Dual-Retired Marriages*|       |      |         |
| Dual-Earner                          | 135   | 1.70 | 5.59*   |
| Dual-Retired                         | 53    | 1.51 |         |

1. Numbers vary due to missing data.

*Significant at the .001 level

dual-earner and dual-retired women in their current patterns (see Table
14.4). Both groups reported traditional patterns. However, their expectations for the division of household responsibility in a dual-retired marriage
differed. Dual-earner women, as compared to dual-retired women, were
significantly less traditional in their expectations for the dual-retired
situation. The women in our sample expected less traditional patterns in
dual retirement, and the dual-earner women's expectations indicated the
most sharing of responsibility.

## FACTORS ASSOCIATED WITH DIVISION OF
## RESPONSIBILITY ORIENTATIONS

Previous research has indicated that age, education, and number of
children are related to women's employment and the division of household
tasks. However, the only factor related to the current division of responsibility pattern reported by dual-earner women was the number of children
living at home (see Table 14.5). In our study, women with more children
living at home reported a more traditional division of responsibility
pattern. This finding corresponds with the Model (1981) and Poloma et al.
(1981) findings. In our sample, most dual-earner women shared the
responsibility for only a few household activities with their husbands.
Those with children living at home were more likely to share responsibility
for fewer household tasks than those without children. Motherhood is thus
related to traditional household patterns.

Timothy H. Brubaker and Charles B. Hennon $\qquad$ 215

TABLE 14.5   Division of Responsibility for Women in Dual-Earner
Marriages (selected correlation coefficients)

|  | Current[1] | Expected |
|---|---|---|
| Age | −.051 | .171* |
| Education | −.042 | .074 |
| Marital situation | −.049 | .025 |
| Number of children at home | −.114** | −.162* |

1. Numbers vary between 133 and 138 cases due to missing data.
*Significant at the .05 level
**Significant at the .01 level

While Albrecht et al. (1979) found some support for a relationship between age and sex-role orientations, they also noted that it was not conclusive. Our findings suggest that age is not related to dual-earner women's current division of responsibility for household tasks. Some younger and older dual earners share responsibility for household tasks, but most report traditional patterns of responsibility. Apparently, the presence of children is more important to dual-earner couples than the age of the wife when dividing responsibility for household tasks.

For these women, their age and the number of children living at home are related to their expectations for dual-retired couples. The older women expect more sharing of responsibility, while those with children expect less. Partial correlation indicates that age remains positively related (r = .132, p < .010) to expectations for retired couples' sharing of responsibility when number of children at home is held constant. Thus, older dual-earner women expect dual-retired couples to share more responsibility for household tasks, regardless of the number of children they have.

Education and number of children at home are the two factors significantly related to the retired women's reported current division of responsibility (see Table 14.6). Since other research (Ericksen et al., 1979) indicates a positive relationship between education and a less traditional sex-role orientation, we expected to find better-educated retired women to have less traditional patterns. Contrary to this expectation, education is inversely related to current household responsibility. The less-educated women are less traditional than the better-educated women. Also, contrary to other research (Model, 1981; Yogev, 1981), the dual-retired women

TABLE 14.6     Division of Responsibility for Women in Dual-Retired
               Marriages (selected correlation coefficients)

|                              | Current  (N = 58)[1] | Expected  (N = 56) |
| ---------------------------- | -------------------- | ------------------ |
| Age                          | −.087                | −.229*             |
| Education                    | −.248*               | .353*              |
| Marital situation            | .115                 | −.054              |
| Number of children at home   | .245*                | .170               |

1. Varying numbers due to missing data.
*Significant at the .05 level

with more children living at home reported *more* sharing of household responsibilities.

Since neither of these relationships appears in other research, it is difficult to explain their direction. It may be that less-educated dual-retired women experience more sharing of responsibility in their marriages because they retired after their husbands and that their husbands had begun to accept responsibility for household tasks before their wives retired. However, timing of the wives' and husbands' retirements was not included in this study. Another factor that was not included in this study that may be crucial is the health status of the household members. The retired women may share household responsibility because they are ill. Their husbands may be more responsible because they are the caretakers of their wives. It is clear that these relationships are unique for women in dual-retired marriages, since opposite relationships were found for dual-earner wives. In any case, additional research is needed to clarify the relationship between education, number of children in the household, and the division of responsibility in dual-retired couples.

Age and education are related to the traditionalism of the expected division of responsibility for a dual-retired couple (see Table 14.6). Age is inversely related. The younger dual-retired women are less traditional. They expect more sharing of household tasks in a dual-retired marriage. Education is positively related. The better-educated women expect less traditional divisions of household labor. Controlling for the number of children at home and marital situation does not affect these zero-order correlations.

## SUMMARY AND CONCLUSIONS

The findings of this study indicate that dual-earner women have traditional divisions of responsibility for household tasks within their marriages and that those with children at home tend to be more traditional. These women expect more sharing of responsibility in dual-retired marriages. Also, dual-retired women report a traditional pattern in their marriages and expect more sharing in dual-retired marriage. Thus, there is an incongruency between perceived actual behavior and expectations for both dual-earner and dual-retired women.

This discrepancy has important implications for retirement programs and policymakers. First, preretirement programs could include discussion of what husbands and wives expect to do within the household after they retire. Employed women who expect more sharing of responsibility for household tasks in their marriages after retirement need to examine these expectations *before* they retire. For many couples, the pattern of household task allocation established during the working years continues into retirement (Keating and Cole, 1980). If dual-earner women are not sharing responsibility for household activities while working, they probably will not share after they retire. Preretirement programs and counselors could encourage dual-employed couples to examine their expectations. Awareness of optional ways to divide responsibility for household tasks could be created. A key issue is whether the discrepancy between their behavior and expectations is detrimental to their life or marital satisfaction. Our data do not address this issue, but preretirement counselors and educators may wish to ask dual-earner women if such a discrepancy is important to them. If it is, the dual-employed women should be urged to discuss their expectations of responsibility for household tasks with their husbands before they retire. It is important to recognize that there is little evidence of a change in these patterns after retirement.

A second implication relates to retired women who expect more sharing of the responsibility for household tasks. Dual-retired women, similar to dual-earner women, are encouraged to examine this discrepancy and determine if it is important to their life or marital satisfaction. Self-awareness and educational programs could be useful in senior centers, churches, cooperative extension, and other community organizations. These activities could stimulate discussion of options within the household. Dual-retired women may thus be able to decrease the discrepancy between what they expect and what they do in the area of household tasks. Although husbands are not the focus of this study, we encourage the development of these programs for both wives and husbands.

A third implication is that marriage and family counselors and educators need to consider the division of responsibility for household tasks within dual-retired marriages. Since this issue is neglected in most pre-retirement programs, retired marriages may be enhanced if focus is directed toward behavior and expectations for household tasks. If the discrepancy is important to retired women and those anticipating retirement, the professionals may want to encourage couples to consider this aspect of their marriages.

A fourth implication is directed toward authors of family life textbooks. Retirement is an important event in the family life of men and women. However, little attention is directed toward this topic in family life texts (Dressel and Avant, 1978). For example, Scanzoni and Scanzoni (1981: 614) note only the following concerning household tasks in retired marriage:

> Retirement is experienced as much more demoralizing to males than is the case with females. . . . This might be changing however as more women are becoming committed to careers. . . . But for wives who have been fulltime homemakers, life goes on much the same as before the retirement period, except that husbands are now around the home all the time.

Our data suggest that for wives who have been employed, household life goes on much the same as before the retirement period, except both the husband and wife now spend more time around the home. Family life texts need to alert students to the discrepancies between behavior and expectations of the responsibility for household tasks in dual-earner and dual-retired marriages. The continuity of patterns before and after retirement should be noted.

A final implication concerns research. Research on responsibility for household tasks in dual-retired marriages is necessary to determine if the discrepancies we discovered are replicated and if these discrepancies are related to life satisfaction. Does it matter if dual-retired women's household behavior is more traditional than they want it to be? Additional delineation of the factors associated with the division of household responsibility for dual-retired couples is needed. Is the level of income important? How is health related to the division of labor within older marriages? What about the occupations of the husband and wife? Did the husband

and wife discuss household activities before they retired? The discrepancies between behavior and expectations found in this study may represent a major source of marital conflict among dual-retired couples. If this is the case, both researchers and practitioners will have to pay more attention to the household responsibilities of retirees.

# 15

# CONCLUSION: SERVICE NEEDS OF WOMEN RETIREES

## Maximiliane Szinovacz

**Current retirement policies** and programs are geared toward the needs of male retirees, primarily because so little is known about women's retirement. Cumulative evidence from the studies presented in this volume indicates several issues which need to be addressed in order to ensure successful adaptation to retirement for women. To be sure, many women (as well as men) adjust well to the retirement transition. However, even women who have little to fear from the retirement transition may profit from some programs specifically designed for women retirees.

## ECONOMIC SECURITY

There can be little doubt that many older women face serious financial problems. Several studies presented in this volume further substantiate that women often suffer significant income losses upon their retirement (Chapters 2, 10, 13). One major reason for women's inadequate retirement incomes is the inconsistency in society's approaches to women's roles. Even though more and more women participate in the labor force, society still attributes secondary importance to women's work roles as compared to their family roles. Not only are low-paying jobs overrepresented among typical female industries and occupations, but society also provides few facilitators to ease working wives' and mothers' dual roles at home and in the labor force. Retirement benefits, on the other hand, are primarily tied to individuals' preretirement income and work history. Because many women interrupt their labor force participation to take charge of family needs—and such interruptions are normative—they are later faced with decreased retirement benefits. Survivors' benefits for widows and divorcees are linked to a standard of family stability that has become obsolete. Thus, divorced wives are only entitled to benefits if their marriage lasted for ten years (see Lowy, 1980), and yet divorce statistics indicate the median interval between first marriage and divorce to be seven years and the interval between remarriage and divorce to be even shorter than for first marriages (Eshleman, 1981).

Any attempt to alleviate women retirees' economic problems will require concerted efforts by government agencies, business, and the women themselves (see also Chapter 8). Current Social Security provisions need to be reviewed to eliminate gender-related inequities and to make adjustments for the divergent work patterns of men and women, as well as the ongoing changes in family life patterns. Similarly, private pension plans need to be modified to better fit the needs of retiring women. Since women tend to work in industries with relatively disadvantageous pension plans (Chapter 2), employers and insurance agencies should be encouraged to extend private pension coverage to typical female industries and to coordinate coverage by diverse pension plans in such a way as to minimize the effects of discontinuous work histories and job mobility on benefits. Also, some current provisions in private pension plans which lead to lower benefits for women as compared to men ought to be altered to enhance women retirees' economic security. For instance, some pension plans adjust benefits for gender-related differences in life expectancies by reducing women's benefits. However, women may be much better off paying more into their retirement plans while they are still working rather than experiencing significant income losses at retirement.

Another step which needs to be taken to achieve adequate retirement incomes for women is to change the apparently widely held belief that a wife can rely on her husband's pension. Unless women take responsibility for their economic security after retirement, they will remain the economic victims of a rapidly changing family system and situational circumstances beyond their control. It is likely that women's reliance on husband's benefits, as well as their inadequate economic preparation for retirement, result to a large degree from lack of information. Employers as well as representatives of retirement insurance companies should be encouraged to provide women with sufficient and easily understandable information on pension coverage and various benefit options. Wives (or their husbands) who quit the labor force for lengthy time periods to take care of family needs might overcome some economic disadvantages of their discontinuous work patterns by continuing payments into pension plans and being given the option to do so.

Lack of economic resources has multiple consequences for women retirees. Not only are they rendered more vulnerable to social and personal economic changes, but research also shows a direct link between financial well-being and diverse non-economic retirement opportunities (Chapters 3, 10, 13). Inadequate financial resources can prevent women retirees from participating in leisure and social activities, curtail their mobility, and reduce their access to adequate medical care.

Programs thus need to be developed to sever the link between low income and lack of non-economic retirement opportunities. While senior citizen centers and other agencies offer various inexpensive leisure programs, retirees are often not aware of their existence or fail to utilize them for other reasons (Szinovacz, 1982a). As is the case with many services for low-income populations, agencies must make special efforts to reach this population group. Personal contacts established by agency personnel or by retirees involved in the programs at the workplace might be one way to enhance information and participation.

In addition, the special circumstances of women retirees have to be considered in program development and delivery. These women may lack transportation, fear to leave their homes at night, or suffer from health problems that restrict their mobility. Their participation in leisure programs would thus be contingent on the provision of transportation or the offering of programs within their immediate neighborhood. Churches and other community organizations could also provide opportunities for lower-income retirees to meet other people and to engage in various leisure activities, including services for these organizations.

Increased options for part-time employment also may offer low-income retirees chances to better their financial situation, as well as to maintain an active life after retirement. In order to enhance such opportunities, both current eligibility requirements for Social Security benefits and age-discrimination in the labor market need to be addressed.

## USE OF TIME

In order to adjust successfully to retirement, it is essential for the retiree to engage in meaningful activities that fill the time previously spent with job activities and to substitute for other gratifications formerly found in gainful work through social contacts and a sense of accomplishment and usefulness. Several chapters in this volume indicate that social contacts and meaningful leisure activities indeed constitute prerequisites for women's retirement satisfaction or attitudes (Chapters 3, 4, 5, 9, 10, 13). Meaningful leisure pursuits after retirement may consist of the continuation of work-related activities, the extension of previous leisure activities, and involvement in new activities. While participation in diverse leisure activities is to a large extent contingent on one's financial resources and physical capabilities (Chapters 3, 10), some programs may generally enhance women's leisure opportunities.

Professional women seem particularly interested in continuing work-related activities (Chapters 7, 8, 11). Employers as well as professional organizations may very well make use of this potential volunteer labor supply. Women who spent many years in professional careers certainly can offer valuable services and may be willing to do so for little or no remuneration. Another way to ease professional women's adaptation to retirement may be through gradual retirement from their jobs. Even though professional women tend toward high work commitment, they may be willing to opt for partial retirement plans that offer them an opportunity to maintain professional activities while relieving them of the heavy workload typical for some professional occupations.

Nonprofessional women appear to profit most from activities that provide them with opportunities to meet new people and at the same time contribute to their feelings of usefulness (Chapters 3, 4, 5, 10, 13). Involvement in various community groups or volunteer work might serve both functions. To attract women retirees, these organizations must advertise their activities and adjust them to the needs of aging women. Retired women appreciate the freedom from rigid work schedules and demanding work. They are therefore unlikely to accept volunteer or community activities that endanger this freedom and flexibility. Indeed, retired women may constitute an important pool for volunteer labor supply. Many retired women are physically capable of and interested in volunteer or community activities, but they lack information on programs they may join or are discouraged by rigid work requirements.

In order to satisfy women retirees' needs for social contacts, senior citizen centers and other organizations could arrange leisure group activities (including trips and tours) for women retirees. Such programs need to be inexpensive and address selected audiences. Research suggests (Chapters 9, 11; Szinovacz, 1982a) that middle-class women show little interest in programs sponsored by such agencies because they perceive these programs to be "just for the poor" and inappropriate for their own needs. Similarly, nonmarried women resent group activities and social events organized for couples and feel too embarrassed to attend them without an escort.

## HOUSEHOLD RESPONSIBILITIES AND MARITAL RELATIONS

In contrast to previous arguments, women retirees' interests do not center on household roles. Problems in this area may occur owing to women's inability to perform heavy household work and repairs or because of unrealistic expectations in regard to the division of labor between spouses (Chapters 10, 13, 14).

There is some evidence that retired women who live alone or with older relatives and friends experience home maintenance difficulties; even minor home repairs and household work that requires some agility may be difficult to perform for older women. Help with such tasks is not easily available unless provided by friends, and hired help is usually quite expensive. While senior citizen centers and other agencies offer home maintenance services, these programs are usually restricted to persons with low incomes. However, even women with higher incomes may not be able to obtain help and/or to afford such help on a relatively regular basis. Extension of currently available services to a larger population group, probably on sliding scale fees, would thus clearly be warranted.

Retiring wives seem to approach retirement with idealistic expectations both in regard to the division of labor between spouses and in regard to marital relations in general. Even though many couples plan retirement together and seem quite satisfied with their postretirement marriages, wives expecting major changes toward a more egalitarian division of labor between spouses and more jointness in activities find themselves disappointed if their hopes are not realized. It is clear that wives do not retire to become full-time housewives in the traditional sense. However, they may find themselves in this role unless both spouses negotiate the division of household responsibilities after retirement prior to this event. Dual-earner couples would therefore profit from preretirement programs that specifically address marital relations after the retirement transition. Such programs should involve both spouses and encourage couples to discuss and negotiate their postretirement relations prior to the transition process.

## RETIREMENT PREPARATION

Successful adaptation to the retirement transition can be enhanced by careful planning for this life event, but many women enter retirement quite unprepared (Chapters 6, 7, 8, 9, 10, 12). At least two factors are responsible for the lack of retirement planning among women: insufficient personal initiative and inadequate access to retirement programs (Chapter 6). Women's retirement preparation seems more contingent than men's on the availability of formal retirement programs offered by employers. However, retirement programs seem more prevalent among typically male than among female industries.

Special efforts are thus necessary to involve women in preretirement programs. One means to increase women's participation is through offering formal programs at their workplace which specifically address women's concerns. Women seem less likely than men to take the initiative in seeking information about retirement, and they may find programs to be of little value to them if they approach retirement planning primarily from a male perspective. It is probably also essential to counteract the ideology that a woman can rely on her husband during the retirement years. Although this information may be painful, female workers must be made aware that they are likely to spend a good part of their retirement life on their own and cannot rely on their husbands for financial security or company.

In order to address potential retirement problems of women adequately, retirement planning programs should include information on at least the following areas and issues: Social Security and private pension benefits, health care and insurance, financial planning and management, available programs for leisure and social activities, other community programs and services for the aged, housing, and marital relations. Since achievement of adequate retirement incomes is contingent on long-term planning, employers should provide detailed information on available pension options and eligibility requirements when women enter a job. Even though such information is included in the pension policies, it is often difficult to understand and not detailed enough to calculate retirement income. Planning programs offered to employees approaching retirement should enable the participants to assess their retirement incomes and expenses and should also provide clear information on medical coverage. Finally, they should include advice on budgeting and on diverse means to reduce expenditures, such as buying patterns and consumer behavior, as well as discount programs and reduced fees for senior citizens. Since employers often lack adequate information on leisure and social programs in the community, personnel from relevant agencies and community groups should either be invited to attend employers' planning programs or provide brochures listing available services and activities. In addition, agencies may further publicize their programs through diverse advertising campaigns.

A similar approach may be used to inform retiring women about housing opportunities and home maintenance services. Their reduced retirement incomes may force some women to give up their more expensive living quarters upon retirement. These women would certainly benefit from information on available housing opportunities in the community, including subsidized housing for retired and senior citizens. Those women who wish to move to other counties or states will require advice on housing options in the areas they choose for retirement residence. National real estate agencies may offer initial information to these women. Given the importance of social contacts to women retirees, they should also be made aware that moving may disrupt their social networks and could result in social isolation, at least for a restricted time period. Such changes in social relations may be more difficult to adjust to if they occur shortly after the retirement transition rather than at a later time.

Finally, as was already pointed out above, planning programs should address marital relations after retirement. Since some wives seem to have unrealistic expectations as to the division of household responsibilities and joint activities between spouses, retirement programs may alert couples in regard to this potential problem and help them to negotiate their post-retirement activities. Economic consequences of the joint or separate retirement of both spouses should also be addressed in such programs. Some wives may opt for early retirement upon the request of their husbands but later find themselves with reduced retirement incomes and lacking meaningful activities, while their spouses pursue personal hobbies and expect their wives to reassume a full-time household role.

## USE OF AND SATISFACTION WITH SERVICES

Even though none of the chapters in this volume specifically dealt with women retirees' use of services, some information on this issue is available from a study by this author (for a description of the sample, see Chapter 9). In this study, a series of questions addressed the service needs of women retirees. Those women indicating specific problems in their lives were asked whether they had sought help from agencies, and if so, how satisfactory this help had been. In addition, a list of programs and services currently available in the community was presented to the subjects, and the women were asked to indicate whether they had participated in these programs, were interested in joining, or had previously heard about them. Further questions addressed the issue of agency advertising.

Data regarding the use of agencies for specific problems suggest that only a very small number of the women (21 percent) who reported some problems went to agencies for help. Information on adequate agencies was often obtained from a senior citizen center, friends or relatives, or the church. Those women who frequented agency services were quite dissatisfied with the help they received. Over three-quarters of the women who went to an agency said they were either moderately or very dissatisfied with the services. Some of the case materials reveal a few reasons for this general dissatisfaction with services. One area of concern centers on the attitude of agency workers, as well as other professionals (e.g., doctors) delivering services:

> I think that the attitude of people within the offices . . . sometimes I think they are not as gracious and as willing to listen as they might be . . . sometimes they fail to realize that you know older people just don't pick up everything like a younger person does [Case 66].

> They sent me this card here last summer saying the first of the year I would be receiving help for glasses and my medicine, but I haven't heard nothing no more. I don't know if my card got lost or what, but I have to pay for all my medicine. I called the social security people and they try to act like they didn't know what I was trying to talk about. . . . You see I only fill out one paper to send it in to medicare and I only got money from it one time. Because Dr. . . . didn't like to fill them out. . . . But the last time I went in there I told him I wanted him to fill (the forms) out. He filled them out and I got nine dollars back. But they want you to get up to sixty dollars before you send it in. I haven't ever been able to get it up to sixty dollars [Case 570].

The latter case demonstrates how especially lower-class subjects easily become lost within bureaucratic rules which are further reinforced by impersonal services on the part of professionals, including Social Security officers who are not patient enough to explain eligibility requirements and procedures, as well as physicians unwilling to fill out forms for "just a few dollars," an amount of money which is obviously not much in their eyes but which may be quite important to a person living at or close to a poverty income level.

Some women also mentioned that the programs were designed for people other than themselves (i.e., for the poor) and/or by people unaware of the needs of the elderly or of women retirees:

> Now I would like to see a place where people with more of the same background that I have could get together on sort of a club-like basis and enjoy each other. . . . But I would like to see things done not just for the needy but for people who can take care of themselves, but would like to take a trip now and then or would like a club-like atmosphere. . . . Sometimes when you got up there to the xxxxx, oh, the smell just knocks you over. It just isn't the type of atmosphere that you enjoy (she talks of a dining service). I have nothing in common with that group [Case 2].

These cases illustrate a need for groups that provide social contacts and entertainment to unattached women, as well as women of middle- to upper-middle-class background.

Finally, women interested in volunteer work complained about the rigidity of some volunteer programs. They feel that if they provide volunteer services for little or no pay, they should not be treated like regular employees. They are willing to help, but at their own choice of time and speed:

> I think they should have a work program that you could work at your own speed and leisure time. You know, to do what you want to do without so many restrictions. Just like I say about my job at the hospital, if you don't want to go (one day), they just should say o.k., then come the next day if you like. I don't think they should give you a hassle. . . . I think it's good to give a person something to do and two dollars an hour, but I don't think they should give you a hassle if you're not feeling well or don't feel like working or want to get off an hour early [Case 404].

In other words, volunteer workers want to be treated as volunteers, particularly since they worked under tight and rigid time schedules for a considerable part of their lives and now want to help, but not to "work" again.

Of the women who did not go to agencies to obtain help for their problems, many indicated that they lacked information on available services (32 percent), didn't require agency help (16 percent), or failed to ask for assistance because of previous negative experiences with agencies (20 percent). State agencies and senior citizen centers are most likely to be considered as sources of potential help, but quite a few women would rather go to friends and relatives for help. Despite their complaints about services, many women were not sure how agencies could improve. Those who suggested specific improvements emphasized better advertising and more programs or programs designed for specific purposes.

Results concerning interest and participation in services and programs for the elderly are shown in Table 15.1. It is quite obvious that women retirees not only rarely go to agencies to obtain help with specific problems, but generally participate little in programs and services for the elderly. The only service that was frequented by more than 10 percent of the subjects was the discount program for senior citizens. In reviewing participation rates, it is further interesting to note that while many women experienced problems with home maintenance, only 5 percent had ever made use of the emergency home maintenance service. Interest in programs is particularly pronounced for discount programs, crime prevention, educational programs, emergency home maintenance, eyeglass referral, volunteer programs, yard work referral, and the public library. One reason why many women may not have become involved in these programs is lack of information. While some programs are generally known (although respondents are not always aware of the exact purposes and eligibility requirements), some services and programs are virtually unknown to at least one-quarter of these women. Over two-fifths of the retirees never heard of the firewood, some medical, and the home maintenance programs. One-third or more indicated lack of information concerning community care, eyeglass referral services, homemaker services, housing and shopping assistance, and social events organized by various agencies. And over one-quarter of the women had never heard of the dining and other activity programs, telephone reassurance, as well as transportation and escort services.

Given these results, there can be little doubt that lack of information about and/or poor advertising of programs leads to some underutilization of available services. Subjects were thus asked to indicate which type of agency announcements they were most likely to see or hear. The findings suggest that TV and newspaper advertisements may reach the largest audience, followed by mailed advertisements and radio announcements. Bulletin boards and the yellow pages, on the other hand, are relatively infrequently consulted (Table 15.2).

**TABLE 15.1  Interest and Participation in Services and Programs for the Elderly**

| | Partici-pates % | Inter-ested % | Heard of program % | Did not hear of program % |
|---|---|---|---|---|
| Programs and services: | | | | |
| community care | 2 | 12 | 48 | 39 |
| counseling | 4 | 2 | 76 | 19 |
| crime prevention | 5 | 20 | 70 | 5 |
| day care | 2 | 8 | 84 | 6 |
| dining, activities | 4 | 6 | 65 | 25 |
| dental referral | 3 | 7 | 41 | 49 |
| discount programs | 12 | 23 | 59 | 6 |
| educational programs | 6 | 17 | 70 | 7 |
| emergency home main-tenance | 5 | 14 | 38 | 44 |
| eyeglass referral | 3 | 12 | 48 | 37 |
| firewood program | 1 | 4 | 32 | 65 |
| food services | 2 | 8 | 74 | 16 |
| friendly visits | 4 | 8 | 51 | 38 |
| hearing referral | 2 | 5 | 53 | 41 |
| home health care | 3 | 6 | 79 | 13 |
| homemaker service | 1 | 7 | 58 | 33 |
| housing assistance | 2 | 4 | 61 | 33 |
| ID cards for senior citizens | 9 | 7 | 71 | 13 |
| library services | 8 | 10 | 69 | 13 |
| meals on wheels | 4 | 4 | 91 | 0 |
| recreational services | 2 | 8 | 81 | 9 |
| volunteer programs | 7 | 14 | 74 | 4 |
| shopping assistance | 2 | 4 | 62 | 32 |
| sitter/companion service | 2 | 4 | 61 | 33 |
| social events | 2 | 8 | 74 | 16 |
| information programs | 2 | 7 | 78 | 13 |
| telephone reassurance | 4 | 6 | 61 | 29 |
| tours and trips | 2 | 12 | 71 | 15 |
| transportation, escort services | 1 | 6 | 64 | 29 |
| yard work referral | 1 | 13 | 44 | 42 |

(N = 115)

TABLE 15.2    Medium Through Which Agency Announcements Most
Likely Seen or Heard (three most likely)

|                      | *Percentage* |
|----------------------|:------------:|
| Medium:              |              |
| television           | 86           |
| radio                | 32           |
| newspaper            | 88           |
| bulletin boards      | 16           |
| yellow pages         | 19           |
| mail                 | 55           |
| (N = 115)            |              |

These data provide clear evidence that available programs and services are only rarely used by women retirees, and those women who used agency help had little positive to say about the services they received. The underutilization of services can thus be attributed to negative experiences on the part of some women, but it also owes itself to a relatively widespread lack of information about available services. Results concerning agency advertisements suggest that TV announcements may reach the largest audience. Other types of advertisements attract women from different population groups, and their use would thus be contingent on the target population.

## SUMMARY

With the increasing labor force participation of middle-aged women and the extension of the time they spend in gainful employment, retirement has become a significant life experience for a large number of older women. Findings presented in this volume provide ample evidence that women's retirement experience differs in various ways from that of men. The importance of family commitments in women's lives renders their employment histories more discontinuous than men's, and this fact, as well as continuing sex discrimination in the labor market, makes women more vulnerable than men to economic loss at retirement, as it may also prevent them from reaching the occupational goals to which they aspired. Furthermore, women retirees could be shown to approach retirement from a different perspective than men (both in regard to attitudes and preretirement planning), and sex differences were also apparent in the circumstances facilitating or hindering adjustment to this life transition. There can also be little doubt that retired women as a group are distinct from older employed women and homemakers. Retirement entails significant changes in a woman's life circumstances and routine, and her life experience as an employee results in situational and personal characteristics that diverge from those of the older homemaker. The widely held assumption that women retirees just become full-time homemakers once they quit work outside the home is clearly not warranted, and it is important to note that major differences exist within the group of women retirees.

Neither research efforts on retirement nor retirement programs have, in the past, paid sufficient attention to this population group. It is now time to acknowledge the problems and needs of women retirees. More research is needed to investigate specific problems encountered by diverse groups of retired women, and programs need to be developed that can help women prepare for and adapt to the retirement transition.

# BIBLIOGRAPHY

ABBOTT, J. (1974) "Covered employment and the age men claim retirement benefits." Social Security Bulletin 35: 5.

ACKER, J. (1973) "Women and social stratification: a case of intellectual sexism." American Journal of Sociology 78: 936-945.

ALBRECHT, S. L., H. M. BAHR, and B. A. CHADWICK (1979) "Changing family and sex roles: an assessment of age differences." Journal of Marriage and the Family 41: 41-50.

ALDOUS, J. (1981) "From dual-earner to dual-career families and back again." Journal of Family Issues 2: 115-125.

American Medical Association (1972) Retirement: A Medical Philosophy and Approach. Chicago: Author.

ANDERSON, K., C. HIGGINS, E. NEWMAN, and S. R. SHERMAN (1978) "Differences in attitudes towards retirement among male and female faculty members and other university professionals." Journal of Minority Aging: 5-13.

ANDERSON, K., R. L. CLARK, and N.D.T. JOHNSON (1980) "Retirement in dual-career families," pp. 109-127 in R. L. Clark (ed.) Retirement Policy in an Aging Society. Durham, NC: Duke University Press.

ANDRÉ, R. (1981) Homemakers: The Forgotten Workers. Chicago: University of Chicago Press.

ANDRISANI, P. J. (1978) "Job satisfaction among working women." Signs 3: 588-607.

ANGRIST, S. S. (1967) "Role constellation as a variable in women's leisure activities." Social Forces 45: 423-431.

ANTONUCCI, T., N. GILLETT, and F. W. HOERR (1979) "Values and self-esteem in three generations of men and women." Journal of Gerontology 34: 415-422.

ARAJI, S. K. (1977) "Husbands' and wives' attitude-behavior congruence on family roles." Journal of Marriage and the Family 39: 309-320.

ARGYLE, M. (1972) The Social Psychology of Work. Middlesex, England: Penguin.

ARLING, G. (1976) "The elderly widow and her family, neighbors and friends." Journal of Marriage and the Family 38: 757-770.

ARNOTT, C. C. and V. L. BENGTSON (1970) "Only a homemaker: distributive justice and role choice among married women." Sociology and Social Research 54: 495-507.

ARRINGTON, Z. A. (1972) "Future implications of increased labor force participation of older women." Presented at the annual meetings of the Gerontological Society, San Juan.

ATCHLEY, R. C. (1969) "Respondents vs. refusers in an interview study of retired women: an analysis of selected characteristics." Journal of Gerontology 24: 42-47.
———— (1971) "Retirement and work orientation." The Gerontologist 11: 29-32.
———— (1972) The Social Forces in Later Life: An Introduction to Social Gerontology. Belmont, CA: Wadsworth.
———— (1974) "The meaning of retirement." Journal of Communications 24: 97-101.
——— (1975a) "Adjustment to loss of job at retirement." International Journal of Aging and Human Development 6: 17-27.
———— (1975b) "Dimensions of widowhood in later life." The Gerontologist 15 (April): 176-178.
———— (1975c) "Sex differences among middle class retired people." Unpublished.
———— (1976a) The Sociology of Retirement. New York: Halsted.
———— (1976b) "Orientation toward the job and retirement adjustment among women," pp. 199-208 in J. F. Gubrium (ed.) Time, Roles, and Self in Old Age. New York: Behavioral.
———— (1976c) "Selected social and psychological differences between men and women in later life." Journal of Gerontology 31: 204-221.
———— (1977) "The leisure of the elderly." The Humanist 37: 14-16.
———— (1979) "Issues in retirement research." The Gerontologist 19: 44-54.
———— (1981) "What happened to retirement planning in the 1970's?" pp. 79-88 in N. G. McCluskey and E. F. Borgatta (eds.) Aging and Retirement. Beverly Hills, CA: Sage.
———— and S. L. CORBETT (1977) "Older women and jobs," pp. 121-125 in L. E. Troll (ed.) Looking Ahead. Englewood Cliffs, NJ: Prentice-Hall.
ATCHLEY, R. C., L. PIGNATIELLO, and E. C. SHAW (1979) "Interactions with family and friends: marital status and occupational differences among older women." Research on Aging 1: 83-95.
BACHRACH, C. A. (1980) "Childlessness and social isolation among the elderly." Journal of Marriage and the Family 42: 627-637.
BACK, K. W. (1974) "Transition to aging and the self-image," pp. 207-215 in E. Palmore (ed.) Normal Aging II. Durham, NC: Duke University Press.
BACK, K. W. (1977) "The ambiguity of retirement," in E. W. Busse and E. Pfeiffer (eds.) Behavior and Adaptation in Late Life. Boston: Little, Brown.
———— and C. S. GUPTILL (1966) "Retirement and self-ratings," pp. 120-129 in I. H. Simpson and J. C. McKinney (eds.) Social Aspects of Aging. Durham, NC: Duke University Press.
BAHR, S. J. (1974) "Effects on power and division of labor in the family," pp. 167-186 in L. W. Hoffman and F. I. Nye (eds.) Working Mothers. San Francisco: Jossey-Bass.
BAILYN, L. (1970) "Career and family orientations of husbands and wives in relation to marital happiness." Human Relations 23: 97-113.
BALDWIN, D. (1978) "Poverty and the older woman: reflections of a social worker." The Family Coordinator 27: 448-450.
BALKWELL, C. (1981) "Transition to widowhood: a review of literature." Family Relations 30: 117-127.
BALLWEG, J. A. (1967) "Resolution of conjugal role adjustment after retirement." Journal of Marriage and the Family 29: 277-281.

BARB, K. H., W. J. GOUDY, and R. D. WARREN (1977) "Aging and changes in the preferred age of retirement." Presented at the annual meetings of the Gerontological Society, San Francisco.

BARFIELD, R. E. and J. N. MORGAN (1978a) "Trends in planned early retirement." The Gerontologist 18: 13-18.

——— (1978b) "Trends in satisfaction with retirement." The Gerontologist 18: 19-23.

BARNETT, R. C. and G. K. BARUCH (1978a) The Competent Woman. New York: Halsted.

——— (1978b) "Women in the middle years: a critique of research and theory." Psychology of Women Quarterly 3: 187-197.

BARRETT, C. J. (1977) "Women in widowhood." Signs 2: 856-868.

BART, P. B. (1971) "Depression in middle-aged women," pp. 163-186 in V. Gornick and B. K. Morgan (eds.) Women in Sexist Society. New York: New American Library.

BEBBINGTON, A. C. (1973) "The function of stress in the establishment of the dual-career family." Journal of Marriage and the Family 35: 530-537.

BECK, E. M., P. M. HORAN, and C. M. TOLBERT II (1978) "Stratification in dual economy: a sectoral model of earnings determination." American Sociological Review 43: 704-720.

BECKMAN, L. J. and B. B. HOUSER (1979) "The more you have, the more you do: the relationship between wife's employment, sex-role attitudes, and household behavior." Psychology of Women Quarterly 4: 160-174.

BEESON, D. (1975) "Women in studies of aging: a critique and suggestion." Social Problems 23: 52-59.

BELANGER, L. (1981) "Sex differences in early retirement decision process." Presented at the annual meetings of the Gerontological Society, Toronto.

BELL, B. D. (1975) "Life satisfaction and symbolic response: toward a comprehensive theory of retirement." Presented at the annual meetings of the Gerontological Society, Louisville.

——— (1976) "Role set orientations and life satisfaction: a new look at an old theory," pp. 148-164 in J. F. Gubrium (ed.) Time, Self, and Roles in Old Age. New York: Behavioral.

——— (1978) "Life satisfaction and occupational retirement: beyond the impact year." International Journal of Aging and Human Development 9: 31-50.

BELLER, D. J. (1980) "Coverage patterns of full-time employees under private retirement plans." Social Security Bulletin 44: 3-10.

BENGTSON, V. L. (1973) The Social Psychology of Aging. Indianapolis: Bobbs-Merrill.

———, P. L. KASSCHAU, and P. K. RAGAN (1977) "The impact of social structure on aging individuals," pp. 237-353 in J. E. Birren and K. W. Schaie (eds.) Handbook of the Psychology of Aging. New York: Van Nostrand.

BENNER, L., R. KLEINER, and H. R. STUB (1981) "Conflict, preretirement planning, and mental and physical health status." Presented at the annual meetings of the Gerontological Society, Toronto.

BERARDO, F. (1968) "Widowhood status in the U.S.: perspective on a neglected aspect of the family cycle." The Family Coordinator 17: 191-203.

BERGHORN, F. J. and D. E. SCHAFER (1981) "The quality of life and older people," pp. 331-352 in F. J. Berghorn et al. (eds.) The Dynamics of Aging. Boulder, CO: Westview Press.

——— and Associates (1981) The Dynamics of Aging. Boulder, CO: Westview.

BERNARD, J. (1972) The Future of Marriage. New York: World.

——— (1981) The Female World. New York: Free Press.

BEST, F. (1979) "The future of retirement and lifetime distribution of work." Aging and Work 2: 173-181.

BEUTNER, G. and A. B. CRYNS (1979) "Retirement: differences in attitudes, preparatory behavior and needs perception among male and female university employees." Presented at the annual meetings of the Gerontological Society, Washington, D.C.

BILD, B. R. and R. J. HAVIGHURST (1976) "Family and social support." The Gerontologist 16: 63-69.

BIRNBAUM, J. (1975) "Life patterns and self-esteem in gifted family oriented and career committed women," in M. Mednick, L. Hoffman, and S. Tangri (eds.) Women: Social Psychological Perspectives. New York: Holt, Rinehart & Winston.

BLALOCK, H. (1972) Social Statistics. New York: McGraw-Hill.

BLAU, F. and C. L. JUSENIUS (1976) "Economists' approaches to sex segregation in the labor market: an appraisal," pp. 181-199 in M. Blaxall and B. Reagan (eds.) Women and the Workplace: The Implications of Occupational Segregation. Chicago: University of Chicago Press.

BLAU, Z. S. (1973) Old Age in a Changing Society. New York: Franklin Watts.

BLAXALL, M. and B. REAGAN [eds.] (1976) Women and the Workplace: The Implications of Occupational Segregation. Chicago: University of Chicago Press.

BLIESZNER, R. and M. E. SZINOVACZ (1979) "Women's adjustment to retirement." Presented at the annual meetings of the Gerontological Society, Washington, D.C.

BLOCK, M. R., J. L. DAVIDSON, J. D. GRAMBS, and K. E. SEROCK (1978) Unchartered Territory: Issues and Concerns of Women Over 40. College Park: University of Maryland.

BLOOD, R. O. and D. M. WOLFE (1960) Husbands and Wives. New York: Free Press.

BLOOD, R. O. and R. L. HAMBLIN (1958) "The effects of the wife's employment on the family power structure." Social Forces 36: 347-352.

BOOTH, A. (1972) "Sex and social participation." American Sociological Review 37: 183-192.

——— and E. HESS (1974) "Cross-sex friendship." Journal of Marriage and the Family 36: 38-47.

BORGATTA, E. F. and R. G. FOSS (1979a) "Correlates of age: the NORC general social survey." Research on Aging 1: 253-272.

——— (1979b) "Correlates of sex among the aged: the NORC general social survey." Research on Aging 1: 516-531.

BOWER, J. (1954) "The retail salespersons: men and women," in R. J. Havighurst and E. A. Friedmann (eds.) The Meaning of Work and Retirement. Chicago: University of Chicago Press.

BOYLE, R. (1970) "Path analysis and ordinal data." American Journal of Sociology 75: 461-480.

BRODY, E. M. (1974) "Aging and family personality: a developmental view." Family Process 13: 23-37.

——— (1978) "The aging of the family." Annals of the American Academy of Political and Social Sciences 438: 13-27.

——— and G. SPARK (1966) "Institutionalization of the aged: a family crisis." Family Process 5: 76-90.

BRODY, S. J. (1976) "Public policy issues of women in transition." The Gerontologist 16: 181-182.

BROWN, A. S. (1974) "Satisfying relationships for the elderly and their patterns of disengagement." The Gerontologist 14: 258-262.

BROWN, P., L. PERRY, and E. HARBURG (1977) "Sex role attitudes and psychological outcomes for black and white women experiencing marital dissolution." Journal of Marriage and the Family 39: 549-561.

BRUBAKER, T. H. and L. E. SNEDEN (1978) "Aging in a changing family context." The Family Coordinator 27(4): 301 302.

BRUBAKER, T. H., C. L. COLE, C. B. HENNON, and A. L. COLE (1978) "Forum on aging and the family: discussions with F. Ivan Nye, Bernice L. Neugarten, David and Vera Mace." The Family Coordinator 27: 436-444.

BRYSON, R., J. B. BRYSON, and M. F. JOHNSON (1978) "Family size, satisfaction and productivity in dual-career couples." Psychology of Women Quarterly 3: 167-177.

BULL, C. N. and J. B. AUCOIN (1975) "Voluntary association participation and life satisfaction: a replication note." Journal of Gerontology 30: 73-76.

BULTENA, G. L. (1969) "Life continuity and morale in old age." The Gerontologist 9: 251-253.

——— and R. OYLER (1971) "Effects of health on disengagement and morale." Aging and Human Development 2: 142-148.

Bundesinstitut fuer Bevoelkerungsforschung (1979) Materialen zur Bevoelkerungswissenschaft 11: differierende Haltungen und Auswirkungen vor und nach der Pensionierung. Wiesbaden.

BURGESS, E. (1960) Aging in Western Societies. Chicago: University of Chicago Press.

BURKE, R. and T. WEIR (1976) "Relationship of wives' employment status to husband, wife, and pair satisfaction and performance." Journal of Marriage and the Family 38: 279-287.

BURKHAUSER, R. V. (1979) "Are women treated fairly in today's Social Security system?" The Gerontologist 19: 242-249.

BURR, W. R. (1970) "Satisfaction with various aspects of marriage over the life cycle: a random middle-class sample." Journal of Marriage and the Family 32: 29-37.

BUTLER, R. N. (1977) Statement before the Subcommittee on Retirement, Income and Employment of the Select Committee on Aging. Washington, DC: Government Printing Office.

BYNUM, J. E., B. L. COOPER, and F. G. ACUFF (1978) "Retirement reorientation: senior adult education." Journal of Gerontology 33: 253-261.

CAMPBELL, A. (1981) The Sense of Well-Being in America. New York: McGraw-Hill.

——, P. E. CONVERSE, and W. L. RODGERS (1976) The Quality of American Life. New York: Russell Sage.

CAMPBELL, S. (1979) "Delayed mandatory retirement and the working woman." The Gerontologist 19: 257-263.

CANDY, S.E.G. (1977) "What do women use friends for?" pp. 106-111 in L. E. Troll et al. (eds.) Looking Ahead. Englewood Cliffs, NJ: Prentice-Hall.

——, L. W. TROLL, and S. O. LEVY (1981) "A developmental exploration of friendship functions in women." Psychology of Women Quarterly 5: 456-472.

CANTOR, M. H. (1979) "Neighbors and friends: an overlooked resource in the informal support system." Research on Aging 1: 434-463.

CANTOR, M. N. (1975) "Life space and the social support system of the inner city elderly of New York." The Gerontologist 15: 23-27.

CARP, F. M. (1972) Retirement. New York: Behavioral.

—— (1966) The Retirement Process: Report of a Conference. Bethesda, MD: National Institute of Child Health and Human Development.

CASADY, M. (1976) "Senior syndromes." Human Behavior 5: 46-47.

CAVAN, R. S. (1962) "Self and role in adjustment during old age," pp. 526-536 in A. M. Rose (ed.) Human Behavior and Social Process. Boston: Houghton Mifflin.

—— (1973) "Speculations on innovations to conventional marriage in old age." The Gerontologist 13: 409-411.

—— (1978) "Role of the old in personal and impersonal societies." The Family Coordinator 27: 315-320.

CHAPMAN, J. R. (1976) Economic Independence for Women: The Foundation for Equal Rights. Beverly Hills, CA: Sage.

—— and M. GATES (1977) Women into Wives: The Legal and Economic Impact of Marriage. Beverly Hills, CA: Sage.

CHAPPELL, N. L. and B. HAVENS (1980) "Old and female: testing the double jeopardy hypothesis." Sociological Quarterly 21: 157.

CHARLES, D. C. (1971) "Effect and participation in a pre-retirement program." The Gerontologist.

CHARTOCK, P. (1980) "Factors in the retirement decision: comparisons between men and women." Presented at the annual meetings of the Gerontological Society, San Diego, California.

CHATFIELD, W. F. (1975) "Environmental factors associated with life satisfaction of the aged." Ph.D. dissertation, West Virginia University.

—— (1977) "Economic and sociological factors influencing life satisfaction of the aged." Journal of Gerontology 32: 593-599.

CHENOWETH, L. C. and E. MARET (1980) "The career patterns of mature American women." Sociology of Work and Occupations 7: 222-251.

CHOWN, S. M. (1977) "Morale, careers, and personal potentials," pp. 672-691 in J. E. Birren and K. W. Schaie (eds.) Handbook of the Psychology of Aging. New York: Van Nostrand Reinhold.

CHU, K. W. and E. SOLBERG (1977) "Early retirement vs. labor force participation of the aged: the impact on Social Security financing." Presented at the annual meetings of the Gerontological Society, San Francisco.

CHUDACOFF, H. P. and T. K. HAREVEN (1979) "From the empty nest to family dissolution: life course transitions into old age." Journal of Family History 4: 69-83.

CICIRELLI, V. (1980) "Social services and the kin network: views of the elderly." Journal of Home Economics 72: 34-37.

CLARK, M. and B. ANDERSON (1967) Culture and Aging. Springfield, IL: Charles C Thomas.

CLARK, R. L. (1980) Retirement Policy in an Aging Society. Durham, NC: Duke University Press.

——— and J. J. SPENGLER (1980) The Economics of Individual and Population Aging. Cambridge: Cambridge University Press.

CLARK, R. L., T. JOHNSON, and A. A. McGERMED (1980) "Allocation of time and resources by married couples approaching retirement." Social Security Bulletin 43: 3-17.

CLAVAN, S. (1978) "The impact of social class and social trends on the role of grandparent." The Family Coordinator 27: 351-358.

COELHO, J. V., D. A. HAMBURG, and J. E. ADAMS (1974) Coping and Adaptation. New York: Basic Books.

COHEN, J. and P. COHEN (1975) Applied Multiple Regression/Correlation Analysis for the Behavioral Sciences. Hillsdale, NJ: Erlbaum.

COHN, R. M. (1979) "Age and the satisfactions from work." Journal of Gerontology 34: 264-272.

COLEMAN, P. G. (1975) "Great Britain: a review of recent and current research." The Gerontologist 15: 219-229.

College of Business Administration (1969) Preretirement Counseling, Retirement Adjustment and the Older Employee. Eugene: Oregon University Press.

CONNER, K. A., E. A. POWERS, and G. L. BULTENA (1979) "Social interaction and life satisfaction: an empirical assessment of late-life patterns." Journal of Gerontology 34: 116-121.

COSER, R. L. and G. ROKOFF (1971) "Women in the occupational world: social disruption and conflict." Social Problems 18: 535-54.

COTTRELL, W. F. and R. C. ATCHLEY (1969) Women in Retirement: A Preliminary Report. Oxford, OH: Scripps Foundation.

COYLE, J. and M. FULLER (1977) "Women's work and retirement attitudes." Presented at the annual meetings of the Gerontological Society, San Francisco.

CRIBIER, F., M. L. DUFAU, and C. RHEIN (1978) "Work history and career patterns of a cohort of Parisian female retired persons." Gerontologie et Sociologie 6: 137-165.

CRONBACH, L. J. (1951) "Coefficient alpha and the internal structure of tests." Psychometrika 16: 297-334.

CUMMING, E. (1969) "The multigenerational family and the crisis of widowhood," in W. Donahue et al. (eds.) Living in the Multigenerational Family. Ann Arbor, MI: Institute of Gerontology.

CUMMING, E. and W. E. HENRY (1961) Growing Old: The Process of Disengagement. New York: Basic Books.

CUTLER, S. J. (1972) "The availability of personal transportation, residential location, and life satisfaction among the aged." Journal of Gerontology 27: 383-389.

——— (1973) "Voluntary association participation and life satisfaction: a cautionary research note." Journal of Gerontology 28: 96-100.

———— (1975) "Transportation and changes in life satisfaction." The Gerontologist 15: 155-159.

———— (1976) "Age profiles of membership in sixteen types of voluntary associations." Journal of Gerontology 31: 462-470.

———— (1977) "Aging and voluntary association participation." Journal of Gerontology 32: 470-479.

DAHLIN, M. (1980) "Perspectives on the family life of the elderly in 1900." The Gerontologist 20: 99-107.

DARNLEY, F. (1975) "Adjustment to retirement: integrity or despair." The Family Life Coordinator 24: 217-225.

DATAN, N. and L. H. GINSBERG (1975) Life-span Developmental Psychology: Normative Life Crises. New York: Academic Press.

DATAN, N. and N. LOHMANN (1980) Transitions of Aging. New York: Academic Press.

DeBURGER, J. E. (1977) "Relations of elderly parents with their offspring." International Journal of Sociology of the Family 7: 61-76.

DECARLO, T. J. (1974) "Recreation participation patterns and successful aging." Journal of Gerontology 29: 416-422.

DEPNER, C. and B. INGERSOLL (1980) "Social support in the family context." Presented at the annual meetings of the Gerontology Society, San Diego, California.

DOHRENWEND, B. P. and B. S. DOHRENWEND (1977) "The conceptualization and measurement of stressful life events: an overview," in J. S. Strauss et al. (eds.) Proceedings of the Conference on Methods of Longitudinal Research in Psychopathology. New York: Plenum.

DONAHUE, W., H. L. ORBACH, and O. POLLAK (1960) "Retirement: the emerging social pattern," pp. 330-397 in C. Tibbitts (ed.) Handbook of Social Gerontology. Chicago: University of Chicago Press.

DONO, J. E., C. M. FALBE, B. L. KAIL, E. LITWAK, R. H. SHERMAN, and D. SIEGEL (1979) "Primary groups in old age: structure and function." Research on Aging 1: 403-433.

DOOGHE, G. and J. HELANDER (1979) Family Life in Old Age. The Hague: Martinus Nijhoff.

DOOLITTLE, J. C. (1977) "Predictors of media use among retired older adults." Presented at the annual meetings of the Gerontological Society, San Francisco.

DORFMAN, M. S. (1981) The Use and Non-use of Tax-deferred Annuities as a Means of Savings for Retirement: Research Report. Washington, DC: NRTA-AARP Andrus Foundation.

DREHER, G. (1970) "Auseinandersetzungen mit dem bevorstehenden Austritt aus dem Berufsleben," pp. 118-124 in R. Schubert (ed.) Geroprophylaxe, Infektions- und Herzkrankheiten: Rehabilitation und Sozialstatus im Alter. Darmstadt: Steinkopff.

DRESSEL, P. L. (1980) "Assortive mating in later life: some initial considerations." Journal of Family Issues 1: 379.

———— and W. R. AVANT (1978) "Aging and college family textbooks." The Family Coordinator 27: 427-435.

DRESSLER, D. M. (1973) "Life adjustment of retired couples." The International Journal of Aging and Human Development 4: 335-349.

DUBIN, R. (1956) "Industrial workers' world: a study of the central life interests of industrial workers." Social Problems 3: 131-142.

DUNCAN, D. D. (1966) "Path analysis: sociological examples." American Journal of Sociology 72: 1-16.

EARP, J. L. (1976) "Older married women and work: the effect of employment status on self-perceived psychological stress." Presented at the NCFR annual meetings, New York.

EDMUNDS, E. P. and J. W. ELIAS (1979) "Middle-aged workers' retirement expectations: implications for retirement planning." Presented at the annual meeting of the Gerontological Society, Washington, D.C.

EDWARDS, J. N. and D. L. KLEMMACK (1973) "Correlations of life satisfaction: a re-examination." Journal of Gerontology 28: 497-502.

EDWARDS, R. C., M. REICH, and D. M. GORDON (1975) Labor Market Segmentation. Lexington, MA: D. C. Heath.

EISDORFER, C. (1972) "Adaptation to loss of work," pp. 245-264 in F. M. Carp (ed.) Retirement. New York: Behavioral.

——— and F. WILKIE (1977) "Stress, disease, aging and behavior," pp. 251-275 in J. E. Birren and K. W. Schaie (eds.) Handbook of the Psychology of Aging. New York: Van Nostrand Reinhold.

EKERDT, D. J. and C. L. ROSE (1975) "Preference for later retirement: a longitudinal analysis." Presented at the annual meetings of the Gerontological Society, Louisville.

EKERDT, D. J. and R. BOSSE (1977) "Rejection of retirement." Presented at the annual meetings of the Gerontological Society, San Francisco.

——— and J. M. MOGEY (1980) "Concurrent change in planned and preferred age for retirement." Journal of Gerontology 35: 232-240.

ELDER, G. and R. ROCKWELL (1976) "Marital timing in women's life patterns." Journal of Family History 1: 34-54.

ELWELL, F. and A. MALTBIE-CRANNEL (1981) "The impact of role loss upon coping resources and life satisfaction of the elderly." Journal of Gerontology 36: 223-232.

EMERSON, A. R. (1959) "The first year of retirement." Occupational Psychology 33: 197-209.

EPSTEIN, C. F. (1970) Woman's Place: Options and Limits in Professional Careers. Berkeley: University of California Press.

EPSTEIN, L. A. and J. H. MURRAY (1968) "Employment and retirement," in B. Neugarten (ed.) Middle Age and Aging. Chicago: University of Chicago Press.

ERAN, M. and D. JACOBSON (1976) "Expectancy theory prediction of the preference to remain employed or to retire." Journal of Gerontology 31: 605-610.

ERICKSEN, J. A., W. L. YANCEY, and E. P. ERICKSEN (1979) "The division of labor." Journal of Marriage and the Family 41: 301-313.

ESHLEMAN, J. R. (1981) The Family: An Introduction. Boston: Allyn & Bacon.

ESTES, C. L. (1980) The Aging Enterprise. San Francisco: Jossey-Bass.

ETENG, W. (1973) Adjustment to Retirement and Aging Transitions in Wisconsin. Ph.D. dissertation, University of Wisconsin.

FANDETTI, D. V. and D. E. GELFAND (1976) "Care of the aged: attitudes of white ethnic families." The Gerontologist 16: 544-549.

FARKAS, G. (1976) "Education, wage rates, and the division of labor between husband and wife." Journal of Marriage and the Family 38: 473-483.

FENGLER, A. P. (1975) "Attitudinal orientations of wives toward their husbands' retirement." International Journal of Aging and Human Development 6: 139-152.

FENGLER, A. P. and N. GOODRICH (1979) "Wives of elderly disabled men: the hidden patients." The Gerontologist 19: 175-184.

FERBER, M. and J. HUBER (1979) "Husbands, wives and careers." Journal of Marriage and the Family 41: 315-325.

FILLENBAUM, G. G. (1971a) "On the relation between attitude to work and attitude to retirement." Journal of Gerontology 26: 244-248.

——— (1971b) "Retirement planning programs—at what age and for whom?" The Gerontologist 11: 33-36.

——— (1979) "The longitudinal retirement history study: methodological and substantive issues." The Gerontologist 19: 203-209.

——— and G. L. MADDOX (1974) "Work after retirement." The Gerontologist 14: 418-424.

FILSINGER, E. and W. J. SAUER (1978) "An empirical typology of adjustment of aging." Journal of Gerontology 33: 437-445.

FISCHER, J., S. CARLTON-FORD, and B. BRILES (1978) "Life-cycle career patterns: a typological approach to female status attainment." Presented at the annual meetings of the Gerontological Society, Dallas.

FLANAGAN, J. C. (1977) "The relation between work history and retirement plans for a national sample." Presented at the annual meetings of the Gerontological Society, San Francisco.

FOGARTY, M. P., R. RAPOPORT, and R. N. RAPOPORT (1971) Sex, Career and Family. Beverly Hills, CA: Sage.

FONER, A. and K. SCHWAB (1981) Aging and Retirement. Monterey, CA: Brooks/ Cole.

FOOTE, N. N. (1956) "Matching of husband and wife in phases of development." Chicago: University of Chicago, Family Study Center.

FOSTER, H. H. and D. J. FREED (1977/78) "Spousal rights in retirement and pension benefits." Journal of Family Law 16: 187-211.

FOX, A. (1979) "Findings from the retirement history study." Social Security Bulletin 42: 17-40.

FOX, J. H. (1977) "Effects of retirement and former work life on women's adaptation in old age." Journal of Gerontology 32: 196-202.

FRIEDMAN, E. A. and R. J. HAVIGHURST (1954) The Meaning of Work and Retirement. Chicago: University of Chicago Press.

FRIEDMAN, E. A. and H. L. ORBACH (1974) "Adjustment to retirement," in S. Arieti (ed.) American Handbook of Psychiatry, Vol. 1. New York: Basic Books.

FRIEDMAN, J. and J. SJOGREN (1981) "Assets of the elderly as they retire." Social Security Bulletin 44: 16-31.

FRIEDMAN, N. (1981) "Orientation and adjustment of women to retirement." Presented at the annual meetings of the Gerontological Society, Toronto.

FULGRAFF, B. (1978) "Social gerontology in West Germany: a review of recent and current research." The Gerontologist 18: 42-58.

GARCIA, A. (1981) "The elderly Chicano female and Social Security." Presented at the annual meetings of the Gerontological Society, Toronto.

GARDNER, M. (1981) "Retirement, the new beginning." The Christian Science Monitor, September 22, 23, 24.

GELF, D. E., J. K. OLSEN, and M. R. BLOCK (1978) "Two generations of elderly in the changing American family: implications for family services." The Family Coordinator 27: 395-404.

GEORGE, L. (1980) Role Transitions in Later Life. Monterey, CA: Brooks/Cole.

GEORGE, L. K. (1979) "The happiness syndrome: methodological and substantive issues in the study of social psychological well-being in adulthood." The Gerontologist 19: 210-216.

——— and G. L. MADDOX (1977) "Subjective adaptation to loss of the work role: a longitudinal study." Journal of Gerontology 32: 456-462.

GIBSON, R. C. (1981) Retirement patterns of black women: a comparative analysis." Presented at the annual meetings of the Gerontological Society, Toronto.

GIESEN, C. B. and N. DATAN (1980) "The competent older woman," pp. 57-74 in N. Datan and N. Lohmann (eds.) Transitions of Aging. New York: Academic Press.

GILFORD, R. (1974) "Marital satisfaction in retirement." Presented at the annual meetings of the Gerontological Society, Portland.

GILMORE, A. (1973) "Attitudes of the elderly to marriage." Gerontologia Clinica 15: 124-132.

GINZBERG, E. (1966) Life Styles of Educated Women. New York: Columbia University Press.

GLAMSER, F. D. (1976) "Determinants of a positive attitude toward retirement." Journal of Gerontology 31: 104-107.

——— (1981) "The impact of preretirement programs on the retirement experience" Journal of Gerontology 36: 244-250.

——— and G. F. DeJONG (1975) "The efficacy of preretirement preparation programs for industrial workers." Journal of Gerontology 30: 595-600.

GLASER, B. and A. STRAUSS (1967) The Discovery of Grounded Theory. Chicago: Aldine.

GLICK, P. C. (1979) "The future marital status and living arrangements of the elderly." The Gerontologist 19: 301-309.

GOEBEL, K. and C. B. HENNON (1981) "An empirical investigation of the relationship among wife's employment status, stage in the family life cycle, meal preparation time, and expenditures for meals away from home." Journal of Consumer Studies and Home Economics.

GOODE, W. J. (1960) "A theory of role strain." American Sociological Review 25: 483-496.

GORDON, C., C. M. GAITZ, and J. SCOTT (1976) "Leisure and lives: personal expressivity across the life span," pp. 310-341 in R. H. Binstock and E. Shanas (eds.) Handbook of Aging and the Social Sciences. New York: Van Nostrand Reinhold.

GORDON, H. A. and K.C.W. KAMMEYER (1980) "The gainful employment of women with small children." Journal of Marriage and the Family 42: 327-336.

GOTTLIEB, N. "The older woman," pp. 280-319 in N. Gottlieb (ed.) Alternative Social Services for Women. New York: Columbia University Press.

GOUDY, W. J., E. A. POWERS, and P. M. KEITH (1975) "Work and retirement: a test of attitudinal relationships." Journal of Gerontology 30: 193-198.

——— and R. A. REGER (1980) "Changes in attitudes toward retirement: evidence from a panel study of older males." Journal of Gerontology 35: 942-948.

GOVE, W. and M. GEERKEN (1977) "The effect of children and employment on the mental health of married men and women." Social Forces 56: 66-67.

GRANEY, M. J. (1971) Social Participation of the Elderly. Ph.D. dissertation, University of Minnesota.

——— (1974) "Media use as a substitute activity in old age." Journal of Gerontology 29: 322-324.

——— (1975) "Happiness and social participation in aging." Journal of Gerontology 30: 701-706.

——— and D. M. COTTAM (1981) "Labor force nonparticipation of older people: United States, 1890-1970." The Gerontologist 21: 138-141.

GRANT, C. H. (1969) "Age differences in self-concept from early childhood through old age." Proceedings of the 77th Annual Convention of the American Psychological Association 4: 717-718.

GREENE, M. R., H. C. PYRON, U. V. MANION, and H. WINKLEVOSS (1969) Pre-Retirement Counseling, Retirement Adjustment and the Older Employee. Washington, DC: ADA.

GUIN, H. (1980) "Retirement planning: suggestions for management." Aging and Work 3: 203-209.

GUBRIUM, J. F. (1974) "Marital desolation and the evaluation of everyday life in old age." Journal of Marriage and the Family 36: 107-113.

GUTTMANN, D. (1978) "Life events and decision making by older adults." The Gerontologist 13: 462-467.

———, J. D. SINNOTT, Z. CARRIGAN, and N. HOLAHAN (1977) A Survey of the Impact of Needs, Knowledge, Ability, and Living Arrangements on the Decision Making of the Elderly. Washington, DC: Catholic University Press.

HALLER, M. and L. ROSENMAYR (1971) "The pluridimensionality of work commitment." Human Relations 24: 501-518.

HAMPE, G. D., A. L. BLEVINS, and S. NYHUS (1979) "The influence of rural-urban residence and perceptions of health on retirement satisfaction." Presented at the annual meetings of the Gerontological Society, Washington, D.C.

HANSSEN, A. M., N. J. MEIMA, L. M. BUCKSPAN, B. E. HENDERSON, T. L. HELBIG, and S. H. ZARIT (1978) "Correlates of senior center participation." The Gerontologist 18: 193-200.

HARDCASTLE, D. A. (1981) "Getting along after retirement: an economic inquiry," pp. 151-168 in F. J. Berghorn et al. (eds.) The Dynamics of Aging. Boulder, CO: Westview Press.

HARMON, L. W. (1967) "Women's working patterns related to their SVIB housewife and 'own' occupational scores." Journal of Consulting Psychology 14: 299-301.

HARRIS, L. and Associates (1975) The Myth and Reality of Aging in America. Washington, DC: National Council on Aging.

HAVENS, B. J. (1968) "An investigation of activity patterns and adjustment in an aging population." The Gerontologist 8: 201-206.

HAVIGHURST, R. J. and E. SHANAS (1953) "Retirement and the professional worker." Journal of Gerontology 8: 81-85.

HAVIGHURST, R. J., B. L. NEUGARTEN, and S. S. TOBIN (1963) "Disengagement, personality, and life satisfaction," pp. 319-324 in P. F. Hansen (ed.) Age with a Future. Copenhagen: Munksgaard.

HAVIGHURST, R. J., J.M.A. MUNNICHS, B. L. NEUGARTEN, and H. THOMAE (1969) Adjustment to Retirement: A Cross National Study. Assen: Van Gorkum.

HAVIGHURST, R. J., W. J. McDONALD, L. MAEULEN, and J. MAZEL (1979) "Male social scientists: lives after sixty." The Gerontologist 19: 55-60.

HAWKINS, B. D. (1976) A Comparative Study of the Social Participation of the Black Elderly Residing in Public Housing in Two Communities. Ph.D. dissertation, Brandeis University.

HEIDBREDER, E. M. (1972) "Factors in retirement adjustment: white-collar/blue-collar experience." Industrial Gerontology 12: 69-79.

HEISE, D. K. (1969) "Problems in path analysis and causal inference," in E. F. Borgatta (ed.) Sociological Methodology. San Francisco: Jossey-Bass.

HENDRICKS, J. A. (1977) "Women and leisure," pp. 114-120 in L. E. Troll et al. (eds.) Looking Ahead. Englewood Cliffs, NJ: Prentice-Hall.

——— and C. D. HENDRICKS (1977) Aging in Mass Society. Myths and Realities. Cambridge: Winthrop.

HENRETTA, J. C. and A. M. O'RAND (1980) "Labor-force participation of older married women." Social Security Bulletin 43: 10-15.

——— (1981) "Conjugal role structure and joint retirement." Presented at the annual meetings of the Gerontological Society, Toronto.

HERALD, A. C. (1976) "Needs of sisters in preretirement and retirement years." Presented at the annual meetings of the Gerontological Society, New York.

HESS, B. B. (1979) "Sex roles, friendship, and the life course." Research on Aging 1: 494-515.

——— and E. W. MARKSON (1980) Aging and Old Age. New York: Macmillan.

HESS, B. B. and J. M. WARING (1978a) "Changing pattern of aging and family bonds in later life." The Family Coordinator 27: 303-314.

——— (1978b) "Parent and child in later life," pp. 241-273 in R. M. Lerner and G. N. Spanier (eds.) Child Influences on Marital and Family Interaction: A Life-span Perspective. New York: Academic Press.

HESSE, S. J. (1979) "Women working: historical trends," pp. 35-62 in K. W. Feinstein (ed.) Working Women and Families. Beverly Hills, CA: Sage.

HEYMAN, D. K. and F. C. JEFFERS (1968) "Wives and retirement: a pilot study." Journal of Gerontology 23: 488-496.

HICKEY, T. and R. L. DOUGLASS (1981) "Neglect and abuse of older family members: professionals' perspectives and case experiences." The Gerontologist 21: 171-176.

HILDRETH, G. J., G. van LAANEN, E. KELLEY, and T. DURANT (1980) "Participation in and enjoyment of family maintenance activities by older women." Family Relations 29: 386-390.

HOFFMAN, L. (1963) "Parental power relations and the division of household tasks," pp. 215-230 in F. I. Nye and L. W. Hoffman (eds.) The Employed Mother in America. Chicago: Rand McNally.

——— and F. I. NYE (1974) Working Mothers. San Francisco: Jossey-Bass.

HOLDEN, K. C. (1978) "Comparability of the measure of labor force of older women in Japan and the United States." Journal of Gerontology 33: 422-426.

——— (1979) "The inequitable distribution of OASI benefits among homemakers." The Gerontologist 19: 250-256.

HOLLEY, M. R. (1978) "Components of life satisfaction of older Texans: a multi-dimensional model." Ph.D. dissertation, North Texas State University.

HOLLINGSHEAD, A. B. (1965) A Two-Factor Index of Social Position. New Haven, CT: Yale University Press.

——— and M. REDLICH (1958) Social Class and Mental Illness. New York: John Wiley.

HOLMSTROM, L. L. (1972) The Two-Career Family. Cambridge: Schenkman.

HOOKER, K. A. (1981) "Work ethic, daily activities, and their relationship to satisfaction in retirement." Presented at the annual meetings of the Gerontological Society, Toronto.

HORNUNG, C. A. and B. C. McCULLOUGH (1981) "Status relationships in dual-employment marriages: consequences for psychological well-being." Journal of Marriage and the Family 43: 125-141.

HOUSE, J. S. (1981) Work, Stress and Social Support. Reading, MA: Addison-Wesley.

HOYT, D. R., M. A. KAISER, G. A. PETERS, and N. BABCHUK (1980) "Life satisfaction and activity theory: a multidimensional approach." Journal of Gerontology 35: 935-941.

HURST, C. E. and D. A. GULDIN (1981) "The effects of intra-individual and inter-spouse status consistency on life satisfaction among older persons." Journal of Gerontology 36: 112-121.

HUSTON-STEIN, A. and A. HIGGINS-TRENK (1978) "Development of females from childhood to adulthood: career and feminine role orientations," pp. 258-297 in P. B. Baltes (ed.) Life-span Development and Behavior. New York: Academic Press.

HUTCHISON, I. W. (1975) "The significance of marital status for morale and life satisfaction among lower income elderly." Journal of Marriage and the Family 37: 287-293.

International Social Security Administration (1979) "Retirement age practices in ten industrial societies." Studies and Research 14: Geneva.

IRELAN, L. (1972a) "Retirement history study: introduction." Social Security Bulletin 35: 3-8.

——— (1972b) "Working wives in the pre-retirement years." Presented at the annual meetings of the Gerontological Society, San Juan.

——— and D. B. BELL (1971) "Understanding subjectively defined retirement." Presented at the annual meetings of the Gerontological Society, Houston.

IRELAN, L. M. and D. K. MOTLEY (1971) "Health on the threshold of retirement." Presented at the annual meetings of the Gerontological Society, Houston.

JACKSON, J. J. (1972) "Marital life among aging blacks." The Family Coordinator 21: 21-22.

JACOBS, R. H. (1976) "A typology of older American women." Social Policy 7: 34-39.

JACOBSON, C. J. (1974) "Rejection of the retiree role: a study of female industrial workers in their 50's." Human Relations 27: 477-492.

JANIS, I. L. (1974) "Vigilance and decision-making in personal crisis," pp. 139-175 in G. V. Coelho et al. (eds.) Coping and Adaptation. New York: Basic Books.

JASLOW, P. (1976) "Employment, retirement, and morale among older women." Journal of Gerontology 31: 212-218.

JEDLICKA, D. (1978) "Sex inequality, aging, and innovation in preferential mate selection." The Family Coordinator 27: 137-140.

JEWSON, R. H. (1978) "After retirement: an exploratory study of the professional woman." Ph.D. dissertation, University of Minnesota.

JOHNSON, C. K. and S. PRICE-BONHAM (1980) "Women and retirement: a study and implications." Family Relations 29: 380-385.

JOHNSON, E. S. (1978) "Good relationships between older mothers and their daughters: a causal model." The Gerontologist 18: 301-306.

——— and B. J. BURSK (1977) "Relationships between the elderly and their adult children." The Gerontologist 17: 90-96.

JOHNSON, L. and G. B. STROTHER (1962) "Job expectations and retirement planning." Journal of Gerontology 17: 418-432.

KAHANA, E. (1976) "The older woman: implications of research for social policy." Presented at the annual meetings of the American Sociological Association.

——— and A. KIYAK (1977) "The nitty-gritty of survival," pp. 172-177 in L. E. Troll et al. (eds.) Looking Ahead. Englewood Cliffs, NJ: Prentice-Hall.

KAHANA, E., J. LIANG, and B. J. FELTON (1980) "Alternative models of person-environment fit: prediction of morale in three homes for the aged." Journal of Gerontology 35: 584-495.

KAHN, R. L. and T. C. ANTONUCCI (1980) "Convoys over the life course: attachment, roles and social support," in P. B. Baltes and G. G. Brim (eds.) Life-Span Development and Behavior. New York: Academic Press.

KALT, N. C. and M. H. KOHN (1975) "Pre-retirement counseling: characteristics of programs and preferences of retirees." The Gerontologist 15: 179-181.

KANTER, R. M. (1977) Work and Family in the United States. New York: Russell Sage.

KAPLIN, J. (1975) "The family in aging." The Gerontologist 15: 385.

KART, C. S. and B. B. MANARD (1976) Aging in America. Readings in Social Gerontology. New York: Alfred.

KAUFMAN, I. (1976) "Marital adaptation in the aging." Journal of Geriatric Psychiatry 9: 161-176.

KEATING, N. and J. MARSHALL (1979) "The process of retirement: the situation of the rural self-employed." Presented at the annual meetings of the Gerontological Society, Washington, D.C.

KEATING, N. and L. J. SPILLER (1981) "Variations on a theme: definitions of leisure in retirement." Presented at the annual meetings of the Gerontological Society, Toronto.

KEATING, N. C. and P. COLE (1980) "What do I do with him 24 hours a day? Changes in the housewife role after retirement." The Gerontologist 20: 84-89.

KEITH, P. M. (1979) "Life changes and perceptions of life and death among older men and women." Journal of Gerontology 34: 870-878.

——— and T. H. BRUBAKER (1977) "Sex-role expectations associated with specific household tasks: perceived age and employment differences." Psychological Reports 41: 15-18.

——— (1979) "Male household roles in later life: a look at masculinity and marital relationships." The Family Coordinator 28: 497-502.

——— (1980) "Adolescent perception of household work: expectations by sex, age and employment situation." Adolescence 15: 171-182.

KEITH, P. M., E. A. POWERS, and W. J. GOUDY (1981) "Older men in employed and retired families." Alternative Lifestyles 4: 228-241.

KEITH, P. M., C. D. DOBSON, W. J. GOUDY, and E. A. POWERS (1981) "Older men: occupation, employment status, household involvement, and well-being." Journal of Family Issues 2: 336-349.

KELL, D. and C. V. PATTON (1978) "Reaction to induced early retirement." The Gerontologist 18: 173-180.

KERCKHOFF, A. C. (1964) "Husband-wife expectations and reactions to retirement." Journal of Gerontology 19: 510-516.

——— (1966) "Family patterns and morale in retirement," pp. 173-192 in I. M. Simpson and J. C. McKinney (eds.) Social Aspects of Aging. Durham, NC: Duke University Press.

KERLINGER, F. N. and E. PEDHAZUR (1973) Multiple Regression in Behavioral Research. New York: Holt, Rinehart & Winston.

KEYS, M. (1979) "Women and retirement income—legislative initiatives and congressional action." Aging and Work 2: 266.

KIDWELL, J. I. and A. BOOTH (1977) "Social distance and intergenerational relations." The Gerontologist 17: 412-420.

KILTY, K. M. and J. H. BEHLING (1980) The Professional Worker, Work Alienation, and Pre-retirement Planning and Attitudes: Research Report. Washington, DC: Andrus Foundation.

KIMMEL, D. C. (1974) Adulthood and Aging. New York: John Wiley.

——— K. F. PRICE, and J. W. WALKER (1978) "Retirement choice and retirement satisfaction." Journal of Gerontology 33: 575-585.

KING, C. E. and W. H. HOWELL (1965) "Role characteristics of flexible and inflexible retired persons." Sociology and Social Research 49: 153-165.

KIRKPATRICK, K. (1979) "Women and retirement income—comparison of social security provisions benefitting women." Aging and Work 2: 268.

KIVETT, V. R. (1978) "Loneliness and the rural widow." The Family Coordinator 27: 389-394.

——— (1979) "Discriminators of loneliness among the rural elderly: implications for intervention." The Gerontologist 19: 108-115.

KLINE, C. (1975) "The socialization process of women: implications for a theory of successful aging." The Gerontologist 15: 486-492.

KOBRIN, F. E. (1981) "Family extension and the elderly: economic, demographic and family cycle factors." Journal of Gerontology 36: 370-377.

KOLODRUBETZ, W. W. and D. M. LANDAY (1973) "Coverage and vesting of full-time employees under private retirement plans." Social Security Bulletin 36: 20-36.

KOMAROVSKY, M. (1974) "Patterns of self-disclosure of male undergraduates." Journal of Marriage and the Family 36: 677-686.

KRAUSS, I. K., H. DENNIS, K. Y. MARSHALL, and B. ERVIN (1981) "Individual differences in reactions to retirement." Presented at the annual meetings of the Gerontological Society, Toronto.

KREPS, J. M. (1963) Employment, Income, and Retirement Problems of the Aged. Durham, NC: Duke University Press.

KUTNER, B., D. FANSHEL, A. TOGO, and T. LAUGNER (1956) Five Hundred Over Sixty. New York: Russell Sage.

KUYPERS, J. A. and V. L. BENGTSON (1973) "Social breakdown and competence: a model of normal aging." Human Development 14: 181-201.

LABOVITZ, S. (1967) "Some observations on measurement and statistics." Social Forces 56: 151-160.

LAND, K. C. (1969) "Principles of path analysis," in E. R. Borgatta (ed.) Sociological Methodology. San Francisco: Jossey-Bass.

LANE, W. (1980) "I always considered myself to be a professional woman: academic women in retirement." Presented at the annual meetings of the Gerontological Society, San Diego.

——— and E. A. FRIEDMAN (1979) "Faculty retirement: locals, cosmopolitans, and professional commitment." Presented at the annual meetings of the Gerontological Society, Washington, D.C.

LANGNER, T. S. (1962) "A twenty-two item screening score of psychiatric symptoms indicating impairment." Journal of Health and Human Behavior 3: 269-276.

LaROCCO, J. M., J. S. HOUSE, and J.R.P. FRENCH (1980) "Social support, occupational stress, and health." Journal of Health and Social Behavior 21: 202-218.

LARSON, R. (1978) "Thirty years of research on the subjective well-being of older Americans." Journal of Gerontology 33: 109-125.

LAURENCE, M. W. (1961) "Sources of satisfaction in the lives of working women." Journal of Gerontology 16: 163-167.

LAWTON, M. (1972) "The dimensions of morale," pp. 144-165 in D. P. Kent et al. (eds.) Research, Planning and Action for the Elderly. New York: Behavioral.

LEE, G. R. (1978) "Marriage and morale in later life." Journal of Marriage and the Family 40: 131-142.

——— (1979) "Children and the elderly: interaction and morale." Research on Aging 1: 335-360.

——— and M. IHINGER-TALLMAN (1980) "Sibling interaction and morale: the effects of family relations on older people." Research on Aging 2: 367-391.

LEE, G. R. and M. L. LASSEY (1980) "Rural-urban differences among the elderly: economic, social, and subjective factors." Journal of Social Issues 36: 62-74.

LEHR, U. (1977) Psychologie des Alterns. Heidelberg: Quelle und Meyer.

——— (1978) "Die Situation der aelteren Frau: psychologische und soziale Aspekte." Zeitschrift fuer Gerontologie 11: 6-26.

——— and G. DREHER (1968) "Psychologische Probleme der Pensionierung," pp. 234-252 in Kongressbericht der Deutschen Gesellschaft fuer Gerontologie. Darmstadt: Steinkopff.

——— (1969) "Determinants of attitudes toward retirement," in R. J. Havighurst et al. (eds.) Adjustment to Retirement: A Cross-national Study. Assen, the Netherlands: Van Gorkum.

LEMON, B. W., V. L. BENGTSON, and J. A. PETERSON (1972) "An exploration of the activity theory of aging, activity types, and life satisfaction among inmovers to a retirement community." Journal of Gerontology 27: 511-523.

LESTER, B. and S. TINE (1975) "Quality of life as defined by older persons." Presented at the annual meetings of the Gerontological Society, Louisville.

LEVY, S. M. (1980) "The adjustment of older women: effects of chronic ill health and attitudes toward retirement." International Journal of Aging and Human Development 12: 93-110.

LEWIS, M. W. and R. N. BUTLER (1972) "Why is women's lib ignoring old women?" International Journal of Aging and Human Development 3: 223-231.

LEWIS, R. A. (1978) "Transitions in middle age and aging families: a bibliography from 1940 to 1977." The Family Coordinator 27: 457-476.

LIANG, J., L. DVORKIN, E. KAHANA, and F. MAZIAN (1980) "Social integration and morale: a re-examination." Journal of Gerontology 35: 746-757.

LIDZ, T. (1976) The Person: His or Her Development Throughout the Life Cycle. New York: Basic Books.

LIEBERMAN, M. A. (1975) "Adaptive processes in late life," in N. Datan and L. H. Ginsberg (eds.) Life-span Developmental Psychology: Normative Life Crises. New York: Academic Press.

LINDEMAN, R. H., P. F. MERENDA, and R. Z. GOLD (1980) Introduction to Bivariate and Multivariate Analysis. Glenview, IL: Scott, Foresman.

LINDENSTEIN-WALSHOK, M. (1979) "Occupational values and family roles: women in blue-collar and service occupations," pp. 63-84 in K. W. Feinstein (ed.) Working Women and Families. Beverly Hills, CA: Sage.

LIPMAN, A. (1960) "Marital roles of the retired aged." Merrill Palmer Quarterly 6: 192-195.

——— (1961) "Role conceptions and morale of couples in retirement." Journal of Gerontology 16: 267-271.

LITTLE, V. C. (1980) The Older Woman. Storrs, CT: University of Connecticut, School of Social Work.

——— (1981a) "Retirement roles of women: use of time and self." Presented at the International Congress of Sociology, Hamburg.

——— (1981b) "The older woman in retirement." Presented at the annual meetings of the Gerontological Society, Toronto.

LIVSON, F. B. (1976) "Patterns of personality development in middle-aged women: a longitudinal study." International Journal of Aging and Human Development 7: 107-115.

——— (1977) "Coming out of the closet: marriage and other crises of middle age," pp. 81-92 in L. E. Troll et al. (eds.) Looking Ahead. Englewood Cliffs, NJ: Prentice-Hall.

LOCKSLEY, A. (1980) "On the effects of wives' employment on marital adjustment and companionship." Journal of Marriage and the Family 42: 337-347.

LOETHER, H. J. (1967) Problems of Aging. Belmont, CA: Dickenson.

LOHMANN, N. (1980) "Life satisfaction research in aging: implications for policy development," pp. 27-40 in N. Datan and N. Lohmann (eds.) Transitions of Aging. New York: Academic Press.

LONGINO, C. F. and J. C. BIGGAR (1981) "The impact of retirement migration on the South." The Gerontologist 21: 283-290.

LONGINO, C. F. and A. LIPMAN (1981) "Married and spouseless men and women in planned retirement communities: support network differentials." Journal of Marriage and the Family 43: 169-178.

LOPATA, H. Z. (1966) "The life cycle of the social role of the housewife." Sociology and Social Research 51: 5-22.

——— (1969) "Social psychological aspects of role involvement." Sociology of Social Research 53: 295-298.
——— (1971a) Occupation Housewife. New York: Oxford University Press.
——— (1971b) "Widows as a minority group." The Gerontologist 11: 67-77.
——— (1973) Widowhood in an American City. Cambridge, MA: Schenkman.
——— (1975) "Widowhood: societal factors in life-span disruptions and alternatives," in N. Datan and L. H. Gindsberg (eds.) Life-span Developmental Psychology. New York: Academic Press.
——— (1977a) "The meaning of friendship in widowhood," pp. 93-105 in L. E. Troll et al. (eds.) Looking Ahead. Englewood Cliffs, NJ: Prentice-Hall.
——— (1977b) "Widows and widowers." The Humanist 37: 25-28.
——— (1978a) "The absence of community resources in support systems of urban widows." The Family Coordinator 27: 383-388.
——— (1978b) "Contributions of extended families to the support systems of metropolitan area widows: limitations of the modified kin network." Journal of Marriage and the Family 40: 355-366.
——— (1979) Women as Widows: Support systems. New York: Elsevier.
——— and K. F. NORR (1980) "Changing commitments of American women to work and family roles." Social Security Bulletin 43: 3-13.
LOPATA, H. Z. and F. STEINHART (1971) "Work histories of American women." The Gerontologist 11: 27-36.
LOWENTHAL, M. F. (1972) "Some potentials of a life-cycle approach to the study of retirement," pp. 307-336 in F. M. Carp (ed.) Retirement. New York: Behavioral.
——— (1975) "Psychosocial variations across the adult life course: frontiers for research and policy." The Gerontologist 15: 6-12.
——— (1977) "Toward a sociopsychological theory of change in adulthood and old age," pp. 116-127 in J. E. Birren and K. W. Schaie (eds.) Handbook of the Psychology of Aging. New York: Van Nostrand Reinhold.
——— and P. L. BECKMAN (1967) Aging and Mental Disorder in San Francisco. San Francisco: Jossey-Bass.
LOWENTHAL, M. F. and D. CHIRIBOGA (1973) "Social stress and adaptation: toward a life perspective," In C. Eisdorfer and M. P. Lawton (eds.) The Psychology of Adult Development and Aging. Washington, DC: American Psychological Association.
LOWENTHAL, M. F. and C. HAVEN (1968) "Interaction and adaptation: intimacy as a critical variable," pp. 390-400 in B. L. Neugarten (ed.) Middle Age and Aging. Chicago: University of Chicago Press.
LOWENTHAL, M. F. and B. ROBINSON (1976) "Social networks and isolation," pp. 432-456 in R. H. Binstock and E. Shanas (eds.) Handbook of Aging and the Social Sciences. New York: Van Nostrand Reinhold.
LOWENTHAL, M. F., M. THURNHER, and D. CHIRIBOGA (1975) Four Stages of Life: A Comparative Study of Women and Men Facing Transitions. San Francisco: Jossey-Bass.
LOWY, L. (1980) Social Policies and Programs on Aging. Lexington, MA: D. C. Heath.
MAAS, S. and J. KUYPERS (1975) From Thirty to Seventy: A Forty-Year Longitudinal Study of Adult Life Styles and Personality. San Francisco: Jossey-Bass.

MACCOBY, E. and C. JACKLIN (1974) The Psychology of Sex Differences. Stanford, CA: Stanford University Press.

MADDOX, G. L. (1963) "Activity and morale: a longitudinal study of selected elderly subjects." Social Forces 42: 195-204.

——— (1966) "Persistence of life style among the elderly: a longitudinal study of patterns of social activity in relation to life satisfaction." Proceedings of the 7th International Congress of Gerontology, Vienna.

——— (1977) "Getting old." Minneapolis Star, December 5: 3B.

——— (1979) "Sociology of later life." Annual Review of Sociology 5: 113-135.

——— and E. B. DOUGLASS (1974) "Aging and individual differences: a longitudinal analysis of social, psychological, and physiological indicators." Journal of Gerontology 29: 555-563.

MADDOX, G. and C. EISDORFER (1962) "Some correlates of activity and morale among the elderly." Social Forces 40: 254-260.

MALLAN, L. B. (1974) "Women born in the early 1900's: employment, earnings, and benefit levels." Social Security Bulletin 37: 3-24.

MANCINI, J. A. (1979) "Family relationships and morale among people 65 years of age and older." American Journal of Orthopsychiatry 49: 292-301.

MANCINI, J. A. (1980) "Friend interaction, competence, and morale in old age." Research on Aging 2: 416-431.

MANION, U. V., M. GREENE, H. PYRON, and H. WINKELVOSS (1969) Preretirement Counseling, Retirement Adjustment and the Older Employee. Eugene: University of Oregon.

MARKIDES, K. S. and H. W. MARTIN (1979) "A causal model of life satisfaction among the elderly." Journal of Gerontology 34: 86-93.

MARTIN, J. and A. DORAN (1966) "Perception of retirement: time and season." Unpublished manuscript, University of Liverpool.

MASNICK, G. and M. J. BANE (1980) The Nation's Families: 1960-1990. Cambridge, MA: Joint Center for Urban Studies of MIT and Harvard University.

MATTHEWS, A. M. and K. H. BROWN (1981) "Economic and social welfare of the recently retired: factors which contribute to the perception of crisis." Presented at the International Congress of Gerontology, Hamburg, West Germany.

MATTHEWS, S. H. (1979) The Social World of Old Women. Beverly Hills, CA: Sage.

McCLELLAND, D. C. (1961) The Achieving Society. New York: D. Van Nostrand.

McLAUGHLIN, S. D. (1978) "Sex differences in the determinants of occupational status." Sociology of Work and Occupations 5: 5-30.

McPHERSON, B. and N. GUPPY (1979) "Pre-retirement life-style and the degree of planning for retirement." Journal of Gerontology 34: 254-263.

MEDLEY, M. L. (1976) "Satisfaction with life among persons sixty-five years and older: a causal model." Journal of Gerontology 31: 448-455.

——— (1977) "Marital adjustment in the post retirement years." The Family Coordinator 26: 5-12.

MEDNICK, M.T.S., S. TANGRI, and L. W. HOFFMAN (1975) Women and Achievement. New York: Halsted.

MEIER, E. L. and E. KERR (1976) "Capabilities of middle-aged and older workers: a survey of the literature." Industrial Gerontology 3: 147-156.

MIDLARSKY, E. and W. SUDA (1978) "Some antecedents of altruism in children: theoretical and empirical perspectives." Psychological Reports 43: 187-208.

MILHOJ, P. (1968) "Work and retirement," pp. 288-319 in E. Shanas et al. (eds.) Old People in Three Industrial Societies. New York: Atherton.

MILLER, M. B., H. BERNSTEIN, and H. SHARKEY (1975) "Family extrusion of the aged patient: family homeostasis and sexual conflict." The Gerontologist 15: 291-296.

MILLER, S. J. (1965) "The social dilemma of the aging leisure participants," in A. Rose and W. Peterson (eds.) Older People and Their Social World. Philadelphia: Davis.

MINDEL, C. H. (1979) "Multigenerational family households: recent trends and implications for the future." The Gerontologist 19: 456-463.

MITCHELL, W. L. (1972) "Lay observations on retirement," pp. 199-217 in F. M. Carp (ed.) Retirement. New York: Behavioral.

MODEL, S. (1981) "Housework by husbands: determinants and implications." Journal of Family Issues 2: 225-237.

MONK, A. (1971) "Factors in the preparation for retirement by middle-aged adults." The Gerontologist 11: 348-351.

——— (1979) "Family supports in old age." Social Work 24: 533.

MONNIER, A. (1979) "Les limites de la vie active et la retraite." Population 34: 301-823.

MOREY, A. and J. A. PETERSON (1975) "Factors related to retirement satisfaction of university faculty." Presented at the annual meetings of the Gerontological Society, Louisville.

MORGAN, L. A. (1976) "A re-examination of widowhood and morale." Journal of Gerontology 31: 687-695.

——— (1977) "Toward a formal theory of life course continuity and change." Presented at the annual meetings of the Gerontological Society, San Francisco.

——— (1980) "Work in widowhood: a viable option?" The Gerontologist 20: 581.

MORRISON, M. H. (1976) "Planning for income adequacy in retirement: the expectations of current workers." The Gerontologist 16: 538-543.

MOSS, M. S., L. E. GOTTESMAN, and L. I. KLEBAN (1976) "Informal social relationships among community aged." Presented at the annual meetings of the Gerontological Society, New York.

MULLER, C. F. (1980) "Economic roles and the status of the elderly," pp. 17-41 in E. F. Borgatta and N. G. McCluskey (eds.) Aging and Society. Beverly Hills, CA: Sage.

MURAKAMI, E. and J. PYNOOS (1981) "Effect of marital status on living arrangements and housing preferences of retired women professionals." Presented at the annual meetings of the Gerontological Society, Toronto.

MYERHOFF, B. (1978) Number Our Days. New York: Simon & Schuster.

——— and A. SIMIC (1978) Life's Career—Aging. Beverly Hills, CA: Sage.

NAEGELE, G. (1979) "Social situation of aged women living alone in the Federal-Republic of Germany." Zeitschrift fuer Gerontologie 12: 274-289.

National Institute on Aging (1978) Summary of Conference on "The Older Woman: Continuities and Discontinuities." Washington, DC: U.S. Department of Health, Education and Welfare.

NEUGARTEN, B. L. (1964) Personality in Middle and Later Life. New York: Atherton.

——— (1968) Middle Age and Aging. Chicago: University of Chicago Press.

——— (1974) "Age groups in American society and the rise of the young old." Annals of the American Academy of Political and Social Sciences 415: 187-198.

——— (1977) "Personality and aging," pp. 626-649 in J. E. Birren and K. W. Schaie (eds.) Handbook of the Psychology of Aging. New York: Van Nostrand Reinhold.

——— and N. DATAN (1974) "Sociological perspectives on the life cycle," pp. 53-69 in P. B. Baltes and K. W. Schaie (eds.) Life-span Developmental Psychology. Personality and Socialization. New York: Academic Press.

——— (1975) "The middle years," pp. 592-608 in S. Arieti (ed.) American Handbook of Psychiatry, Vol. 1. New York: Basic Books.

NEUGARTEN, B. L., and R. J. HAVIGHURST (1961) "Disengagement reconsidered in cross-national context," in R. J. Havighurst et al. (eds.) Adjustment to Retirement. Assen, The Netherlands: Van Gorcum.

NEUGARTEN, B. L. and K. K. WEINSTEIN (1972) "The changing American grandparent." Journal of Marriage and the Family 26: 199-206.

NEUGARTEN, B. L., J. W. MOORE, and J. C. LOWE (1975) "Age norms, age constraints, and adult socialization." American Journal of Sociology 70: 710-717.

NOBERINI, M. and B. L. NEUGARTEN (1975) "A follow-up study of adaptation in middle-aged women." Presented at the annual meetings of the Gerontological Society, Louisville.

O'RAND, A. M. (1981) "Socioeconomic status and poverty," D. Mangen and W. L. Peterson (eds.) Handbook of Research Instruments in Gerontology, Vol. 2. Minneapolis: University of Minnesota Press.

——— and J. C. HENRETTA (1981) "Early family and work careers, industrial pension structure and early retirement among unmarried women." Unpublished manuscript, Duke University.

OAKLEY, A. (1974) The Sociology of Housework. New York: Pantheon.

OPPENHEIMER, V. K. (1970) The Female Labor Force in the United States: Demographic and Economic Factors Governing Its Growth and Changing Composition. Berkeley: University of California Press.

OSAKO, M. M. (1979) "Aging and family among Japanese Americans: the role of ethnic tradition in the adjustment to old age." The Gerontologist 19: 448-455.

OSMOND, M. W. and P. Y. MARTIN (1975) "Sex and sexism: a comparison of male and female sex-role attitudes." Journal of Marriage and the Family 37: 744-758.

OXLEY, H. G. (1974) Mateship in Local Organization. Australia: University of Queensland Press.

PALMORE, E. (1965) "Differences in the retirement patterns of men and women." The Gerontologist 5: 4-8.

——— (1971) "Why do people retire?" International Journal of Aging and Human Development 2: 269-283.

——— (1979) "Stress and adaptation in later life." Journal of Gerontology 34: 841-851.

——— and V. R. KIVETT (1975) "Change in life-satisfaction among the middle-aged." Presented at the annual meetings of the Gerontological Society, Louisville.

——— (1977) "Change in life satisfaction: a longitudinal study of persons aged 46-70." Journal of Gerontology 32: 311-316.

PALMORE, E. and G. LUIKART (1972) "Health and social factors related to life satisfaction." Journal of Health and Social Behavior 13: 68-80.

PAMPEL, F. C. (1981) Social Change and the Aged. Lexington, MA: Lexington Books.

PARNES, H., A. V. ADAMS, P. ANDRISANI, et al. (1976) Dual Careers: A Longitudinal Analysis of the Labor Market Experience of Women. Columbus: Ohio State University Press.

PARNES, H., C. L. JUSENIUS, F. BLAU, G. NESTEL, R. SHORTHLIDE, Jr., and S. SANDELL (1975) Dual Careers: A Longitudinal Analysis of the Labor Market Experience of Women, Vol. 4. Columbus: Ohio State University Press.

PARRON, E. M. and L. E. TROLL (1978) "Golden wedding couples: effects of retirement on intimacy in long-standing marriages." Alternative Lifestyles 1: 447-464.

PATTON, C. V. (1977) "Early retirement in academia: making the decision." The Gerontologist 17: 347-354.

PAYNE, B. P. and F. WHITTINGTON (1976) "Older women: examination of popular stereotypes and research evidence." Social Problems 23: 288-504.

PEPITONE-ROCKWELL, F. (1980) Dual-Career Couples. Beverly Hills, CA: Sage.

PEPPERS, L. G. (1976) "Patterns of leisure and adjustment to retirement." The Gerontologist 16: 441-446.

PERETTI, P. O. and C. WILSON (1973) "Voluntary and involuntary retirement of aged males and their effect on emotional satisfaction, usefulness, self-image, emotional stability, and interpersonal relations." International Journal of Aging and Human Development 6: 131-138.

PERUN, P. J. (1976) "Academic women social scientists and retirement." Presented at the annual meetings of the Gerontological Society, New York.

PETROWSKY, M. (1976) "Marital status, sex and the social networks of the elderly." Journal of Marriage and the Family 38: 749-756.

PFEIFFER, E. and G. C. DAVIS (1974) "The use of time and leisure in middle life," pp. 232-242 in E. Palmore (ed.) Normal Aging II. Durham, NC: Duke University Press.

PIHLBLAD, T. and D. ADAMS (1972) "Widowhood, social participation, and life satisfaction." International Journal of Aging and Human Development 3: 323-330.

PILISUK, M. and M. MINKLER (1980) Supportive Networks, Life Ties for the Elderly. The Journal of Social Issues 36: 95.

PLECK, J. H. (1977) "The work family role system." Social Problems 24: 417-427.

PLONK, M. A. and M. A. PULLEY (1977) "Financial management practices of retired couples." The Gerontologist 17: 256-261.

POLACHEK, S. W. (1975) "Discontinuous labor force participation and its effects on women's market earnings," pp. 20-122 in C. B. Lloyd (ed.) Sex, Discrimination and the Division of Labor. New York: Columbia University Press.

POLLMAN, A. W. (1971) "Early retirement: relationship to variation in life satisfaction." The Gerontologist 11: 43-47.

POLOMA, M. M., B. F. PENDLETON, and T. N. GARLAND (1981) "Reconsidering the dual-career marriage: a longitudinal approach." Journal of Family Issues 2: 205-224.

POWELL, B. (1977) "The empty nest, employment, and psychiatric symptoms in college educated women." Psychology of Women Quarterly 2: 34-43.

POWERS, E. A. (1971) "The effect of the wife's employment on household tasks among post-parental couples: a research note." International Journal of Aging and Human Development 2: 284-287.

——— and G. L. BULTENA (1976) "Sex differences in intimate friendships in old age." Journal of Marriage and the Family 38: 739-747.

POWERS, E. A. and W. H. GOUDY (1971) "Examination of the meaning of work to older workers." International Journal of Aging and Human Development 2: 38-45.

PRENTIS, R. S. (1980) "White-collar working women's perception of retirement." The Gerontologist 20: 90-95.

President's Commission on Pension Policy (1980) Interim Report, May, 1980. Washington, DC: Government Printing Office.

PRESTON, C. E. and O.K.S. GUDIKSEN (1966) "A measure of self-perception among older people." Journal of Gerontology 21: 63-71.

PRICE, K. F., W. WALKER, and D. C. KIMMEL (1979) "Retirement timing and retirement satisfaction." Aging and Work 2: 235-245.

PROTHERO, J. (1981) "Retirement: expectations and intentions of older workers, male and female." Presented at the annual meetings of the Gerontological Society, Toronto.

PRUCHNO, R. (1981) "Obeying the social clock: timing of retirement and well-being in old age." Presented at the annual meetings of the Gerontological Society, Toronto.

QUADAGNO, J. S. (1978) "Career continuity and retirement plans of men and women physicians: the meaning of disorderly careers." Sociology of Work and Occupations 5: 55-74.

QUAM, J. K. (1980) "Is not the housekeeper happier than the working woman? An examination of the roles of older women." Presented at the Meetings of the Gerontological Society, San Diego.

RAGAN, P. K. (1977) "Socialization for the retirement role: cooling the mark out." Presented at the annual meetings of the American Psychological Association, San Francisco.

——— (1979) Aging parents. Los Angeles: University of Southern California, Andrus Gerontology Center.

——— (1980) Work and Retirement. Los Angeles: University of Southern California, Andrus Gerontology Center.

RAPOPORT, R. and R. N. RAPOPORT (1975a) Leisure and the Life Cycle. London: Routledge & Kegan Paul.

——— (1975b) "Men, women, and equity." The Family Coordinator 24: 421-432.

——— (1976) Dual-Career Families: Re-examined. New York: Harper & Row.

RATHBONE-McCUAN, E. (1976) "Geriatric day care: a family perspective." The Gerontologist 16: 517-521.

REBELSKY, F. (1975) Life: The Continuing Process. New York: Knopf.

RENO, V. P. (1972) "Compulsory retirement among newly entitled workers: survey of new beneficiaries." Social Security Bulletin 34: 3-17.

——— (1973) "Women newly entitled to retired worker benefits." Washington, DC: U.S. Social Security Administration, Office of Research and Statistics.

——— (1976) "Social security and the two-earner couple." Presented at the annual meetings of the Gerontological Society, New York.

RICHARDSON, J. G. (1979) "Wife occupational superiority and marital troubles: an examination of the hypothesis." Journal of Marriage and the Family 41: 41-50.

RIDLEY, J. C., C. A. BACHRACH, and D. A. DAWSON (1979) "Recall and reliability of interview data from older women." Journal of Gerontology 34: 99-105.

RIEGEL, K. F. (1975) "Adult life crises: a dialectical interpretation of development," in N. Datan and L. H. Ginsberg (eds.) Life-Span Developmental Psychology: Normative Life Crises. New York: Academic Press.

――― R. M. RIEGEL, and G. MEYER (1968) "The prediction of retest resisters in research on aging." Journal of Gerontology 23: 270-237.

RILEY, M. and A. FONER (1968) Aging and Society: An Inventory of Research, Vol. 2. New York: Russell Sage.

RILEY, M. W., M. E. JOHNSON, and S. S. BOOCOCK (1963) "Women's changing occupational role: a research report." The American Behavioral Scientist 6: 33-37.

RILEY, M. W., M. E. JOHNSON, and A. FONER (1972) Aging and Society: A Sociology of Age Stratification, Vol. 3. New York: Russell Sage.

ROBERTS, W. L. and A. E. ROBERTS (1975) "Factors in life styles of couples married over 50 years." Presented at the annual meetings of the Gerontological Society, Louisville.

――― (1980) "Significant elements in the relationship of long-married couples." The International Journal of Aging and Human Development 10: 265.

ROBERTSON, J. F. (1976) "Significance of grandparents: perceptions of young adult grandchildren." The Gerontologist 16: 137-140.

――― (1977) "Grandmotherhood: a study of role conceptions." Journal of Marriage and the Family 30: 165-176.

――― (1978) "Women in mid-life crises, reverberations, and support networks." The Family Coordinator 27: 375-382.

ROBINSON, B. and M. THURNHER (1979) "Taking care of aged parents: a family cycle transition." The Gerontologist 19: 586-593.

ROBINSON, J. P. (1977) Changes in Americans' Use of Time, 1965-75: A Progress Report. Cleveland: Cleveland State University, Communication Research Center.

ROLLINS, B. C. and H. FELDMAN (1970) "Marital satisfaction over the family life cycle." Journal of Marriage and the Family 32: 20-28.

ROMAN, P. and P. TAIETZ (1967) "Organizational structure and disengagement: the emeritus professor." The Gerontologist 7: 147-152.

ROSEN, A. (1981) "Retirement and general well-being of women." Presented at the annual meetings of the Gerontological Society, Toronto.

ROSEN, D. H. (1973) "Social relationships and successful aging among the widowed aged." Ph.D. dissertation, Brandeis University.

ROSENBERG, G. S. (1970) The Worker Grows Old. San Francisco: Jossey-Bass.

ROSENFELD, J. P. (1979) "Old age, new beneficiaries—kinship, friendship and disinheritance." Sociology and Social Research 64: 86.

ROSENFELD, R. A. (1979) "Women's occupational careers." Sociology of Work and Occupations 6: 283-311.

ROSENKAIMER, D., A. SAPERSTEIN, B. ISHIZAKI, and D. MacBRIDE (1976) "Coping with old age—sex differences." Presented at the annual meetings of the Gerontological Society, New York.

ROSOW, I. (1967) Social Integration of the Aged. New York: Free Press.
——— (1973) "The social context of the aging self." The Gerontologist 13: 82-87.
——— (1974) Socialization to Old Age. Berkeley: University of California Press.
ROSS, H. and I. SAWHILL (1975) Time of Transition: The Growth of Families Headed by Women. Washington, DC: The Urban Institute.
ROSS-FRANKLIN, J. (1981) "Five stages of retirement marriage: an exploratory test." Presented at the annual meetings of the Gerontological Society, Toronto.
ROSSI, A. S. (1980) "Life span theories and women's lives." Signs 6: 4-33.
ROTMAN, A. (1979) "Married working women in retirement." Journal of Social Work 1: 311-320.
ROWE, A. R. (1976) "Retired academics and research activity." Journal of Gerontology 31: 456-461.
RUBIN, L. (1973) "Assessment of differential contributions of demographic and employment history characteristics to Social Security benefits: a comparison of black and white workers newly entitled to retirement benefits." Presented at the annual meetings of the Gerontological Society, Miami Beach.
——— (1976) Worlds of Pain. Life in the Working-Class Family. New York: Basic Books.
——— (1979) Women of a Certain Age. The Midlife Search for Self. New York: Harper & Row.
SALES, E. (1978) "Women's adult development," in E. Sales et al. (eds.), Women and Sex Roles: A Social Psychological Perspective. New York: W. W. Norton.
SAMUELS, V. (1975) "Nowhere to be found: a literature review and annotated bibliography on white working class women." New York: Institute on Pluralism and Group Identity.
SANDERS, L. T. and W. C. SEELBACH (1981) "Variations in preferred care alternatives for the elderly: family versus nonfamily sources." Family Relations 30: 447-451.
SATSCHUK, N. N., N. V. PANINA, G. M. MOSKALEZ, S. EITNER, and A. EITNER (1979) "Soziologische Aspekte der Vorbereitung auf die Pensionierung sowie des Freizeitverhaltens der Rentner." Zeitschrift fuer Alternsforschung 34: 549-555.
SAUER, W. J. (1975) "Morale of the urban aged: a regression analysis by race." Ph.D. dissertation, University of Minnesota.
SCANZONI, L. D. and J. SCANZONI (1981) Men, Women and Change (2nd ed.). New York: McGraw-Hill.
SCHNEIDER, C. (1964) Adjustment of Employed Women to Retirement. Ph.D. dissertation, Cornell University.
SCHNORE, M. M. and J. B. KIRKLAND (1981) "Sex differences in adjustment to retirement." Presented at the annual meetings of the Gerontological Society, Toronto.
SCHULZ, J. H. (1980) The Economics of Aging. Belmont, CA: Wadsworth.
——— and B. L. FRIEDMAN (1977) "Private pension coverage for women." Presented at the annual meetings of the Gerontological Society, San Francisco.
SCHULZ, J. H., T. D. LEAVITT, and L. KELLY (1979) "Private pensions fall short of preretirement income levels." Monthly Labor Review: 28-32.
SCHWAB, K. and L. M. IRELAN (1981) "The Social Security Administration's retirement history study," pp. 15-30 in N. G. McCluskey and E. F. Borgatta (eds.) Aging and Retirement: Prospects, Planning, and Policy. Beverly Hills, CA: Sage.

SCOTT, J. P. and V. R. KIVETT (1980) "The widowed black, older adult in the rural South." Family Relations 29: 83-90.

SEARS, L. V. (1975) "Selected environmental factors related to life satisfaction of black senior citizens." Ph.D. dissertation, Michigan State University.

SEELBACH, W. C. (1977) "Gender differences in expectations for filial responsibility." The Gerontologist 17: 421-425.

——— (1978) "Correlates of aged parents—filial responsibility expectations and realizations." The Family Coordinator 27: 341-350.

——— and C. J. HANSEN (1980) "Satisfaction with family relations among the elderly." Family Relations 29: 91-98.

SEELBACH, W. C. and W. J. SAUER (1977) "Filial responsibility expectations and morale among aged parents." The Gerontologist 17: 492-499.

SELTZER, M. M. (1975) "Women and sociogerontology." The Gerontologist 15: 484.

——— (1976) "Suggestions for the examination of time-disordered relationships," pp. 111-125 in J. F. Gubrium (ed.) Time, Roles, and Self in Old Age. New York: Behavioral.

——— (1979) "The older woman: fact, fantasies, and fiction." Research on Aging 1: 139-154.

——— and R. C. ATCHLEY (1971) "The impact of structural integration into the profession on work commitment, potential for disengagement and leisure preference among social workers." Sociological Focus 5: 9-17.

Senior Citizens in Great Cities (1976a) "The case of Chicago Chapter IX: life satisfaction." The Gerontologist 16: 70.

Senior Citizens in Great Cities (1976b) "The case of Chicago Chapter X: knowledge and use of services." The Gerontologist 16: 76.

Senior Citizens in Great Cities (1976c) "The case of Chicago Chapter VIII: family and social support." The Gerontologist 16: 63.

SHANAS, E. (1962) The Health of Older People: A Social Survey. Cambridge, MA: Harvard University Press.

——— (1968) "The meaning of work," pp. 320-346 in E. Shanas et al. (eds.) Old People in Three Industrial Societies. New York: Atherton.

——— (1972) "Adjustment to retirement: substitution or accommodation," pp. 219-243 in F. M. Carp (ed.) Retirement. New York: Behavioral.

——— (1973) "Family kin networks and aging in cross cultural perspective." Journal of Marriage and the Family 35: 505-511.

——— (1977) 1975 Survey of the Aged. Chicago: University of Illinois Press.

——— (1979a) "Social myth as hypothesis: the case of the family relations of old people." The Gerontologist 19: 3-10.

——— (1979b) "The family as a social support system in old age." The Gerontologist 19: 169-174.

——— (1980) "Older people and their families: the new pioneers." Journal of Marriage and the Family 42: 9-15.

——— and M. B. SUSSMAN (1977) Family, Bureaucracy, and the Elderly. Durham, NC: Duke University Press.

SHAPIRO, S. A., S. A. MURRELL, and W. M. USUI (1980) "Formal and social activity related to life satisfaction among older men and women: replication and extension of a causal model." Presented at the annual meetings of the Gerontological Society, San Diego.

SHELDON, A., P.J.M. McEWAN, and C. P. RYSER (1975) Retirement: Patterns and Predictions. Rockville, MD: National Institute of Mental Health.

SHEPPARD, H. L. (1976) "Work and retirement," pp. 286-309 in R. H. Binstock and E. Shanas (eds.) Handbook of Aging and the Social Sciences. New York: Van Nostrand Reinhold.

SHERMAN, S. R. (1974) "Labor-force status of nonmarried women on the threshold of retirement." Social Security Bulletin 37: 3-13.

SIEGEL, J. S. (1976) "Demographic aspects of aging and the older population." Current Population Reports, Series P-23, No. 59. Washington, DC: U.S. Bureau of the Census.

SIMOS, B. G. (1973) "Adult children and their aging parents." Social Work 18: 78-85.

SIMPSON, I. H. and P. ENGLAND (1981) "Conjugal work roles and marital solidarity." Journal of Family Issues 2: 164-179.

SIMPSON, I. H. and J. C. McKINNEY (1966) Social Aspects of Aging. Durham, NC: Duke University Press.

SIMPSON, I. H., K. W. BACK, and J. C. McKINNEY (1966a) "Work and retirement," pp. 45-54 in I. H. Simpson and J. C. McKinney (eds.) Social Aspects of Aging. Durham, NC: Duke University Press.

——— (1966b) "Orientations toward work and retirement, and self-evaluation in retirement," pp. 75-89 in I. H. Simpson and J. C. McKINNEY (eds.) Social Aspects of Aging. Durham, NC: Duke University Press.

——— (1966c). "Continuity of work and retirement activities and self-evaluation," pp. 106-119 in I. H. Simpson and J. C. McKinney (eds.) Social Aspects of Aging. Durham, NC: Duke University Press.

——— (1966d) "Exposure to information on preparation for and self-evaluation in retirement," pp. 90-105 in I. H. Simpson and J. C. McKinney (eds.) Social Aspects of Aging. Durham, NC: Duke University Press.

SKOGLUND, J. (1979) "Job deprivation in retirement: Anticipated and experienced feelings." Research on Aging 1: 481-493.

SLATER, P. E. (1970) The Pursuit of Loneliness. Boston: Beacon Press.

SLAVICK, F. and S. L. WOLFBEIN (1960) "The evolving work life pattern." In C. Tibbitts (ed.) Handbook of Gerontology: Social Aspects of Aging. Chicago: University of Chicago Press.

SMITH, K. and A. LIPMAN (1972) "Constraint and life satisfaction." Journal of Gerontology 27: 77-82.

SMITH, P. C., L. M. KENDALL, and C. L. HULIN (1969) The Measurement of Satisfaction in Work and Retirement: A Strategy for the Study of Attitudes. Chicago: Rand McNally.

SOBOL, M. G. (1974) "Commitment to work," pp. 63-80 in L. W. Hoffman and F. I. Nye (eds.) Working Mothers. San Francisco, CA: Jossey-Bass.

SOKOLOWSKA, M. (1965) "Some reflections on the different attitudes of men and women toward work." International Labor Review, 92: 35-50.

SOMMERS, T. (1976) Aging in America: Implications for Women. Oakland, CA: National Commission on Aging.

SPECTOR, W. D. (1979) "Women's retirement income," pp. 247-276 in K. W. Feinstein (ed.) Working Women and Families. Beverly Hills, CA: Sage.

SPENCE, D. and T. LONNER (1971) "The 'Empty Nest': a transition within motherhood." The Family Coordinator 20: 369-375.

SPORAKOWSKI, M. J. and G. A. HUGHSTON (1978) "Prescriptions for happy marriage, adjustments and satisfactions of couples married for 50 or more years." The Family Coordinator 27: 321-328.

SPREITZER, E. and E. E. SNYDER (1974) "Correlates of life satisfaction among the aged." Journal of Gerontology 29: 454-458.

SRB, J. H. (1981) Women and Pensions in the United States. Presented at the annual meetings of the Gerontological Society, Toronto.

STEARNS, P. (1980) "Old women: some historical observations." Journal of Family History 5: 44-57.

STINNETT, N., J. COLLINS, and J. E. MONTGOMERY (1970) "Marital need satisfaction of older husbands and wives." Journal of Marriage and the Family 32: 428-434.

STINNETT, N., L. M. CARTER, and J. E. MONTGOMERY (1972) "Older persons' perceptions of their marriages." Journal of Marriage and the Family 34: 665-670.

STOKES, R. G. and G. L. MADDOX (1967) "Some social factors on retirement adaptation." Journal of Gerontology 22: 329-333.

STRAUSS, H. D., B. W. ALDRICH, and A. LIPMAN (1976) "Retirement and perceived status loss," pp. 220-235 in J. F. Gubrium (ed.) Time, Roles, and Self in Old Age. New York: Behavioral.

STREIB, G. F. (1965) Longitudinal Study of Retirement: Final Report to the Social Security Administration. Ithaca, NY: Cornell University Press.

——— and R. M. BECK (1980) "Older families: a decade review." Journal of Marriage and the Family 42: 937-956.

STREIB, G. F. and C. J. SCHNEIDER (1971) Retirement in American Society: Impact and Process. Ithaca, NY: Cornell University Press.

STREIB, G. F. and R. B. STREIB (1979) "Retired persons and their contributions: exchange theory," in H. Orimo et al. (eds.) Recent Advances in Gerontology. Amsterdam.

STUEVE, A. and C. S. FISCHER (1978) "Social networks and older women." Berkeley: University of California, Institute of Urban and Regional Development.

SUSSMAN, M. B. (1972) "An analytical model for the sociological study of retirement," pp. 29-74 in F. M. Carp (ed.) Retirement. New York: Behavioral.

——— (1976) "The family life of old people," pp. 218-243 in R. H. Binstock and E. Shanas (eds.) Handbook of Aging and the Social Sciences. New York: Van Nostrand Reinhold.

SWEET, J. A. (1973) Women in the Labor Force. New York: Seminar Press.

SZALAI, A. (1972) The Use of Time. The Hague: Mouton.

SZINOVACZ, M. (1977) "Role allocation, family structure, and female employment." Journal of Marriage and the Family 39: 781-791.

——— (1978) "Female retirement: personal and marital consequences—a case study." Presented at the annual meetings of the Gerontological Society, Dallas.

——— (1979a) The Situation of Women in Austria: Economic and Family Issues. Vienna: Federal Ministry of Social Affairs.

——— (1979b) "Women employed: effects on spouses' division of household work." Journal of Home Economics 71: 42-45.

——— (1980) "Female retirement: effects on spousal roles and marital adjustment." Journal of Family Issues 1: 423-440.

——— (1982a) Women's Adjustment to Retirement: Final Report to the NRTA-AARP Andrus Foundation. Tallahassee: Florida State University.

——— (1982b) "Beyond the hearth: older women and retirement from the labor force," in E. W. Markson (ed.) Older Women: Issues and Prospects. Lexington, MA: Lexington Books.

TAYLOR, C. (1972) "Developmental conceptions and the retirement process," pp. 75-116 in F. M. Carp (ed.) Retirement. New York: Behavioral.

TERIET, B. (1978) "Gliding out: the European approach to retirement." Personnel Journal 57: 368-370.

THOENNES, N. A., R. CHAPMAN, and K. FLAMING (1978) "Sex, role theory and retirement." Presented at the annual meetings of the Gerontological Society, Dallas.

THOMAE, H. (1970) "Theory of aging and cognitive theory of personality." Human Development 13: 1-16.

THOMPSON, E. (1980) "The values of employment to mothers of small children." Journal of Marriage and the Family 42: 551-566.

THOMPSON, G. B. (1971) "Work experience and income of the population aged 60 and older, 1971." Social Security Bulletin 35: 3-20.

——— (1972) "Adjustments in retirement: a causal interpretation of factors influencing morale of retired men." Ph.D. dissertation, Brandeis University.

——— (1973) "Work versus leisure roles: an investigation of morale among employed and retired men." Journal of Gerontology 28: 339-344.

THOMPSON, W. E. (1958) "Pre-retirement anticipation and adjustment in retirement." Journal of Social Issues 14: 35-45.

——— and G. F. STREIB (1969) "Meaningful activity in a family context," pp. 177-212 in R. W. Kleemeir (ed.) Aging and Leisure. New York: Oxford University Press.

——— and J. KOSA (1960) "The effect of retirement on personal adjustment: a panel analysis." Journal of Gerontology 15: 165-169.

THURNHER, M. (1974) "Goals, values, and life evaluation at the preretirement stage." Journal of Gerontology 29: 85-96.

TIGER, L. (1969) Men in Groups. New York: Random House.

TISSUE, T. (1979) "Low-income widows and other aged singles." Social Security Bulletin 42: 3-10.

TOBIN, S. and B. NEUGARTEN (1961) "Life satisfaction and social interaction in the aging." Journal of Gerontology 16: 344-346.

TOSELAND, R. and J. SYKES (1977) "Senior citizens center participation and other correlates of life satisfaction." The Gerontologist 17: 235-241.

TOWNSEND, P. (1957) The Family Life of Old People. London: Routledge & Kegan Paul.

TREAS, J. (1975) "Aging and the family," pp. 92-108 in D. S. Woodruff and J. E. Birren (eds.) Aging: Scientific Perspectives and Social Issues. New York: Van Nostrand Reinhold.

——— (1977) "Family support systems for the aged: some social and demographic considerations." The Gerontologist 17: 486-491.

——— (1981) "The great American fertility debate: generational balance and support of the aged." The Gerontologist 21: 98.

––– and A. Van HILST (1976) "Marriage and remarriage rates among older Americans." The Gerontologist 16: 132-136.

TRELA, J. E. and D. J. JACKSON (1979) "Family life and community participation in old age." Research on Aging 1: 233-251.

TRILLING, R. (1977) "Retirement and voter turnout: an exploratory study." Presented at the annual meetings of the Gerontological Society, San Francisco.

TROLL, L. E. (1971) "The family of later life: a decade review," pp. 187-214 in C. B. Broderick (ed.) A Decade of Family Research and Action. Minneapolis: National Council on Family Relations.

––– and B. TURNER (1979) "Sex differences in problems of aging," in E. Gomberg and V. Franks (eds.) Gender and Disordered Behavior. New York: Brunner/Mazel.

TROLL, L. E. and V. BENGTSON (1979) "Generations in the family," pp. 127-161 in W. R. Burr et al. (eds.) Contemporary Theories About the Family, Vol. 1. New York: Free Press.

TROLL, L. E., J. ISRAEL, and K. ISRAEL (1977) Looking Ahead: A Woman's Guide to the Problems and Joys of Growing Older. Englewood Cliffs, NJ: Prentice-Hall.

TROLL, L. E., S. J. MILLER, and R. C. ATCHLEY (1979) Families in Later Life. Belmont, CA: Wadsworth.

TURNER, B. F. (1979) "The self-concepts of older women." Research on Aging 1: 464-480.

UHLENBERG, P. (1979) "Challenge to design constructive roles." The Gerontologist 19: 236-241.

––– and M.A.P. MYERS (1981) "Divorce and the elderly." The Gerontologist 21: 276-282.

U.S. Bureau of the Census (1973) Detailed Characteristics: United States Summary, Series PC(1)D1. Washington, DC: Government Printing Office.

––– (1974) General Population Characteristics: United States Summary, Series PC(1)B1. Washington, DC: Government Printing Office.

––– (1976) Current Population Reports, Series P-23, No. 59. Washington, DC: Government Printing Office.

––– (1978a) Census of the Population, 1970: General Social and Economic Characteristics. Washington, DC: Government Printing Office.

––– (1978b) Demographic Aspects of Aging and the Older Population in the United States. Current Population Reports, Series P-23, No. 59. Washington, DC: Government Printing Office.

U.S. Department of Commerce (1976) Statistical Abstract of the United States. Washington, DC: Government Printing Office.

U.S. Department of Labor (1975) Handbook on Women Workers. Washington, DC: Government Printing Office.

––– (1980) Employment and Training Report of the President. Washington, DC: Government Printing Office.

USHER, C. E. (1981a) "Delayed retirement: a matter of necessity or preference?" Presented at the annual meetings of the Gerontological Society, Toronto.

––– (1981b) "Work or retirement: a decision for older American women." Presented at the annual meetings of the Gerontological Society, Toronto.

Van DUSSEN, R. A. and E. B. SHELDON (1976) "The changing status of American women: a life-cycle perspective." American Psychologist 31: 106-116.

VEROFF, J., R. KULKA, and E. DOUVAN (1981) Mental Health in America. New York: Basic Books.

VIDEBACK, R. and A. B. KNOX (1965) "Alternative participatory response to aging," in A. M. Rose and W. A. Peterson (eds.) Older People and Their Social World. Philadelphia: F. A. Davis.

VINICK, B. H. (1978a) "Remarriage in old age." Journal of Geriatric Psychiatry 11: 75-78.

——— (1978b) "Remarriage in old age." The Family Coordinator 27: 359-364.

WALKER, J. W. and K. F. PRICE (1975) "Retirement choice and retirement satisfaction." Presented at the annual meetings of the Gerontological Society, Louisville.

WALKER, K. E. and M. E. WOODS (1976) Time Use: A Measure of Household Production of Family Goods and Services. Washington, DC: American Home Economics Association.

WALSH, J. A. and N. M. KIRACOFE (1980) "Change in significant other relationships and life satisfaction in the aged." The International Journal of Aging and Human Development 10: 273.

WALTHER, R. J. (1975) "Money income, age, and work status." Presented at the annual meetings of the Gerontological Society, Louisville.

WAPNER, S. (1980) Transition to Retirement. Washington, DC: The NRTA-AARP Andrus Foundation.

WARD, R. A. (1978) "Limitations of the family as a supportive institution in the lives of the aged." The Family Coordinator 27: 365-374.

——— (1979) "The meaning of voluntary association participation to older people." Journal of Gerontology 34: 438-445.

WEISS, R. S. and N. M. SAMUELSON (1958) "Social roles of American women: their contribution to a sense of usefulness and importance." Marriage and Family Living 20: 358-366.

WELCH, S. and A. BOOTH (1977) "The effect of employment on the health of married women with children." Sex Roles 3: 385-397.

WEXLEY, K. N., J. L. McLAUGHLIN, and H. L. STERNS (1973) "A study of perceived need fulfillment and life satisfaction before and after retirement." Journal of Vocational Behavior 7: 81-87.

WOLF, W. C. and R. ROSENFELD (1978) "Sex structure of occupations and job mobility." Social Forces 56: 823-844.

Women's Studies Program and Policy Center (1980) Older Women: The Economics of Aging. Washington, DC: George Washington University Press.

WOOD, V. and J. F. ROBERTSON (1978) "Friendship and kinship interaction: differential effect on the morale of the elderly." Journal of Marriage and the Family 40: 367-375.

WOOD, V., M. WYLIE, and B. SHEAFOR (1969) "An analysis of a short self-report measure of life satisfaction: correlation with rater judgments." Journal of Gerontology 24: 465-469.

WRIGHT, H. W., R. O. BENNETT, and J. A. TERESI (1976) "Family roles as factors in the retirement adjustment of women." Presented at the annual meetings of the Gerontological Society, New York.

WYLIE, M. (1970) "Life satisfaction as a program impact criterion." Journal of Gerontology 25: 36-40.

Yearbook of Labor Statistics (1979) Geneva: International Labour Office.

YOGEV, S. (1981) "Do professional women have egalitarian marital relationships?" Journal of Marriage and the Family 43: 865-871.

ZANDER, M. L., F. K. KALLAN, and J. S. SAINER (1973) "Previous social conditioning as barrier or enhancement to new roles in retirement." Presented at the annual meetings of the Gerontological Society, Miami Beach.

ZEGLEN, M. E. (1976) "The impact of primary relationships on life satisfaction of the elderly." Ph.D. dissertation, Washington State University.

ZIBBELL, R. A. (1971) "Activity level, future time perspective and life satisfaction in old age." Ph.D. dissertation, Boston University.

# ABOUT THE CONTRIBUTORS

**ROBERT C. ATCHLEY** is Director of the Scripps Foundation Gerontology Center, Miami University, Oxford, Ohio. His books in the field of aging include *The Social Forces in Later Life* (3rd ed.), as well as numerous journal articles and book chapters. He is editor of *Gerontological Monographs* for the Gerontological Society of America.

**MARILYN R. BLOCK** is Director of the National Policy Center on Women and Aging, University of Maryland, College Park. Prior to assuming this role, she was affiliated with the Center on Aging at the University of Maryland, where she conducted research on a variety of issues related to the female aging process. Since coming to the NPCWA, she has expanded her research efforts to incorporate public policy concerns that evolve out of the social, psychological, biological, and economic aspects of normative female aging.

**TIMOTHY H. BRUBAKER** is an Associate Professor in the Department of Home Economics and Consumer Sciences and a Fellow of the Scripps Foundation Gerontology Center, Miami University, Oxford, Ohio. He received his Ph.D. from Iowa State University. His research interests focus on family relationships in later life, attitudes toward the elderly, and service delivery to the elderly and their families.

**CHARLENE DEPNER** is Assistant Research Scientist, Survey Research Center, the University of Michigan. Her research is focused on role-related stressors, their outcomes, and mediators of the stress/strain relationship. Her recent work examines role-related stress from a life-course perspective.

**CHARLES B. HENNON** is Family Life Education Extension Specialist in Family Living Education, University of Wisconsin-Extension, and Associate Professor of Child and Family Studies in the School of Family

Resources and Consumer Sciences, University of Wisconsin-Madison. He earned his Ph.D. in sociology from Case Western University. In addition to his research on developing personalized stress management and conflict management strategies, he is currently doing a study of marriage role expectations and behaviors among older Americans.

**JOHN C. HENRETTA** is Associate Professor of Sociology at the University of Florida, Gainesville. His research, which has appeared in the *American Journal of Sociology, American Sociological Review,* and other journals, deals with women's retirement, income of the elderly, and home ownership.

**CLAIRE E. HIGGINS** is a former Director of the Schenectady Inner City Ministry Enriched Housing Program. She is currently analyzing data on familism in community housing of the elderly.

**BERIT INGERSOLL** is a Ph.D. candidate in social work and psychology at the University of Michigan. Her primary area of interest is in gerontology. She has written several articles in this area that focus on gender differences, social support, and therapeutic issues.

**RUTH HATHAWAY JEWSON** has served as Executive Officer of the National Council on Family Relations since 1956. She was the first recipient of the NCFR's annual Distinguished Service to Families Award. She was the author of chapters about the NCFR in *A Decade of Family Research and Action—the Seventies* and in *A Decade of Family Research and Action, 1960-1969,* both published by the NCFR. Her research interests are in the areas of retirement.

**CAROLYN KITCHINGS JOHNSON** received her Master's degree in the Department of Child and Family Development, University of Georgia. She is presently employed at the DeKalb County Council on Aging, Atlanta, Georgia.

**PAT M. KEITH** is Professor of Sociology at Iowa State University. Primary research interests are in social gerontology and sex roles. Recent efforts include a study of work and family roles over the life cycle, household involvement of men and women in later life, and factors associated with depression in the two-job family.

**NAOMI KROEGER** is an Associate Professor in the Department of Sociology, Hunter College–CUNY, New York and is also associated with the Brookdale Center on Aging of Hunter College. Her areas of interest include industrial sociology, the sociology of work, and midlife and aging.

**EVELYN S. NEWMAN** is Associate Director of the Ringel Institute of Gerontology, School of Social Welfare, Rockefeller College, State University of New York at Albany. Her current research interests are long-term care of the elderly and the elderly offender.

**ANGELA O'RAND** is Assistant Professor of Sociology at Duke University. Her current research interests include life-span models of women's lives and the relationship of institutional structures to career trajectories across different occupational and professional groups.

**SHARON PRICE-BONHAM** is Associate Professor in the Department of Child and Family Development, University of Georgia, Athens. Her research has focused on the changing roles of women, decision making in marriages, family members' perceptions, and divorce.

**CAROL CUTLER RIDDICK** is Assistant Professor of Recreation at the University of Maryland. Her current research is focused on how leisure roles affect the health of older persons, and on age differences and age changes regarding leisure values and leisure meanings. She is currently at work on a book tentatively titled *Leisure Services for the Aging Population.*

**SUSAN R. SHERMAN** is Associate Professor in the School of Social Welfare, State University of New York at Albany. Her current research interests include sex roles and retirement, sex role stereotypes of the middle-aged and the elderly, and environments for the well and the frail elderly.

**MAXIMILIANE SZINOVACZ** is Assistant Professor of Sociology, Florida State University. Her research interests and publications focus on marital power and decision making, effects of female employment on the family, and women's retirement. She is co-author of *Family Decision-Making: A Developmental Sex Role Model* (with John Scanzoni).